Wittgenstein's *Investigations* 1–133

D1594059

'It is a genuinely important book ... there is nothing I know of in print which goes into such sophisticated detail as Lugg in getting Wittgenstein right.'

Burton Dreben, *Harvard and Boston Universities*

One of the greatest works of twentieth-century philosophy, Ludwig Wittgenstein's *Philosophical Investigations* is also one of the most controversial. *Wittgenstein's* Investigations *1–133* provides a clear and concise introduction to the crucial early sections of this classic work.

Andrew Lugg discusses in detail what Wittgenstein says about meaning, metaphysics and philosophy in sections 1–133 of the *Philosophical Investigations*. Besides making Wittgenstein's thought accessible to a general audience and explaining its philosophical significance, the book develops a radical interpretation of his remarks. It takes Wittgenstein's text to epitomize his philosophical outlook and applies Wittgenstein's philosophical strategy to his own words.

Wittgenstein's Investigations *1–133* will be a valuable resource for anyone interested in Wittgenstein, language and the history of twentieth-century philosophy.

Andrew Lugg is Professor of Philosophy at the University of Ottawa.

For Lynne Cohen, fellow traveller and partner for the best part of a lifetime.

Wittgenstein's
Investigations 1–133
A guide and interpretation

Andrew Lugg

Routledge
Taylor & Francis Group

LONDON AND NEW YORK

First published 2000
by Routledge
11 New Fetter Lane, London EC4P 4EE
Paperback edition published in 2004

Simultaneously published in the USA and Canada
by Routledge
29 West 35th Street, New York, NY 10001

Routledge is an imprint of the Taylor & Francis Group

©2000, 2004 Andrew Lugg

Typeset in Times by Taylor & Francis Books Ltd
Printed and bound in Great Britain by Biddles Ltd, Guildford and
King's Lynn

British Library Cataloguing in Publication Data
A catalogue record for this book is available from the British Library

Library of Congress Cataloging-in-Publication Data
Lugg, Andrew
Wittgenstein's investigations 1–133: a guide and interpretation /
Andrew Lugg.
p. cm.
Includes index.
1. Wittgenstein, Ludwig, 1889–1951. Philosophische Untersuchungen.
1–133. 2. Meaning (Philosophy). 3. Metaphysics. 4. Philosophy.
I. Title: Wittgenstein's investigations one through one hundred
thirty-three.
II. Title.

B3376.W563 P529 2000
192–dc21
                                                    99–089678

ISBN 0–415–23245–7 (CASED)
ISBN 0–415–34902–8 (LIMP)

Contents

Preface to paperback edition - December 2003

I have taken the opportunity of this reprinting to make small editorial revisions, clarify the discussion of several paragraphs and correct a few passages that misreport Wittgenstein's remarks. What has not changed is my conception of Wittgenstein's aims and tactics. I continue to believe that §§1-133 of the Investigations serve as an object lesson in how philosophical issues should, as Wittgenstein saw it, be handled and there is no better introduction to his philosophy.

Preface to hardback edition

Ludwig Wittgenstein is mainly known for two great works of philosophy, the *Tractatus Logico-Philosophicus*, published in 1921, and the *Philosophical Investigations*, published posthumously in 1953. In the earlier work Wittgenstein purports to solve all the problems of philosophy; in the later work he rethinks some of the same problems and explores issues that he had previously overlooked, failed to appreciate properly or dismissed as unimportant. Though just as ambitious as the *Tractatus*, the *Investigations* is very different in form and spirit. It too deals with central problems of philosophy, but it is not as abstract or dogmatic. Here Wittgenstein does greater justice to the appeal and depth of past philosophy and devotes much more time and effort to exposing and confronting the grip of philosophical ideas on our thinking.

The first 133 sections of the *Investigations*, the subject of the present work, deal with topics central to Wittgenstein's later philosophy. They are some of the most carefully worked out sections of the book, and had Wittgenstein written nothing else they would still merit our attention. The philosophy of the rest of the *Investigations* is of the highest order, but §§1–133, which constitute about a fifth of the book, deserve special attention (and are more than enough to consider in a single volume). Also §§134–142 are somewhat technical, and at §143 Wittgenstein embarks on a more detailed examination of a variety of issues, some of which are touched on in the sections we shall be considering. It is not by chance that §§1–133 deal with the themes they do; Wittgenstein took what he says here to be fundamental for what he was trying to achieve in the *Investigations* and elsewhere.

My discussion is in the form of a commentary. I go through §§1–133 a paragraph at a time, sometimes even line by line, and relegate discussion of how the text should be understood to interspersed interludes. Wittgenstein's remarks are exceptionally compressed, and it is easy to misconstrue what he is saying if one allows oneself the liberty of skipping from section to section and disregards how they are arranged. Few authors were more reluctant to go into detail than Wittgenstein, and the further we stray from the text, the more likely we are to misconstrue him. While reading the *Investigations* from the beginning is not a panacea, it is a useful antidote to common misinterpretations of what he is saying. Half the battle, it seems to me, is to refrain from trying to make his remarks more perspicuous by reorganizing them and to avoid assuming he intended us to fill what appear to be gaps in his exposition in this or that particular way (or at all). Instead of regarding the *Investigations* as an arcane document that can be understood only by imposing an interpretation on it, we should try to meet it on its own terms and struggle to figure out what each of its sentences actually says.

I have three main goals. First to provide a clear and concise introduction to §§1–133 of the *Investigations*, one accessible to those unfamiliar with Wittgenstein's philosophy. Secondly to remedy what I take to be mistaken ways in which individual sections are often read. And thirdly to draw attention to what, for want of a better phrase, might be called Wittgenstein's philosophical outlook. I believe it possible to do all three things at once since I believe what Wittgenstein is trying to say is best appreciated by working through his text from the beginning. In fact I am persuaded that the power and importance of the *Investigations* becomes clear only when it is studied section by section in the order Wittgenstein intended. To understand him one has to follow the trail he pioneers and explore the issues he takes up along with him. Grappling with the text is not one option among many, never mind a first step towards a philosophically more sophisticated account of Wittgenstein's remarks. It is the only way to grasp what he is trying to convey.

My strategy in what follows is somewhat similar to Wittgenstein's own strategy. Just as Wittgenstein labours to clear away what he takes to be misleading ways of thinking about the world and our place in it, so I bend my energies to clearing away misleading ways of reading his text. In Wittgenstein's view we are led for a variety of reasons to see things other than they are, and I believe we are swayed by equally extraneous factors to regard him as saying something he does not say. Also in much the same way as Wittgenstein attempts to get us to see what is in front of our very eyes, I try to get us to read the words on the page. In my opinion the *Investigations* has to be appreciated in the spirit of Wittgenstein himself, and we must resist the temptation to overinterpret and overstructure his remarks. At any rate the reader should bear in mind that I intend to apply what I take to be a central lesson of Wittgenstein's philosophy to his own writing.

I do not mean to suggest I am the first to have realized that Wittgenstein's remarks have to be wrestled with to be understood. This has often been stressed, and it would be preposterous at this late date to claim to have found a new way of interpreting the *Investigations*. My purpose is rather to clarify and develop an approach to Wittgenstein's book that I take to be insufficiently appreciated. Where I mainly differ from others who take there to be no alternative to working through the text is over what this entails. I see myself as treating the idea more seriously than usual and as showing in greater detail what it amounts to in practice. Wrestling with Wittgenstein's text is easier said than done, and one has to guard against falling back on the easy option of summarizing what he is saying instead of working out the details. Throughout I have tried to avoid putting words into Wittgenstein's mouth in favour of letting him speak for himself.

Readers familiar with the secondary literature on the *Investigations* will notice that I forego much of the critical apparatus commentators usually deploy. I do not speak of Wittgenstein as attacking the 'Augustinian picture' nor do I take him to be engaged in a discussion with an imaginary opponent, 'the interlocutor', who expresses a point of view he finds seductive and wishes to combat. This is not the way I began, but the more I pondered the text, the less I found myself needing such paraphernalia. In fact I gradually came to think it better to read Wittgenstein as challenging a range of interconnected pictures and to regard him as doing battle with a range of opponents. It now seems to me preferable to use the non-technical language Wittgenstein himself favoured and to avoid even the slightest suggestion that he is examining a well-defined philosophical position. As I see it, the power and drama of the *Investigations* resides largely in the way Wittgenstein digs out and comes to terms with philosophical conceptions that grip us, and it subverts what he is attempting to achieve to belittle the diversity of the intuitions he is at pains to combat.

Acknowledgements

I have profited greatly from reading what others have written about §§1–133 of the *Investigations* whether or not I ended up agreeing with their interpretations. Garth Hallett's and Gordon Baker and Peter Hacker's commentaries on the *Investigations* have saved me from many errors, and I have learned a great deal from Stanley Cavell's, Juliet Floyd's and Edward Minar's papers on Wittgenstein's philosophy. My greatest intellectual debts, however, are to Burton Dreben and Warren Goldfarb. Goldfarb's papers on some of the sections I discuss influenced my thinking more than anyone else's, and Dreben helped me, as he helped so many others, better understand the nature of the philosophical endeavour. In addition I am indebted to Lynne Cohen and Paul Forster for the time and energy they expended going over this book with a fine-toothed comb, to Nadine Faulkner for useful comments on virtually every section of the book, and to Puqun Li and Joseph McDonald for their work on an earlier draft. Burton Dreben and Juliet Floyd also gave me much good advice, and Warren Ingber, Klaus Jahn, Tessa McWatt and Tara Sigouin were kind enough to help me with specific sections of Wittgenstein's book. Were it not for the assistance I received from these friends, colleagues and students, my discussion would be much less clear and much less faithful to the text. Finally thanks are due to the editorial and production-editorial staff at Routledge (Anna Gerber, Brie Allio, Muna Khogali and Allison Bell) for their efforts on my behalf and to Basil Blackwell Ltd for granting me permission to reproduce material from Ludwig Wittgenstein, *Philosophical Investigations*, edited by G.E.M. Anscombe and R. Rhees, translated by G.E.M. Anscombe, 2nd edition (Basil Blackwell: Oxford, 1958).

Introduction

Nearly everything about Wittgenstein's remarks in the *Investigations* is controversial – how to read them, how they relate one to another, what they are meant to convey individually and collectively, and whether they are of enduring importance. Beyond acknowledging that the book concerns meaning, thought and related topics and that Wittgenstein believes we are all too prone to be misled by language, readers and commentators agree on very little. His remarks have been appropriated by thinkers of very different philosophical persuasions and have been promoted and criticized on a bewildering variety of grounds. Even those sympathetic to Wittgenstein's later philosophy are at odds about its main aims and how it contributes to philosophy. Indeed it sometimes seems as though there are as many interpretations of the *Investigations* as there are readers.

One major division among the augurs is over the question of whether Wittgenstein intends to develop and defend answers to the problems of philosophy or aims instead to disabuse us of our feeling that these problems are serious problems in need of serious solutions. On the one side there are those who read him as advancing definite philosophical views and as putting forward more or less good reasons in support of these views. On the other side there are those who regard him as questioning whether philosophical questions are genuine and as inviting us to adopt an attitude towards them different from the one most of us find natural and plausible. The contrast, which is more easily grasped than characterized, is between reading the *Investigations* as making a positive contribution to knowledge and reading it as attempting to put a brake on philosophical speculation. For one group of readers Wittgenstein is making philosophical claims (and giving advice about how to think about philosophical issues); for the other group he is trying to get us to scrutinize more closely our philosophical biases and predictions.

There is a lot to be said for both ways of reading the *Investigations*. In support of the view that Wittgenstein meant to propose and defend a philosophical position, there is the fact that he seems to adumbrate theses about language, thought and the world, to expound philosophical distinctions regarding these matters, and to promote methods for resolving (or dissolving) philosophical problems about them. It is easy to find passages in the *Investigations* to bolster the suggestion that Wittgenstein defends a theory of meaning based on the use of words, distinguishes sharply between conceptual and empirical truths, recommends that we regard metaphysical theses as grammatical remarks, and much else besides. In fact the *Investigations* is riddled with what for all the world look like philosophical pronouncements of one sort or another.

But then again much of what Wittgenstein says points in the opposite direction. The second way of reading him squares well with his inclination to debate issues back and forth without coming to any clear resolution and with what he himself says about his philosophy. The book does not look or read like a textbook, even less like a treatise in which a particular viewpoint is propounded and defended. In fact Wittgenstein's use of the tactic of give and take and other rhetorical devices reminds one of nothing so much as the strategies we use when we try to get others to change their ways. And why if his aims are theoretical and explanatory, does he deprecate the conception of philosophy as promoting theories, deny that the distinctions he makes have any special force, and disclaim that he is putting forward a new philosophical method? Scattered throughout his writings are remarks that strongly suggest he does not intend to put forward a theory of language, accords no special weight to the distinction between conceptual and empirical truth and does not think metaphysical theses can be dispensed with by viewing them as grammatical rules.

Evaluating these two approaches to what Wittgenstein is doing in the *Investigations* is no easy matter. Neither can be demonstrated or refuted by the simple expedient of noting a fact or two about the content or tone of his remarks. Those who take Wittgenstein to be propounding positive views can argue that he uses a dialectical approach to establish theoretical and methodological conclusions and can discount his negative remarks about philosophical speculation on the grounds that they extend only so far. Similarly those who read him as mainly trying to get us to forego philosophical speculation can insist that the claims he seems to be making, including those regarding the correct method in philosophy, have to be understood as so many way-stations in an on-going discussion rather than as settled opinions. For better or worse, there is plenty of room for each side to manoeuvre. Wittgenstein provides both groups of commentators with abundant resources to turn back their opponents' objections.

To avoid prejudicing the outcome, I propose to consider what Wittgenstein says in the *Investigations*, and how he says it, without assuming in advance whether or not he is making substantive philosophical claims. I do not scour the text for passages in support of either view but work through the text allowing both for the possibility that he means to promote one or more philosophical doctrines and for the possibility that he is, to the contrary, antipathetic to philosophical doctrines of every description. If Wittgenstein's text contains definite theses, distinctions or methods, we should encounter them sooner or later. And if not, not. Indeed it seems to me both sides should welcome a careful examination of the text. Proponents of the first approach should be pleased since it sidelines the objection that Wittgenstein's remarks have to be considered in context – this is how they are being considered. And proponents of the second approach should appreciate that their view is being given an airing rather than ruled out of court at the outset.

If the first way of reading Wittgenstein is right, we ought to find him expounding and defending specific views about the world, language, the mind and such like. Since he is, by all accounts, a major philosopher, what he says should not be old-fashioned, preposterous or easily refuted, nor should his arguments be weak, hackneyed or incoherent. He should not say one thing one minute and another thing the next, still less first defend views, then criticize them (at least not without acknowledging the fact). Nor again should we expect to discover his aversion to philosophical speculation permeating his thinking. However he characterizes his own philosophy, it ought to be clear that he intends to make a substantive contribution – if only a negative one – to philosophy.

If, on the other hand, the second way of reading Wittgenstein is correct, we should find him questioning our philosophical presuppositions and encouraging us to adopt a different attitude to philosophical problems. At every stage, we should have the sense that we are being led along by the dialectical cut and thrust of his discussion, and the interest of his thoughts should seem to us to reside more in the manner in which he deals with issues than in any definite conclusions he may seem to be drawing. We should feel that we are gaining insight rather than information and find ourselves doubting whether there is a complete story to be told about the book. In this regard the *Investigations* should seem like a great work of art, and the idea that we can get to the bottom of it, even the idea that it has a bottom, should come to seem shallow. In particular we should end up thinking that its title – *Philosophical Investigations* – is especially apt.

No single examination of the *Investigations* can be expected to resolve the question of how the book should be read once and for all, let alone an examination of one part of it. Still a close study of §§1–133 of the sort that follows should provide a good indication of where the truth lies. If we find Wittgenstein advancing philosophical theses, stressing the importance of philosophical distinctions, defending one or more methods of dealing with philosophical problems, or pronouncing in a similarly definitive way on some other philosophical matter, we shall be well on the way to showing the book to be a philosophical treatise of a relatively familiar sort. And if we find that he does not make any such claims, we shall have good reason to conclude that his aims are different from those of most great philosophers of the past. To resist this conclusion we would have to maintain that Wittgenstein gets around to presenting his view only later in the book, which is highly unlikely, or argue that he does not present them systematically because of the difficulty of the subject he is dealing with, which is even less probable.

I have already indicated that I believe that Wittgenstein aims to nudge us into regarding philosophical issues differently from the way we usually regard them rather than to provide information about language, the mind or anything else. Indeed I shall suggest that he is best read as pursuing this goal in an especially uncompromising way. I do not, however, begin by assuming that this is the right way to read the *Investigations*; this is something I should like to think emerges in the course of the discussion rather than something assumed at the start. The object of the exercise is to figure out what Wittgenstein is saying in §§1–133 and hence to come to see how these sections should be read, not to show that they can be orchestrated in accordance with what I take to be Wittgenstein's basic philosophical perspective. My aim is to show that Wittgenstein's text has to be grappled with and to demonstrate by example what it means to say it is the cumulative effect of his remarks that counts. If this is right, the question of what Wittgenstein is trying to convey in the book and why his remarks are important should pretty much answer itself.

Wittgenstein's Preface

Wittgenstein begins his Preface by telling us that the remarks of the *Investigations* are the result of inquiries in which he has been engaged for the 'last sixteen years' (p. ix).[1] By this he means that the ideas of the book began to take shape after he returned to philosophy in the late 1920s. He had studied philosophy with Bertrand Russell in Cambridge between 1911 and 1913 and had written the *Tractatus* during the First World War while serving in the Austrian army. After his release from a prisoner-of-war camp in 1919 he taught in an elementary school in Austria and worked on the design and construction of a mansion for one of his sisters. Although not completely cut off from philosophy during the 1920s, he was not, as he had been for most of the previous decade, preoccupied by it. It was not until 1929, when he returned to Cambridge, that he again dedicated himself fully to philosophical work. Only then did he seriously rethink his earlier views and begin the inquiries that led to the *Investigations*.

What prompted Wittgenstein to return to philosophy is difficult to say. There can, however, be little doubt that at around this time he came to realize that the *Tractatus* contained 'grave mistakes' (p. x). His second thoughts, coupled with the criticisms of those with whom he discussed his ideas – notably the philosopher Frank Ramsey and the economist Piero Sraffa – convinced him that he needed to reconsider the issues he had taken himself to have resolved. Whether this meant that he came to repudiate the aim of the *Tractatus* (as is usually supposed) or came to question the means he had used in this book (as I am inclined to believe) is not something that needs discussing here. The important thing is that the *Investigations* differs radically from the *Tractatus* in its style and tone.

Wittgenstein says it helps when reading the *Investigations* to compare what he says with what he wrote in the *Tractatus*. There is a lot of truth to this, and I shall from time to time mention Wittgenstein's 'old thoughts' to clarify his new ones (p. x). But it is not at all obvious that his new thoughts can 'be seen in the right light only by contrast with and against the background of [his] old ways of thinking'. Besides the awkward fact that the *Tractatus* is extraordinarily difficult to understand, focussing on the similarities and differences between the two works can make Wittgenstein's target seem narrower than it is. We should not assume that in the *Investigations* Wittgenstein challenges only the shortcomings of one particular book. He takes issue with the thinking that animates past and present philosophy, even the very enterprise of philosophy itself.

The 'thoughts' of the *Investigations* were culled from notebooks, manuscripts and typescripts (p. ix). Wittgenstein fashioned this work by pruning, supplementing and reorganizing his reflections, and we are to think of its '*remarks*' as the 'precipitate' of his philosophical inquiries. (Here and throughout this book the italics are Wittgenstein's.) Initially Wittgenstein seems to have hoped he could present his ideas 'in a natural order and without breaks', but he soon came to think they would be 'crippled' if he 'tried to force them on in any single direction against their natural inclination'. This was, he tells us, not accidental but 'connected with the very nature of the investigation'. Given what he was attempting to accomplish, he had to 'travel over a wide field of thought criss-cross in every direction'. He could not expect to provide more than 'a number of sketches of the landscape' he had covered in the course of his 'long and involved journeyings'.

While the *Investigations* may be 'really only an album', it is not a hodgepodge (p. ix). It is no more a miscellany of aphorisms than a typical family album is a jumble of unrelated pictures. Wittgenstein does, it is true, frequently 'make a sudden change, jumping from one topic to another', and there can be no denying that 'the same or almost the same points' are 'always being approached afresh from different directions'. But the way the remarks of the book are grouped together is hardly haphazard. (Unlike most other volumes of Wittgenstein's writings, the arrangement of the sections of the *Investigations* discussed here is Wittgenstein's own, not that of an editor.) Wittgenstein carefully considered how he could best provide 'a picture of the landscape', and we should not assume that he could have presented his ideas in a more conventional form had he tried or that somebody else could have done better. The safest policy, at least to start with, is to take Wittgenstein at his word and allow that his way of proceeding may be, as he says, integrally 'connected' with what he is trying to communicate.

A particularly striking feature of the 'Preface' is its high moral tone and its pessimism. Wittgenstein was deeply bothered by what seemed to him to be his moral failings, and there is no reason to doubt he deplored his 'vanity' about his 'results' being circulated 'variously misunderstood, more or less mangled or watered down' (pp. ix–x). Nor should his remarks about the 'poverty' and 'darkness' of the times be discounted (p. x). Besides being troubled by the dreadful situation in Europe at the time he was writing, he was profoundly antipathetic to the modern world with its emphasis on technological novelty and scientific progress. It was not for nothing that he chose as a motto for his book the nineteenth-century Viennese playwright Johann Nestroy's observation (omitted from the monolingual English edition of the *Investigations*): 'In general progress looks much greater than it really is'. (This is not the place to discuss Wittgenstein's personal opinions, his private struggles and his relations with others. I shall only say that his life story makes for fascinating reading.[2])

Wittgenstein imposed enormous demands on himself and agonized over whether the *Investigations* was a 'good book' (p. x). He seems to have believed it to be aesthetically inferior to the *Tractatus* but felt, at least partly for the reasons he details in his Preface, that he could not produce a better book. All he could do – and all he did between January 1945, the date of the Preface, and April 1951, the date of his death – was polish what he had already written. (Between 1945 and 1951 Wittgenstein revised and added new material to part I of the *Investigations*, wrote the material that appears as part II, and drafted other work, nearly all of which has been published; §§1–133 were mostly drafted early in the 1930s and all but a few of them had been written by 1937.) Perhaps in 1945 he believed he could meet his own exceptionally high standards only by reworking and refining everything from beginning to end, and the time for that, in his own mind at least, was well and truly past.

Sections 1 and 2: The shopkeeper and the builders

In these sections Wittgenstein explains and examines a simple philo-sophical conception of language. He expresses his thoughts succinctly, and it is important to remember he does not wish to spare us 'the trouble of thinking' (p. x). Elsewhere he says: 'Sometimes a sentence can be understood only if it is read at the *right tempo*. My sentences are all supposed to be read *slowly*'.[1]

Section 1

Wittgenstein begins with a quotation from Augustine's *Confessions*, a work he greatly admired. Augustine observes that he learnt words by watching and hearing his elders name objects. 'When they (my elders) named some object', he tells us, 'I grasped that the thing was called by the sound they uttered'. This idea – that we learn words by coming to understand 'what objects they signif[y]' – should be familiar. Most people are inclined to think we learn language by learning the names of things.

In the paragraph following the quotation, Wittgenstein introduces a 'particular picture of the essence of human language' that Augustine's remarks 'give us' and isolates an 'idea' that has its 'roots' in this picture. Simply stated, the 'picture' takes language to consist of sentences comprising words that name objects, while the 'idea' adds that the meaning of a word is the thing with which it is correlated. Consider 'Spot is black'. According to the picture, this sentence essen-tially comprises two names, 'Spot' and 'black'. According to the idea, the meaning of 'Spot' is a certain dog with this name and the meaning of 'black' a certain colour. If I were to ask you what you mean by 'Spot' and 'black' you would doubtless refer me to a particular dog and a particular colour.

Wittgenstein is drawing our attention to a picture of language that 'seems to [him]' to be 'give[n]' by Augustine's autobiographical remarks. He is not suggesting that Augustine stated – or even would have recognized – this picture. It is unimportant that the picture makes no mention of the way language is learnt and is silent about the teacher's gestures, expressions and tone of voice. Nor is it significant that Augustine does not explicitly state that sentences are combinations of names, the meanings of which are the objects they stand for. Wittgenstein only claims that Augustine can be read as assuming that naming is central to language. All that matters is that he could have had this conception of language in mind when he spoke of himself as having grasped that certain things were 'called by' certain sounds and as having come to understand what words 'signified'. In another discussion of Augustine's remarks, Wittgenstein speaks of him as having taken '*[n]aming* [to be] the foundation, the be all and end all of language'.[2]

Similarly it is irrelevant that most philosophical accounts of language are more sophisticated than the one Wittgenstein takes Augustine's remarks to give us. He knows he is not doing full justice to what philosophers have said – he has not forgotten that what he says about language in the *Tractatus* is much more subtle. The picture he sketches in §1 is simply one he thinks philosophers and others interested in language more or less unquestioningly take to be a good basis on which to build a full-fledged theory. What concerns him are our first thoughts, not our last ones. He is interested in our preconceptions about the nature of language and how it functions, not in how philosophers refine and embellish them.

Next Wittgenstein observes that Augustine focusses on names at the expense of other kinds of words. If you take words to name objects, you are probably thinking of people's names and of nouns like 'table', 'chair' and 'bread'. It is unlikely you are thinking of verbs such as 'sing', which name actions, or adjectives such as 'heavy', which name properties of things, to say nothing of prepositions such as 'with'. In the case of the sentence 'Spot is black', you are likely to do as I did – fasten onto the proper name 'Spot' and the noun 'black' and ignore the word 'is'. In an earlier work Wittgenstein wrote: 'He [i.e. Augustine] does not primarily think of such words as "today", "not", "but", "perhaps" '.[3]

Wittgenstein is not suggesting that philosophers who focus 'primarily' on nouns and names do not know what they are doing, even less implying that they are wrong to focus on them. He is reminding us that people who think like Augustine usually treat verbs and adjectives 'secondarily' and regard 'the remaining kinds of words as something that will take care of itself'. He knows it is widely thought to be a good policy in philosophy, as in science, to begin with simple cases, and he confines himself to underlining that this is what philosophers tend to think. His object is to get us to recognize that proper names and nouns are usually taken to play a central role in language and to consider whether we are right to focus on them initially to the exclusion of everything else.

Having noted that those who think of words as Augustine does are thinking primarily of names and proper names, Wittgenstein introduces a particular use of language, one in which a shopkeeper fills an order on a slip of paper for five red apples. This use of language is easy to visualize – a film director would have no difficulty directing a scene in accordance with Wittgenstein's description. We are to imagine the shopkeeper going to a drawer marked 'apples', checking what the word 'red' corresponds to on a colour chart, and counting out apples that match the colour on the chart: one, two, three, four, five. This is not how shopkeepers normally fill orders, but it is one way they could fill them. As Wittgenstein says: 'It is in this and similar ways that one operates with words'.

Wittgenstein does not say that the example of the shopkeeper accords with or conflicts with the picture of sentences as comprising names. Nor does he explain how it relates to the idea that the meanings of words are the objects for which they stand; he only asks us to consider the example as a 'use of language'. He introduces the shopkeeper's use of words for the purpose of exploring the picture of language he takes to be given by Augustine's remarks (and the idea he takes to be associated with this picture). His hope is that everyone will agree that the example of the shopkeeper fills the bill.

It is tempting to think Wittgenstein's description of the interchange between the shopkeeper and the shopper is incomplete. Certainly those who take sentences to comprise names and the meanings of words to be what they stand for are likely to think Wittgenstein should have added that the shopkeeper knows 'where and how he is to look up the word "red" and what he is to do with the word "five"'. It seems obvious that the shopkeeper acts as he does because he knows 'five' names a specific number, 'red' a specific colour, and 'apple' a specific sort of fruit. And it seems equally undeniable that what the shopkeeper is determining when he looks up the word 'red' in his table is its meaning.

Wittgenstein resists this line of argument. It is, he suggests, far from clear that his description is incomplete. There is no need to invoke the picture of words as naming objects to understand the exchange between the shopper and the shopkeeper (or to invoke the idea that their meanings are the objects they stand for). Adding that 'five' is correlated with the number five, 'red' with the colour red, and 'apple' with such-and-such sort of fruit does not illuminate anything. It is enough to observe that the shopkeeper opens the drawer marked 'apples', checks which colour 'red' corresponds to in his table, and counts out five apples of the required colour. Nothing is gained by saying the shopkeeper is determining the meaning of the word 'red' when he consults his chart. There does not have to be anything he does besides look up the word 'red' in his table and find the colour sample next to it.

But is this really all there is to it? Nobody looking for an account of how 'one operates with words' will accept Wittgenstein's laconic response that the shopkeeper '*acts* as ... described'. While Wittgenstein can claim to have described how the shopkeeper acts, he cannot claim to have explained how this person manages to do what he does. It is no answer to the question of how the shopkeeper succeeds in filling the shopper's order that 'explanations come to an end somewhere'. The crucial question is not whether explanations must always come to end but whether in the particular case of the shopkeeper they come to an end so quickly. Surely the more reasonable view is that he manages to fill the shopper's order because the words on the slip he has been given mean something. What is needed, it would seem, is an account of 'the essence of human language' comparable to the account Wittgenstein discerns in Augustine's remarks.

Wittgenstein probes the suggestion that more needs to be said about the shopkeeper by considering the question '[W]hat is the meaning of the word "five"?'. (While this question does not appear in quotation marks, the dash makes it clear that it is to be understood as a response to what has just been said.) You must, Wittgenstein imagines someone responding, concede that the shopkeeper would not have proceeded as he did – ignoring the possibility of chance – had he not known the meaning of the word 'five' (and the meanings of the other two words on the shopper's slip). Moreover is it not indisputable that the shopkeeper knows the meaning of 'five' only if he has memorized the cardinal numbers, one, two, three, etc.? Presumably to know this series one must know the numbers 'by heart'.

Wittgenstein again dismisses what is being suggested. He insists that we can understand the shopkeeper's actions without assuming he knows what 'five' means (and what 'red' and 'apple' mean). 'No such thing was in question here', he declares, 'only how the word "five" is used'. It is pointless to note that the shopkeeper knows the meanings of the words on the slip. Nothing is gained by stating that he is able to fill the order successfully because he knows that the first word on the shopper's slip means five, the second red and the third apples. Once it has been pointed out what the shopkeeper does (open the drawer marked 'apples', etc.) everything that needs to be said has been said.

None of this implies that Wittgenstein has refuted the idea that language essentially comprises names, the meanings of which are the objects they stand for. Many other considerations may be advanced to bolster this idea. The picture that Augustine's autobiographical remarks give us is extremely powerful, and Wittgenstein would not for a minute claim to be able to dislodge it by a brief examination of a single example. This is his opening salvo.

Section 2

Wittgenstein first mentions two ways of regarding 'the philosophical concept of meaning' that he discerns in Augustine's remarks. We may think of this concept as having 'its place in a primitive idea of the way language functions'. Or we may think of it as 'the idea of a language more primitive than ours', one that has many fewer resources than languages like English and German.

A language for which 'the description given by Augustine is right' is the language used by a group of builders to get their assistants to fetch building-stones. In this example, as in the example of the shopkeeper, Wittgenstein concentrates on language used to order someone to do something. We are to imagine the builder's assistant bringing a block when the builder calls out 'Block!', a pillar when he calls out 'Pillar!', a slab when he calls out 'Slab!' and a beam when he calls out 'Beam!'. Here and in the discussion of the shopkeeper in §1, Wittgenstein is concerned with how people operate with words, not with how they acquire language. He will return later to Augustine's conception of how we learn to speak.

By 'the description given by Augustine' Wittgenstein means the idea of language introduced in §1. It is unimportant that there is no combination of names in the builders' language (apart from simple sequences of commands), and irrelevant that Augustine describes how he came to understand the meanings of words. Wittgenstein takes Augustine's description to be right for the builders' language because the words of this language can be regarded as correlated with objects along the lines Augustine mentions. It is, Wittgenstein wants us to agree, reasonable to think of the words 'block', 'pillar', 'slab' and 'beam' as naming different kinds of building-stone. One might even go so far as to say 'every word [of the builder's language] has a meaning', '[t]his meaning is correlated with the word', and 'the object for which the word stands' is its meaning (§1).

Wittgenstein urges us to regard the builders as speaking 'a complete primitive language'. We are not to think of them as signalling machines and their assistants as responding to calls in the way that a door responds to being pushed but to think of them as using language in much the same way as the shopkeeper and shopper. In this respect, I take it, Wittgenstein would like us to agree that the builder who calls out 'Slab!' when he wants a block and the assistant who brings a block when told to bring a slab are properly spoken of as having made mistakes. They should not be regarded as having broken down.

Wittgenstein's telling us to '[c]onceive [the builders' language] as a complete primitive language' is rather like a physicist's telling us to conceive a free-falling object as a self-contained system of mechanics. The account of language adumbrated in §1 is no less right for the builders' rudimentary language than the physicist's description is right for the rudimentary physical phenomenon of a free-falling object. Criticizing Wittgenstein for ignoring supposedly essential facts about communication is as inappropriate as criticizing the physicist for ignoring air resistance and the influence of other bodies. (This is not to suggest that Wittgenstein intends us to think of the model of the builder's language as explanatory in the way the physicist's model of a free-falling object is. I am only noting that Wittgenstein's injunction 'Conceive this as a complete primitive language' makes good sense. We do not have to read him as, wittingly or unwittingly, saying something problematic, still less take him to be hoping we shall object that the builder's four words cannot be regarded as a language.)

In sum, Wittgenstein mainly does three things in §§1–2. He introduces a rudimentary philosophical picture of language as essentially comprising names (and an accompanying idea about the meanings of names). He provides a simple example of how we operate with words, the example of the shopkeeper, for which the question of the meaning of words seems out of place. And he outlines a 'complete primitive language', the builders' language, for which the philosophical conception of words as naming objects 'is right'.

Interlude (1): 'No such thing was in question here'

The opening two sections of the *Investigations* are, I think it clear, exploratory and critical. Wittgenstein mainly invites us to reflect on an assumption to which we are inclined to gravitate when we think about language, namely the assumption that sentences comprise names, the meanings of which are the things they name. He wants us to consider whether this way of conceiving how we manage to say things captures 'the essence of human language' (§1) and suggests it is better regarded as a 'primitive idea' or as the idea of a 'primitive language' (§2). Generally speaking, his aim in §§1–2 seems to be twofold: to get us to appreciate the power of a particular 'philosophical conception of meaning' and to get us to ask ourselves whether it is as obvious as it appears at first sight. He would like us to scrutinize this conception with an eye to figuring out why it seems so reasonable and how it might be defended against the criticisms of someone, like himself, who is disinclined to accept it.

Wittgenstein neither endorses nor rejects the 'picture' of language he takes Augustine's remarks to 'give us' (§1). He chides those who take it to clarify the nature of language for forgetting the differences between kinds of words. But he also acknowledges, indeed emphasizes, that languages exist 'for which the description given by Augustine is right' (§2). Even when he discusses the shopkeeper in the last paragraph of §1, he draws no definite conclusions. He mentions an explanation of the transaction between the shopper and the shopkeeper that we are likely to find attractive and challenges the suggestion that this explanation illuminates what transpires between them. He does not provide an alternative explanation of the shopkeeper's use of language, never mind advance a philosophical thesis, either positive or negative, about the meanings of words.

Contrary to what is often suggested, Wittgenstein does not suggest or insinuate in §1 that the meanings of words are identical to their uses. He does, it is true, speak of the use of words when discussing the shopkeeper's actions. But he does not refer to their uses as their meanings. There is nothing in the text to suggest he equates the meaning of the word 'five' with the shopkeeper's use of it, and nothing to indicate that he believes that what the shopkeeper learnt by heart when he learnt its meaning was its use. As a matter of fact, Wittgenstein contrasts the meaning of a word with its use. When discussing the shopkeeper's use of words, he flatly states that '[no] such thing [as the meaning of the word "five"] was in question here, only how the word is used'. All he commits himself to is the anodyne idea that what a word means is connected with how it is used.

Likewise it is a mistake to read Wittgenstein as promoting a philosophical conception about the relative importance of actions and words. When he emphasizes that the shopkeeper '*acts*' in the way he describes and reminds us that 'explanations come to an end somewhere', he is not putting forward a view about the relative importance of words and actions. What he says does not carry this sort of weight. His aim is rather to turn aside the question of how the shopkeeper knows 'where and how he is to look up the word "red" and what he is to do with the word "five" '. He wants us to consider what could possibly be said in addition to what he has already said – except for incidental detail – that would make things clearer. We are not supposed to conclude that actions are more fundamental than words, only come to see that it is far from obvious that the description of the shopkeeper's actions given in §1 is, in any interesting sense, incomplete.

Nor should §§1–2 be regarded as containing an argument against the idea that words have meanings. Wittgenstein is not denying the undeniable but inviting us to scrutinize carefully one important 'philosophical concept of meaning'. What he is challenging is the widespread belief that our linguistic transactions cannot properly be understood without invoking a philosophical conception of meaning of the sort he sketches. He is trying to get us to see that what the word 'five' stands for, if anything, is irrelevant for understanding what the shopkeeper is doing when he fulfils the shopper's order. All that matters is that the shopkeeper 'knows [the cardinal numbers] by heart' and knows 'how the word "five" is used'. Moreover Wittgenstein allows that the meaning of a word may be the object it stands for. Although he questions this for the language we speak with its verbs, adjectives and prepositions, he does not hesitate to characterize the builder's language as 'a language for which the description given by Augustine is right' (§2).

The discussion of the shopkeeper illustrates the sort of critical examination of philosophical theses I take Wittgenstein to favour. In this discussion he explores a rudimentary conception of language and pinpoints a worry that often leads people to embrace it, namely that we cannot understand how people manage to fulfil orders if we do not accept this conception (or something similar). He uses the case of the shopkeeper to probe the philosophical picture of meaning he isolates in §1 in a preliminary and tentative fashion. He does not deny that more can be said on its behalf and would admit that there are many ways a person may respond to what he says that need tracking down – indeed he would insist on it. For instance he would agree that the question of what the shopkeeper is doing when he looks at his table deserves careful scrutiny (this will occupy him later on). In fact I think he would agree he has done no more than discuss in a cursory fashion a couple of objections related to the meaning of the word 'five'.

This is not to suggest we should regard Wittgenstein as disparaging substantive philosophical doctrines. We cannot conclude from what he says in §§1–2 that he opposes philosophical speculation. The most these sections show is that he thinks philosophers go astray because their thinking is dominated by a particular picture of language. At the moment we are in no position to know whether he will continue to explore philosophers' accounts of language or turn to the task of developing his own account. All we can conclude is that Wittgenstein's opening remarks do not encapsulate a philosophical conception of language. To suppose otherwise is to read into them claims that are not there.

Sections 3 to 7: Teaching by training

The five sections in this instalment are devoted to exploring the picture introduced in §1. Wittgenstein stresses that the picture is not so much incorrect as limited, recommends we look at simple examples as an aid to clarifying how we operate with words, and examines the practice of teaching words by pointing to objects. In addition he introduces the idea of a language-game.

Section 3

While Augustine describes 'a system of communication', his description does not apply to all systems of communication. It is, Wittgenstein notes, 'appropriate, but only for [a] narrowly circumscribed region'. To say that the builders' language is a language for which 'the description given by Augustine is right' (§2) is not to say that 'everything we call language is this system'. There are many clear cases to which Augustine's description does not apply. For one thing, as Wittgenstein notes in §1, 'Augustine does not speak of there being any difference between kinds of word'.

Conceiving language as comprising words that name objects is comparable to conceiving games as activities in which pieces are moved on a board in accordance with rules. The person who thinks language consists of names and regards the builders' language as typical is like the person who thinks all games are board games and regards chess as typical. In both cases one sort of example is wrongly taken to epitomize them all.

It is always possible to make definitions 'correct' by 'expressly restricting' them to the cases to which they apply. We can make the definition of language as comprising words that name objects correct by limiting it to languages like the builders' language, and we can make the definition of a game as an activity involving the movement of pieces on a board correct by limiting it to board games like chess and draughts. But this hardly means we should accept the picture of 'the essence of human language' adumbrated in §1 or the conception of 'game' as 'consist[ing] of moving objects about on a surface according to certain rules ...'. There is an enormous difference between singling out what is essential to a system of communication or a game and legislating what counts as one. The shopkeeper's exchange with the shopper is a verbal exchange whatever we choose to call it just as football is a competitive activity whatever we take the word 'game' to cover. While definitions can always be made correct by restricting them, this does not alter the facts. (Wittgenstein's use of the familiar German *du* form of 'you' here and in what follows suggests that he regards himself as close to his opponents and feels the pull of the views they defend. In fact he rarely examines views he does not take seriously.)

Wittgenstein's point is that the philosophical conception of words as names of objects is a caricature of language. Like other caricatures, it highlights some aspects of what is being caricatured but only at the expense of others. There is a grain of truth in the philosophical conception of language sketched in §1 since it fits some systems of communication. But by no stretch of the imagination can it be regarded as delineating 'the essence of human language'.

Section 4

The conception of language as fundamentally comprising names is 'over-simple'. Taking words to be names is comparable to taking the letters of a script to have a single function when they actually have several. It is like taking the letter 'a' of a script 'in which the letters [are] used to stand for sounds, and also as signs of emphasis and punctuation' to stand just for the sound aye. Regarding every word as a name is as much a mistake as regarding letters as standing exclusively for sounds when they may also be used for emphasis and to indicate how they are grouped together.

Section 5

If we examine how the shopkeeper operates with words, we 'get an inkling' of how misleading the 'general notion of the meaning of a word' introduced in §1 can be. This person's use of language comports poorly with the philosophical conception of words as names, the meanings of which are the objects they stand for. The meaning of his words is not 'in question here, only how [the words are] used' (§1). As we saw, there is no need to assume that the shopkeeper must know the meanings of 'five', 'red' and 'apple' to be able to fill the shopper's order.

The conception of words as meaning what they stand for 'surrounds the working of language with a haze which makes clear vision impossible'. To understand 'the aim and functioning of words' we need to lower our sights and consider 'the phenomena of language in primitive kinds of application'. Focussing on simple – actual or imaginary – uses of language where the phenomena are most perspicuous is valuable because it helps disperse 'the fog'. (Compare the suggestion that the essential purpose of society is to protect its citizens from attack. This obscures how societies function, and it helps to disperse the fog to consider how simple – actual or imaginary – social groups operate.)

At the end of the section Wittgenstein returns to the question of how we learn to speak a language. Having focussed in the last four sections on how language is used to communicate, he now directs his attention to how it is learnt in the first place. When learning to talk, he points out, children use 'primitive forms of language' comparable to the shopkeeper's and builders' uses of language described in §1 and §2.

The teaching of language 'is not explanation, but training' – at least initially. (Elsewhere Wittgenstein notes that he is 'using the word "trained" in a way strictly analogous to that in which we talk of an animal being trained to do certain things. It is done by means of example, reward, punishment, and suchlike'.[1]) One cannot explain the meaning of 'red' to a child who does not know any words. To understand the sentence 'This is called "red"', the child must already understand the construction 'This is called ...'. Initially there is no alternative to using gestures, saying words while pointing to the things, and the like.

When Wittgenstein says 'the teaching of language is not explanation, but training', he is not reporting an empirical finding or putting forward a hypothesis about how children learn language. He is simply noting that children initially use 'forms of language' similar to the simple forms of language he has been considering. This is not intended to be novel or surprising. It is worth noting only because it is often overlooked.

Section 6

Wittgenstein observes that we can imagine the builders' language of §2 as 'the *whole* language of A and B; even the whole language of a tribe'. This is not an unreasonable suggestion. As I noted when commenting on §2, conceiving the builders' language 'as a complete primitive language' (§2) is no more outlandish than conceiving of a free-falling object as a self-contained system of mechanics. Wittgenstein's point is that we can get clear about the 'primitive forms of language' children use when learning language by considering how the builders' children would be taught to issue and respond to the calls 'Block!', 'Pillar!', 'Slab!' and 'Beam!'. The important thing to notice is that 'the children are brought up to perform *these* actions, to use *these* words as they do so, and to react in *this* way to the words of others'.

Wittgenstein observes that the builders will train their children by pointing to a block while saying 'block', to a pillar while saying 'pillar', etc. Such teaching is obviously important, and it is not by chance that Augustine should say he 'grasped that the thing was called by the sound [his elders] uttered when they meant to point it out'.

When the builders teach words by pointing to objects, they are engaged in a process of 'ostensive teaching', not one of 'ostensive definition'. They are in no position to define 'block', 'pillar', 'slab' and 'beam' since they lack the words 'this', 'is', 'called' and 'a'. All they can do is train their children using gestures and other non-linguistic means. (Wittgenstein considers the technique of teaching words by pointing to objects and saying 'This is a such and such' or 'This is called "such and such"' later on.)

There is no suggestion here that a child can only be trained by pointing to objects while uttering their names or that ostensive teaching is essential to language learning. Wittgenstein speaks of ostensive teaching as 'part of the training' of the builders' children and explicitly notes that the way children are trained could 'be imagined otherwise'. Nothing he says precludes the possibility of the builders' children learning their language by watching their parents at work or their being born with language or their acquiring it by taking pills. His point is much more modest. He is saying that ostensive teaching is part of the training for people like us, that 'it is so with human beings'.

Having remarked on the importance of ostensive teaching, Wittgenstein notes that this sort of teaching may be thought of as 'establish[ing] an association between the word and the thing'. When children are taught words by being shown objects, they do what Augustine says he did – they learn that words are correlated with what they are shown. They come to appreciate that 'slab' is correlated with one sort of building-stone, 'block' with another sort of building-stone, and so on. This is not to say they come to possess information about these correlations, only to observe that they come to take words to be correlated with things. Initially the children are in no position to formulate such correlations; indeed it is impossible for the builders to express in their language what their four words are correlated with.

To say that ostensive teaching connects words with things can 'mean various things'. One possibility, one we are 'very likely [to think] of first of all', is that it connects words with images. (When asked, people often say that what they mean by a word like 'slab' is a picture of a slab they have in mind.) The thought is that, in the course of learning to speak, the builders' children come to associate 'slab' with a mental picture of a slab, 'block' with a mental picture of block, etc. Their words become connected with images somewhat as keys on a piano are connected with musical tones. The builders are to be regarded as having an image of a slab whenever they hear or say the word 'slab' just as you and I hear a certain sound whenever middle C is struck on a piano. (Also compare the 'over-simple' conception of the script mentioned in §4, the letters of which are correlated with sounds.)

Wittgenstein allows that the builders' words may be connected with images but insists that 'in the language of §2 it is *not* the purpose of the words to evoke images'. The purpose of teaching the builders' children the word 'slab' is to have them respond to the call 'Slab!' by fetching a slab. The images evoked by words, if any, are irrelevant. On the one hand the child who fails to fetch a slab when 'Slab!' is called out cannot be said, all things being equal, to understand the command whatever images he or she has. On the other hand the child who fetches a slab when so commanded is properly regarded, odd situations aside, as understanding the command regardless of the images, if any, he or she has. While a builder who has an image of a slab whenever he hears the call 'Slab' may find it easier to go about his business, this is not the 'purpose' of the call. The 'purpose' of 'Slab!' is to have a slab fetched, not to produce an image of a slab.

The same would be true even if ostensive teaching had the effect of associating words with images, and the word 'Slab!' invariably evoked an image of a slab. It would still be wrong to conclude that words mean the images with which they are associated. You might have an image of a slab every time you hear the call 'Slab!' yet still not know you are supposed to bring a slab. It might prompt you to bring one but then again it might prompt you to sit on one, take one away, fetch some other sort of building-stone or merely nod in agreement. Images no more tell us how they are to be understood than words do. (Wittgenstein will develop this point later on; the thing to notice is that neither the image of a slab nor the call 'Slab!' tells us – by itself – that a slab should be fetched.)

Wittgenstein does not claim to have refuted the 'picture of the essence of human language' sketched in §1. He is aware that Augustine says nothing about images and would agree that a picture of language of the sort he sketches cannot be dislodged by challenging one version of it. Even on Wittgenstein's own reckoning, the idea that words mean the images with which they are associated is only an idea 'one very likely thinks [of] first of all'. Wittgenstein's aim is to give us 'an inkling' of how a 'general notion of the meaning of a word' obscures the way language functions (§5). He is noting that one way of articulating the general picture mentioned in §1 is questionable even for languages, like the builders' language, to which it seems to apply especially well.

Understanding the call 'Slab!' is not to be equated with having a particular sort of image but of 'act[ing] upon [the call] in such-and-such a way'. When the builders' children are taught the word, they are trained to do something – fetch a certain type of building-stone. The requisite 'understanding' is a consequence of the ostensive teaching coupled with 'a particular training'. To get children to fetch slabs, rather than to fetch blocks or nod in agreement, it is not enough to say the word 'slab' while pointing to a slab. One has to encourage them when they bring slabs, show them what to do and the like. It is hardly coincidental that Augustine refers to the expressions on his teachers' faces, the play of their eyes, the movements of other parts of their bodies and the tone of their voices (see §1).

Connecting a word with a thing no more 'effects the understanding of the word' than connecting a rod and a lever sets up a brake. The nature of the connection in the case of words depends on the character of the training just as the nature of the connection in the case of brakes depends on 'the whole rest of the mechanism'. Rods and levers can function very differently given different supports, and '[w]ith different training, the same ostensive teaching of [the builders'] words would have effected a quite different understanding'. A rod and a lever may be 'anything, or nothing' in the absence of the rest of the mechanism, and a word may mean anything, or nothing, in the absence of the support provided by the training.

Section 7

The practice of teaching words ostensively is comparable to the practice of calling out words of things that one wants fetched. A builder's child may learn to speak by saying the words of the language when shown appropriate building-stones or – more simply – by repeating words after a teacher. Both of these processes resemble the builders' use of language, and both are similar to the uses competent speakers make of their language. (Wittgenstein speaks of the process by which children learn language as 'resembling' language – rather than as a form of language – because he is concerned with the child's initial acquisition of words.)

The use of primitive languages like the builders' language and processes 'resembling language' such as learning a language may usefully be regarded as 'language-games'. While speaking and playing games are different in many respects, they are also importantly alike. Neither the practice of learning a language nor the practice of using words to get someone to do something is just a matter of stringing signs together. (Wittgenstein does not compare linguistic practices with games because he takes them to be unimportant or inconsequential. He does so to highlight the fact that language is used. As a matter of fact the German word 'Spiel' covers more than the English word 'game'; it can apply to play and even more generally to doing something.)

Words and actions rarely go together as closely as they do in the children's game of ring-a-ring-a-roses, but go together they do. (In this game, one is supposed to fall down at the words 'all fall down'. 'Ring-a-ring-a-roses' was added by the translator; Wittgenstein uses the word 'Reigenspielen', which literally means 'round dance games', and apparently preferred 'nursery rhymes' as a translation.) As the discussion of the builders makes clear, language-use is not something separate from the rest of what we do. When we use words, we operate with them, and it makes sense to regard 'the whole, consisting of language and the actions into which it is woven' as a 'language-game'.

Concentrating on language-games rather than on words and sentences is helpful because it serves as a counterbalance to philosophical conceptions of language like the one sketched in §1. When we compare the processes in which language is used with games, we are less likely to regard language as essentially comprising combinations of names. It becomes much harder to think of language in isolation and to ignore or discount how it is intertwined in our lives. Moreover Wittgenstein's way of regarding language has the advantage that it makes room for communication that does not involve spoken or written words. Signalling by means of flag movements or bodily gestures is no less reasonably regarded as a language-game than 'the whole process of using words in language (2)'.

Interlude (2): Dispersing the fog

The first seven sections of the *Investigations* set the scene and may be read as a prologue to the book. Wittgenstein extracts a 'picture of the essence of human language' from some of Augustine's remarks (§1), describes a language for which 'the description given by Augustine is right' (§2), observes that the conception of language Augustine described is not so much false as limited (§3 and §4), clarifies the technique of ostensive training, which figures so prominently in the thinking of those who take names to be central to language (§5 and §6), and points out that language consists of actions as well as words (§7). He does not advance a view of language of his own, still less purport to settle the philosophical problem of 'the essence of human language' (§1). He simply introduces one important philosophical view of meaning and brings up – in a preliminary way – some questions about it.

Is this all Wittgenstein is doing in these sections? In the eyes of many readers he is attempting to clear the way for his own philosophical theory of language, and in the eyes of many more he means to insinuate his own theories of meaning and ostensive teaching. In fact §7 is commonly thought to introduce a new view of language, one based on the concept of a language-game. Such a reading of Wittgenstein's remarks, however, labours under enormous difficulty. Not only does Wittgenstein not explicitly commit himself to any particular philosophical account of language in these sections, he is more naturally read as eschewing the idea that language requires philosophical explanation. After all, one of the major themes of the instalment is that an examination of primitive forms of language 'disperses the fog' that prevents our properly appreciating 'the aim and functioning of ... words' (§5).

In this regard it is important to notice that Wittgenstein speaks of 'Augustine's description' as 'over-simple' (§4). As he sees it, the picture Augustine's autobiographical remarks seem to 'give us' (§1) is not so much wrong as misleading. We get into difficulty because we take what is 'appropriate' for a certain 'narrowly circumscribed region' to apply to 'the whole of what [it is said to] describe' (§3). It is not that there are no languages that comprise names that mean what they name. What is objectionable is the easy assumption that all languages are of this sort, and Augustine's description applies to 'everything that we call language' (§3). Wittgenstein even says Augustine's description can be made 'correct' (§3), albeit only at the expense of what seem to be perfectly meaningful ways in which we operate with words. Actually it is striking how infrequently Wittgenstein speaks of philosophers' contentions as being true or false.

Nor should it be forgotten that Wittgenstein allows that the conception of words as meaning what they stand for 'has its place in a primitive idea of the way language functions' (§2). For him the conception sketched in §1 expresses a primitive belief, one that has grown up around our thinking of language over the years. He believes it should be explored and clarified rather than accepted or rejected. It is, he thinks, problematic because it is a primitive belief, one that, like many other primitive beliefs, misconstrues trivialities about a few examples of a phenomenon to be deep truths about the nature of the phenomenon itself. Nobody should regard the conception as false and its opposite as true. The trouble is rather that it misleadingly promotes one aspect of language at the expense of others.

Also reading Wittgenstein as intending to advance a new theory of meaning squares poorly with the fact that he begins by introducing a somewhat nebulous philosophical view of it. If he means to put forward his own theory, why does he focus on a simple 'picture' of the essence of language rather than on an account that philosophers deem interesting (for instance the account he propounded in the *Tractatus*)? And why does he bother to stress the value of studying 'the phenomena of language in primitive kinds of application' (§5)? Surely he is most reasonably regarded as casting his net broadly because he is interested in examining the inchoate intuitions that fuel philosophers' speculations. It is hard to imagine someone who does not have serious qualms about philosophers' theoretical manoeuvrings concentrating on the assumptions underlying philosophical thinking about language as intently as Wittgenstein does.

In any case, I do not think it can seriously be denied that the sections of the *Investigations* considered so far are meant to get us to reflect on the 'picture' of language as comprising names and the 'idea' that names mean what they stand for. Here Wittgenstein mainly warns us against uncritically accepting this notion of language and meaning. He urges us to look at the shopkeeper's language-game or the builders' language-game because he wants us to notice that it 'surrounds the working of language with a haze which makes clear vision impossible' (§5). His aim is to get us to recognize that this notion hinders at least as much as it helps. Why else would he have stressed that it obscures how different training can effect 'a quite different understanding' (§6)? And why else would he have suggested that it distorts our understanding of the way language is 'woven' into action (§7)?

I conclude that the remarks considered so far are nowhere near as substantive as often alleged. There is nothing in §§1–7 that shows Wittgenstein to be concerned with explaining this or that feature of language, never mind the phenomenon of language as such. He does not imply or assume it is possible to develop an account of the nature of language by examining primitive languages such as the builders' language, nor does he put forward a 'theory of language-games'. Just the reverse, he confines himself to encouraging us to consider carefully philosophers' conceptions of how language works. (All he does in §7 is introduce a useful turn of phrase and announce that he will call certain sorts of languages and certain sorts of processes 'language-games'.) Given what we have to go on up to now, we cannot be sure that he is not clearing the ground prior to launching yet another attack on the philosophical problem of how we manage to think and speak meaningfully. What we cannot do, it seems to me, is read §§1–7 as substantive and explanatory. Whatever happens next, these sections are exploratory and critical.

Sections 8 to 17: Primitive applications

Wittgenstein now turns his attention to numerals such as 'one', 'two' and 'three', demonstratives such as 'there' and 'this', and colour samples of the sort the shopkeeper uses to determine the colour of apples. In these ten sections, Wittgenstein examines commands involving these three new types of word in 'primitive kinds of application' (§5).

Section 8

Wittgenstein asks us to consider the builders' language described in §2 supplemented by numerals, demonstratives and colour samples. (Nothing of significance turns on his use of 'a' to signify one, 'b' to signify two, 'c' to signify three and 'd' to signify four. In an earlier version of these sections he used '1', '2', '3' and '4'.) Builders who know the new language can order their assistants to fetch a specified number of building-stones of a particular colour, order them to move an indicated stone to an indicated place, and such like. Thus a builder might call out 'b–slab' to get his assistant to fetch two slabs; call out 'this–there' while pointing to a building-stone and indicating a certain place to get him to move the stone there; and call out 'd–slab–there' while holding up a red colour sample to get him to do the same with four red slabs. In the last case the assistant will take a red slab for each of the letters up to 'd', then bring the slabs he has gathered to where the builder pointed.

Wittgenstein does not think that there is anything unusual about the expanded version of the builders' language, nor does he take himself to be telling us something we do not know. His goal is to clarify 'the aim and functioning' of three new sorts of words, this being something he takes to be obscured by the 'general notion of the meaning of a word' he has been examining (§5). We can, he thinks, get clearer about numerals, demonstratives and colour samples by comparing them with 'slab' and 'block'.

Section 9

Wittgenstein begins his discussion of the language introduced in §8 by considering how numerals and demonstratives are taught and used. (The use of colour samples is considered in §16.) He notes that children may be taught the numerals 'a', 'b', 'c', etc. by a process of ostensive teaching. The teacher counts out letters of the alphabet while pointing to building-stones one after another, and the child comes to know how they are used. This procedure is both similar to the procedure involved in teaching a word like 'slab' and different from it. The similarity is that the teacher points to objects. The difference is that the teacher says a series of words – 'a', 'b', 'c', etc. – which the child learns to repeat in order. (Many philosophers question whether numerals can be taught ostensively since the numbers with which they are correlated cannot be seen, tasted, touched, heard or smelt. For them only things accessible to one or more of the five senses can be defined by pointing.)

There is also a kind of ostensive teaching more like the teaching described in §6, namely the teaching of numerals that 'refer to groups of objects that can be taken in at a glance'. (At the end of the paragraph Wittgenstein notes that this is how children actually learn the use of the first five or six cardinal numerals.) We are to imagine the teacher pointing to two slabs and saying 'b' and the child coming to appreciate that 'b' is used to refer to pairs of things. As in the case of the word 'slab', the child learns the use of a single word rather than a series of words. The only difference is that the letters refer to groups of objects rather than to single objects.

Next Wittgenstein reminds us that demonstratives such as 'there' and 'this' are used very differently from words like 'block' and 'slab'. While 'there' and 'this' are also taught by pointing to things, the use of these words, in contrast to the use of 'block' and 'slab', involves a pointing gesture. If I say 'The slab is heavy', I do not normally have to point to a slab to make clear my meaning. But if I say 'This is heavy', I have to indicate in some way or other what I am speaking about.

Section 10

Wittgenstein now raises the question of what the words of the expanded version of the builders' language introduced in §8 *'signify'*.

One can imagine someone objecting that his remarks, while well and good as far as they go, do not go far enough, and he still owes us an account of how the words of language (8) manage to mean something. In response Wittgenstein declares, as he did in response to a similar question in §1, that he has already described how the words of the language are used. Nothing can be added to what was said in §9 that would clarify their use – apart from more information of the same general sort. It does not make things any clearer to say 'slab' signifies a certain sort of building-stone, 'a' signifies the number one, 'there' signifies a place, and 'red' signifies the colour red. To show what these words signify one has to show 'the kind of use they have'. Though less blunt here than in §1, Wittgenstein is saying much the same thing; he is saying 'Explanations come to an end somewhere. … No such thing [as meaning] was in question here' (§1). And once again few philosophers are likely to concede the point. They will argue that more explanation is both possible and necessary.

It may be helpful to mention that the word 'slab' signifies what we call slabs to someone who thinks it signifies what we call blocks. And when someone thinks that 'a', 'b' and 'c' signify building-stones rather than numbers or that 'c' signifies four rather than three, it may be useful, even necessary, to tell him or her what these letters signify. Still the question raised at the beginning of the section, '[W]hat do the words of [language (8)] *signify?*', remains. Saying that 'a' signifies the number one to remove a mistaken idea about what it signifies does not in any way illuminate the nature of signification and how words mean.

It is one thing to say 'The word ... signifies ...' when 'the kind of *"referring"* ... is already known', quite another to say the same thing when this is not known. If you know everything about the use of the word 'slab' apart from what it happens to signify, my telling you that it signifies what we call slabs might make all the difference. But it would be pointless for me to tell you 'slab' signifies slabs if you did not understand that the word refers to a type of building-stone rather than to a number or a colour.

There is a world of difference between using the phrase 'The word ... signifies ...' to allay misunderstanding and explaining what signification involves. When we use the phrase 'The word ... signifies ...' in everyday life, the person we are addressing normally knows what it means. We are not attempting to say something about the 'essence of human language'. Our aim is not to explain the nature of signification or anything else of philosophical interest, only to put the person right or show that we know what a word means or something equally commonplace.

Nor is it of any philosophical consequence that we can say of every word of language (8) that it signifies something. To allow that each of the words of this language signifies something is not to concede anything to the philosopher who seeks to know what it means to say they '*signify*'. While 'slab' certainly signifies a certain sort of building-stone, 'red' the colour red, 'a' the number one and 'there' an indicated place, the uses of these words could hardly be more different. One speaks of stacking slabs but not of stacking numbers and – as already noted – 'this' differs from 'slab' in that it has to be accompanied by an implicit if not explicit pointing gesture (see §9).

Saying every word of language (8) signifies, though true, only obscures matters. Nothing is gained by regarding the words of this language as all signifying. As Wittgenstein puts it, 'assimilating the descriptions of the uses of words in this way cannot make the uses any more like one another'. There is no escaping the fact that the uses of names for objects, colours, numbers and the like 'are absolutely unlike'.

Section 11

Wittgenstein first develops the point, stressed at the end of §10, about the uses of words being 'absolutely unlike' by comparing them with the uses of tools in a tool-box. ('Tools' is the translator's rendering of 'Werkzeuge' [literally 'work-things']. It is irrelevant that glue-pots, glue, nails and screws are hardware, not tools.) Wittgenstein wants us to notice that the 'functions of words are as diverse as the functions of [tools]'. While there are 'in both cases ... similarities', there are also differences. Words are no more reasonably regarded as having a single use because they all 'signify' than tools are reasonably regarded as having a single function because they all belong in tool-boxes.

'Especially when we are doing philosophy' – and trying to delineate 'the essence of human language' (§1) – we are fooled by the 'uniform appearance' of words. Since their '*application* is not presented to us so clearly', we are apt to think they have the same use. We wrongly take the fact that they look (and sound) much the same to mean they are used in more or less the same way as well. (Elsewhere Wittgenstein says: '[W]hen words in our ordinary language have prima facie analogous grammars we are inclined to try to interpret them analogously; i.e. we try to make the analogy hold throughout'.[1]) On the other hand when we think of words as 'tools' with different uses, we are less likely to be misled by their appearance and less likely to treat language along the lines Wittgenstein canvasses in §1.

Section 12

In addition the diverse uses of words can be compared with handles in the cabin of a locomotive, which also look 'more or less alike'. Words have many uses just as handles do. And, as before, there are similarities. One can no more deny that words are spoken or written than one can deny that handles are handled.

Section 13

Wittgenstein now returns to the question broached in §10 about what words '*signify*'. There he noted there are many circumstances in which it is appropriate to say 'This word signifies *this*'. Now he considers the claim that '[e]very word in language signifies something'. While this looks like a substantive philosophical claim, it is 'so far [to say] *nothing whatsoever*'. It is not enough to declare that words '*signify*'. In the absence of an explanation of what we mean by 'signify', declaring that they signify is empty.

We can always explain 'exactly *what* distinction we wish to make'. If we have in mind the idea that 'slab', 'red' and the other words of language (8) differ from 'brillig', 'Lilliburlero' and other words 'without meaning', we can say so. But this gets us no further ahead. We are not explaining the word 'signify'; we are using it (compare §10). Nothing of philosophical interest is being said about the signification of words.

Section 14

But how clear is it that '[w]hen we say: "Every word in language signifies something" we have so far said *nothing whatsoever*' (§13), that we have said nothing about how words mean? Saying every word signifies something seems no more empty than saying '*all* tools serve to modify something'. (Recall that words are compared with tools in §11.) In response Wittgenstein questions whether all tools are properly spoken of as 'modify[ing] something'. Rulers, glue-pots and nails do not modify anything, at least not in the way that hammers modify the position of nails. (It is no objection that Wittgenstein focuses on 'work-things' and counts glue-pots and nails as tools. A similar point can be made regarding tools. Tools for recording information such as cameras do not modify anything, nor do tools for finding one's way around such as maps, nor do scholarly tools such as books, articles and pamphlets.)

One might object that rulers modify our knowledge of length, glue-pots modify the temperature of the glue, and nails modify the things into which they are pounded. But this too is a useless manoeuvre. Nothing is 'gained by this assimilation of expressions' (also compare the last paragraph of §10.) Stretching the word 'modify' to cover whatever tools are used for only fosters the illusion that they function the same way.

Section 15

Wittgenstein next draws attention to what is 'perhaps the most straightforward way' the word 'signify' is used, namely to refer to the relation between a mark scratched on an object and the object itself. (In this regard it is helpful to remember that footballers are 'signified' by numbers or names on their uniforms.) This is one 'narrowly circumscribed region' where the picture of words as signifying objects is indeed 'appropriate' (compare §3).

In philosophy we need to remind ourselves that 'naming something is like attaching a label to a thing'. We shall then be less likely to forget that most words do not name objects and less puzzled about the way words signify. The closer we scrutinize the way '//' serves to identify a tool with two scratches on it (and '7' serves to identify a particular footballer), the harder it is to accept the idea that words signify in ways other than the uncontroversial ways alluded to in §10 and §13.

Section 16

Wittgenstein now examines the last of the three new devices introduced in §8, that of a colour sample. (Since colour samples are comparable to labels, the topic of §15, this is an appropriate place for him to discuss them.) He asks whether the colour samples the builders show their assistants are 'part of the *language*' and answers 'It is as you please'. We may regard the samples as something other than language since they are not words. But we may also think of them as part of language since they are used by the builders in the course of their linguistic transactions. (Also notice that colour samples are sometimes included in dictionaries to explain the meanings of colour words.) A colour sample can be said to be part of language or not a part of it just as the second occurrence of 'the' in 'Pronounce the word "the"' can be said to be part of this sentence or not a part of it. (The second 'the' is a sample of what is to be pronounced.) As Wittgenstein stresses in §3, the facts remain the same however we choose to describe them.

Still colour samples are better regarded as being 'among the instruments of the language'. While this is not the only way to think of them, 'it is most natural, and causes least confusion'. In particular, reckoning samples this way makes sense given Wittgenstein's concern with 'language and the actions into which it is woven' (§7). Undoubtedly, samples are essential to the language-games of fulfilling orders sketched in §1 and §8.

The parenthetical remark at the end of the section reminds us of the fact that the phrase '*this* sentence' can be regarded two ways in much the same way as colour samples and the word 'the' in 'Pronounce the word "the"'. Consider 'This sentence has five words'. The phrase 'this sentence' in this sentence can be thought of as part of the sentence or as referring to the sentence itself. There is no single correct way to think of it. In some contexts the first way will be superior, in other contexts the second way will be.

Section 17

We can say that language (8) comprises several different sorts of words. It is not wrong to speak of this language – as I did when I introduced it – as comprising numerals, demonstratives and colour samples as well as words for objects. But this does not show there is one correct way of classifying the words of a language. Words can be grouped according to their appearance, how they sound, their grammatical function and in many other ways, none of which is intrinsically better than the others. How we classify the words of a language 'depend[s] on the aim of the classification, – and on our own inclination'.

This becomes clearer if we compare words with tools or chess pieces. A classification of words as names, nouns, demonstratives and the like no more counts as correct in and of itself than a classification of tools according to their usefulness on a building site or a classification of chess pieces according to their point value. In each case different classifications are possible and different ones will be appropriate for different purposes.

Wittgenstein is not claiming to have demonstrated that there is not one ultimate or basic classification of words. He knows the analogy of words with chess can be questioned on the grounds that language is a different sort of phenomenon. And he knows it is possible to accept the analogy without forgoing the idea of an ultimate classification (for one thing classifying chess pieces by point value seems more natural than classifying them according to how they can move). Rather he is sowing a few seeds of doubt. He is noting that language is plausibly compared with chess and trying to get us to see that it is not at all obvious that words are properly classified from just one point of view.

Interlude (3): 'Every word in language signifies something'

§8, §9, §16 and §17 are relatively easy to understand. In these four sections Wittgenstein explores some of the ways in which numerals, demonstratives and colour samples function in language. Reflecting on how we use these three devices, he thinks we can 'perhaps get an inkling how much [the general notion of meaning introduced in §1] surrounds the working of language with a haze which makes clear vision impossible' (§5). Moreover the comparison of words with tools and with handles in the cabin of a locomotive in §11 and §12 is clear enough. Wittgenstein is reminding us of the fact, often overlooked by philosophers, that there are 'differences between kinds of words' (§1). Where difficulties arise is mainly over the question of how the remaining four sections – §10, §13, §14 and §15 – should be understood.

To appreciate what Wittgenstein is driving at we need to know why someone might insist that 'every word in language signifies something' (§13). Presumably nobody needs reminding that words have meanings, or that a sentence like 'Spot is black' says something, or that names designate individuals and nouns denote particular sorts of objects. Nor is it of any philosophical interest to be told that 'slab' means what the dictionary says it means or that it corresponds to the German word 'Platte' and the French word 'dalle'. Nor again is it news that words like 'brillig' and 'Lilliburlero' are very different from words that 'signify' such as 'slab', 'red' and 'there' (see §13). What prompts philosophers to insist that 'every word in language signifies something' is rather that they take 'signification' to be central to language. They are not making a trivial claim; they are isolating what they take to be a deep fact about language.

Philosophers will complain that Wittgenstein has not clarified how the words of language (8) '*signify*' (§10). What they want – and what Wittgenstein conspicuously fails to provide – is an account of how language functions. (Note that while Wittgenstein introduces the question of the nature of signification in connection with language (8), his discussion is not restricted to the words of this language.) Taking it to go without saying that 'slab' has something that 'brillig' does not have – a meaning – and supposing that language works only because its words are backed by meanings, they expect this idea to be developed and clarified. To their way of thinking, the early sections of the

Investigations fail to engage what they are concerned with. Wittgenstein not only does not explain how we are able to think about the world and how we manage to communicate, he does not even address the issue.

To clarify this complaint it helps to distinguish between two ways of explaining what happens when the builders' assistants fetch slabs in response to the builders calling out 'Slab!', one of which is at issue here, one of which is not. Explanations that draw attention to the way in which the builders, or other people, are trained and use the words they learn are utterly uninteresting from a philosophical standpoint. Philosophers who are concerned with how we operate with words seek a very different sort of explanation. They are looking for an explanation of how words signify, one that lays bare the mechanism or principles underlying the functioning of language. In their eyes what we need is an explanation of how the meanings of sentences are related to the meanings of their constituent words and how their constituent words manage to mean (compare the picture of language sketched in §1).

At bottom Wittgenstein's disagreement with the philosopher who wants to know what the words of language (8) '*signify*' turns on the possibility and necessity of a general explanation of language. Wittgenstein never denies that explanations of the meanings of words and sentences are often needed and available – he would not shunt off ordinary requests for explanation with the retort that 'explanations come to an end somewhere' (see §1). What he questions is only the philosopher's demand for a general explanation of language. He wants us to consider whether anything is required or could be provided over and above the mundane explanations of linguistic transaction we occasionally require and provide in everyday life.

In the sections under discussion, then, Wittgenstein is trying to get us to look askance at the apparently anodyne philosophical assumption that language can be – and needs to be – explained by referring to what its words '*signify*'. He stresses that misunderstandings can sometimes be allayed by noting what words signify because we are inclined to forget how different our ordinary notion of signification is from the philosopher's notion (see §10, §13 and §15). He contrasts the uniform appearance of words with the variety of ways in which they are used because we are prone – 'when we are doing philosophy' – to regard all words as names signifying objects (see §10 and §14). And he points out that the sentence 'every word in language signifies something' says '*nothing whatsoever*' to remind us that it is far from obvious that there is anything philosophically interesting to be said about signification (§13).

The important thing to notice is that Wittgenstein is attempting to disperse some of the fog surrounding our thinking about the meaning of words. The purpose of §§8–17 is to encourage us to consider the possibility that the philosopher's search for an explanation of how words '*signify*' may be futile and unnecessary. Wittgenstein discusses language (8) to draw attention to the various ways in which words are used and to underline the point that questions about the ordinary use of the word 'signify' are philosophically uninteresting. What concerns him is the feeling many of us have that there is an important question regarding signification, one that remains even when all the everyday facts about it are taken into account. As he sees it, an examination of the phenomena of language should help disabuse us of the idea that we are saying something philosophically interesting when we aver that 'every word in language signifies something'.

Sections 18 to 20: 'Bring me a slab'

Wittgenstein has been proceeding on the assumption that simple languages like those of §2 and §8 can be used to throw light on a language like English, which is much more complicated. In these three sections he explores some considerations that may seem to put this into question. He confronts the objection that languages (2) and (8) are not complete languages, examines the worry that the words of these languages function very differently from the corresponding words in the language we use in everyday life, and exposes some confusions regarding the relationship between our calls 'Slab!' and 'Bring me a slab'.

Section 18

You may object that our language with its abundance of resources is utterly unlike languages (2) and (8), which consist solely of orders. In response Wittgenstein asks us to consider whether our own language is complete. If you think languages are incomplete whenever they can be added to, you must count English as incomplete 'before the symbolism of chemistry and the notation of the infinitesimal calculus were incorporated in it' even though it served Chaucer and Shakespeare well enough. On the other hand if you allow that languages may be complete even though they may be added to, why think the builders' language is incomplete? The fact that their language is less rich than our own is, in this respect at least, irrelevant.

It is no more reasonable to insist that a language must have resources for raising questions and for making assertions in addition to resources for issuing orders than it is to insist that towns must have so many houses or streets. There are no good grounds for stipulating that towns must have at least, say, ten streets and a thousand houses or that language must have such and such resources. And if you think the builders' language is more like a group of houses than a town, it still seems wrong to regard it as incomplete.

Our language is comparable to an ancient city, which has grown over the years and was never 'incomplete'. Natural languages develop in much the same haphazard way as cities. New language-games appear and old ones disappear in response to our changing needs just as streets and buildings do. And like recent additions to cities, recent additions to language, notably those involving scientific and mathematical terms, are usually more 'regular ... and uniform'. (Here Wittgenstein tries to get us to look at matters differently by means of a metaphor. While this way of proceeding does not result in definite conclusions, it can be very persuasive.)

Section 19

A language might consist solely of orders and reports in battle – e.g. 'Move the first battalion forward' and 'The first battalion has taken the town'. Or it might consist solely of questions and the words 'yes' and 'no' – e.g. 'Is the weather good? Yes'; 'Is the prisoner guilty? No'. Such languages are no more difficult to conceive than the builders' language. Indeed each could be 'the whole language of a tribe' (§6). Moreover imagining a language is tantamount to imaging a form of life. It is to imagine - compare what Wittgenstein says in connection with language games in §7 - 'the whole, consisting of language and the actions into which it is woven'.

But how clear is it that a natural language such as English can be illuminated by considering a primitive language such as the builders' language? It is tempting to argue against Wittgenstein that the builders' language throws no light on English since the meanings of the builders' words are different from the meanings of our words. (In the *Brown Book* Wittgenstein mentions this difficulty immediately after introducing material that now occurs in §2 and §6. He writes: 'Objection: The word "brick" in [the builders' language] has not the meaning which it has in *our* language'.[1]) If the builders' call 'Slab!' is the same as our call 'Slab!', presumably it must correspond to our noun 'slab' or to our one-word sentence 'Slab!'. But it does not seem to correspond to either. It diverges from our word 'slab' since 'slab' is no more a call than the phrase 'a thick piece of stone'. And it diverges from our call 'Slab!' since this is equivalent to 'Bring me a slab', a sentence that includes words the builders do not have: 'bring', 'me' and 'a'. So, lacking any other plausible candidate, we seem forced to conclude that the words of language (2) are disconnected from the words of English.

Unsurprisingly Wittgenstein resists this line of argument. You can, he declares, regard the builders' call as 'a word and also a sentence'. It is – to borrow a phrase from §16 – 'as you please'. What matters is not how we choose to refer to the builders' call but the facts, specifically the role of the call in the language-game (compare §3 and §16). The crucial thing is what goes on when the builders use their words. Indeed we may take the builders' call 'Slab!' to be a limiting case of a sentence, one that comprises a single word. It is just as reasonable to think of their call as a 'degenerate sentence' as it is to think of a straight line, as mathematicians do, as a 'degenerate hyperbola'. 'In fact [the builders' call] *is* our 'elliptical' sentence: "Slab!"'. It is the call that in our language is elliptical for 'Bring me a slab'.

How good is this response? Has Wittgenstein managed to deflect the objection that the builders' call is different from ours? One might doubt it since our call 'Slab!' is elliptical for a sentence that cannot be stated in language (2), specifically 'Bring me a slab'. But this hardly answers Wittgenstein. 'Bring me a slab' may be regarded as long for 'Slab!' just as 'Slab!' may be regarded as short for 'Bring me a slab'. Nothing prevents our equating the builders' call with our command 'Slab!' and taking 'Bring me a slab' to be a roundabout way of saying what the builders say when they call out 'Slab!'.

Up to now Wittgenstein has been considering the objection that the builders' call 'Slab!' is different from our call 'Slab!'. In what follows he shifts his attention away from the builders' use of language to our own use of it and focusses on the question of whether our call 'Slab!' is parasitic on our call 'Bring me a slab'. This makes sense since showing our call 'Slab!' to be subordinate to 'Bring me a slab' would be tantamount to showing that the builders' call 'Slab!' is different from our call 'Slab!'.

It will not do to argue that 'Bring me a slab' must be more fundamental than 'Slab!' because 'if you shout "Slab!" you really mean: "Bring me a slab"'. Imagine calling out 'Slab!'. Do you *mean that* ["Bring me a slab"] while you *say* "Slab!"'? You would if you said 'Bring me a slab!' to yourself while you called out 'Slab!'. But this is not something we normally do; as a rule we do not say anything to ourselves, let alone what we 'really mean'.

Nor is it plausible to think that the sentence 'Slab!' has to be translated into the sentence 'Bring me a slab' before it is possible to say 'what someone means by it' (though, of course, one may provide a translation to clarify one's thoughts). If it were necessary to translate a sentence to understand it, the translation – 'Bring me a slab' – would be understandable only when translated into a third sentence. This sentence would be understandable only when translated into yet another sentence. And so on *ad infinitum*. Far more reasonable, surely, to think we mean the untranslated call 'Slab!' when we say 'Slab!'. Usually we mean what we say. As Wittgenstein puts it: '[I]f you can mean "Bring me a slab", why should you not also be able to mean "Slab!"?'.

Few philosophers who think our call 'Slab!' is parasitic on 'Bring me a slab!' and take 'Slab!' to really mean something other than 'Slab!' will find this convincing. They are likely to retort – I imagine them doing this with some irritation – 'When I call "Slab!", then what I want is, *that [someone] should bring me a slab!*'. But this proves nothing. The fact that I want a slab to be brought to me when I call out 'Slab!' hardly shows that 'Slab!' really means 'Bring me a slab'. My wanting you to bring me a slab need not consist in my having the thought that you should do this, even less in my thinking to myself 'Bring me a slab'. (In the *Brown Book* Wittgenstein asks: '[W]hat reason could we have to assert' that 'while [a builder] says aloud "brick!" he as a matter of fact always says in his mind, to himself, "Bring me a brick"?'.[2]) It is one thing to say 'Slab!' when one wants a slab to be brought, quite another to say it and to think the sentence 'Bring me a slab'. Taking people who say 'Slab!' to be thinking the sentence 'Bring me a slab' is hardly more credible than taking French speakers who say 'Venez ici' to be thinking the English sentence 'Come here'.

So far, then, Wittgenstein has been trying to turn back the objection that the builders' call 'Slab!' is different from our call 'Slab!'. He has been criticizing considerations that may be thought to show that 'if you shout "Slab!" you really mean "Bring me a slab"' (and are 'thinking in some form or other a different sentence from the one you utter'). We should resist the easy assumption that our call 'Slab!' is parasitic on our call 'Bring me a slab'. It is not at all clear that persons who do not have the words 'bring', 'me' and 'a' cannot mean by 'Slab!' the very same thing as we do. Thus – in the absence of further objections – Wittgenstein would seem to be well within his rights using languages (2) and (8) to throw light on our language.

Section 20

The discussion of §19 shows that Wittgenstein's use of the builders' language to illuminate our language can be defended against some apparently compelling objections. But there are still other objections. In this section Wittgenstein considers an important worry that the discussion of the last section might prompt. He again concentrates on the question of whether our words faithfully reflect what we mean.

If – as suggested in §19 – 'Bring me a slab' can be thought of as a 'lengthening' of 'Slab!', it would seem that a person can 'mean this expression [i.e. the expression "Bring me a slab"] as *one* long word corresponding to the single word "Slab!"'. But then are we not forced to concede that 'one can mean [this expression] sometimes as one word and sometimes as four', and is not Wittgenstein obliged to admit that there is more to be said about the meaning of sentences than he is allowing? If I can mean the sentence 'Bring me a slab' as four words or mean it as one long word corresponding to 'Slab!', it would seem that I may either think the sentence itself or think 'in some form or other a different sentence' (§19, last sentence).

Wittgenstein questions this conclusion. If you hold that a person who says 'Bring me a slab' must really mean it either as one long word or as four separate words, you are, he suggests, overlooking the fact that which is meant depends on what the sentence is being compared with. 'Bring me a slab' counts as four words instead of one if it is taken 'in contrast with' similarly complex expressions. In particular we shall 'be inclined to say' that the sentence is meant as four words when it is used in contrast with '*Hand* me a slab', 'Bring *him* a slab', 'Bring *two* slabs', and the like. (It should not be thought Wittgenstein ought to have written 'Bring me *two* slabs' rather than 'Bring *two* slabs'. His point is not that the sentence means four words when used 'in contrast with' other four-word sentences but that it means this when used in contrast with other sentences containing the words of the original command. In the *Brown Book* he says 'One is tempted to answer: [A person] *means* all four words if in his language he uses that sentence [i.e. "Bring me a brick"] in contrast with other sentences in which these words are used, such as, for instance, [the five-word sentence] "Take these two bricks away"'.[3]) In other words asking whether a person who says 'Bring me a slab' really means it as one long word or as four separate words is like asking whether the sentence 'The first is the best' comprises four words or five. The answer depends on what the sentence is being contrasted with. What, if anything, the speaker has in mind is neither here nor there.

Still you might think there is a difference between saying 'Bring me a slab' and meaning it as four words and saying it and meaning it as one word. If the answer to the question of whether the sentence means four words or one depends on what it is being contrasted with, you may argue, there must be something that 'using one sentence in contrast with others consists in', something going on in us that determines that we are using 'Bring me a slab' in contrast with other sentences. But this too is debatable.

Wittgenstein asks us to consider whether we do in fact note the sentences that 'Bring me a slab' is used 'in contrast with'. (The German text has fewer mentalistic overtones than the English translation. In the original Wittgenstein asks whether the comparison sentences are 'noted'; he does not ask whether they 'hover before one's mind'.) Evidently we cannot note every sentence 'containing the separate words of our command in other combinations'. There is no end of such sentences. But if we are only supposed to note some of them, which ones? And are we supposed to note these sentences before or while or after we are saying the sentence itself? (When I consider this, I do not find myself noting any sentences before I speak, nor any as I speak, nor any once I have said what I have said – at least not usually.)

If we attend to what happens when we say 'Bring me a slab', we can 'see that we are going astray'. The comparison sentences, 'Hand me a slab' and such like, do not count as comparison sentences because we note them. They count as such because '*our language* contains the possibility of those other sentences'. What determines that I mean 'Bring me a slab' as four separate words rather than as one long word is that I could have said 'Hand me a slab' or 'Bring him a slab' or 'Bring two slabs' instead of saying 'Bring me a slab'. There does not have to be anything else my 'using one sentence in contrast with others consist[s] in'. To say that certain sentences function as comparison sentences for someone is to say this person knows English, not that he or she notes them.

But is it not undeniable that a foreigner who takes our four-word sentence 'Bring me a slab' to be a one-word sentence would think something different from an English speaker like me who takes it to be a four-word sentence? The foreigner's saying the sentence and my saying it certainly seems to 'consist in' two very different things. If he takes the sentence to be 'one word corresponding perhaps to the word for "building-stone" in his language', he must understand it very differently from how I understand it since I know it 'contains the possibility of those other sentences'. Surely nobody can deny there is 'something different going on in him when he pronounces ["Bring me a slab"], – something corresponding perhaps to the fact that he conceives the sentence as a *single* word'.

Wittgenstein's riposte is short and to the point. 'Either the same thing may go on in [the foreigner]', he says, 'or something different'. To know whether the same thing is going on in him as is going in me, one would have to know what is going on in our respective heads when we say 'Bring me a slab'. But I do not even know what is going on in my own head. (If you are anything like me, you are not at all 'conscious of [the sentence's] consisting of four words *while* you are uttering it'.) The important thing is not whether the same thing 'goes on' in the foreigner as in me but how each of us uses the language.

What differentiates the way I say 'Bring me a slab' from the way a foreigner says it (and what makes us pronounce it differently) '*need* not lie in anything that accompanies the utterance of the command'. My having a 'mastery of [the] language' which a foreigner lacks is not 'something that *happens* while [I am] uttering [a] sentence'. Abilities do not happen or not happen. My ability to speak English no more occurs in me when I speak than my ability to drive occurs in me when I drive. (Here Wittgenstein is making a similar point to the one he made in §6 regarding images. He is saying that what happens in us when we utter a sentence is irrelevant to what we mean. Of course nobody denies there are language-games in which people note something while uttering a sentence.)

The answer to the question Wittgenstein broaches in §19 of what makes a sentence 'elliptical' is thus that 'it is shortened – in comparison with a particular paradigm of our grammar'. 'Slab!' counts as elliptical not because 'it leaves something out that we think when we utter it' but because 'Bring me a slab' functions as a paradigm sentence (and serves as a model or sample sentence for us). What matters is not anything that happens in us, only the possibilities inherent in our language.

One might object that there must be a particular 'sense' or 'meaning' shared by the shortened sentence and the unshortened paradigm, a sense or meaning that has a 'verbal expression'. In response Wittgenstein returns to a theme that first made an appearance in §1. There he said that 'no such thing [is] in question …, only how [a word is] used'. Here he asks '[D]oesn't the fact that the sentences have the same sense consist in their having the same *use*?'. To say the shortened sentence 'Slab!' and the unshortened sentence 'Bring me a slab' have the same 'sense' is simply to say they are used the same way – to get someone to fetch a certain sort of building-stone.

The English speaker who says 'Slab!' is no more plausibly regarded as supplying the unshortened sentence 'Bring me a slab' 'in *thought*' than the Russian who says 'stone red' (in Russian) supplies the longer sentence 'the stone is red' in thought. In the case of the word 'Slab!', as in the case of the Russian sentence, there is no reason to think something has been left out. People who know Russian do not feel that words are missing nor do they silently attach words to what they say. (Those still unconvinced might wish to consider whether they feel they are missing something because English nouns, unlike French nouns, mostly lack genders.)

Interlude (4): Real meaning

Wittgenstein is often assumed to be propounding one or more positive or negative philosophical theses in §§19–20, and debates over the correct interpretation of these sections generally centre on the question of what he is attempting to establish. This is not unreasonable since the discussion is very compressed even by Wittgenstein's standards. Still we should hesitate before jumping to conclusions. For one thing it is hard to find a single thesis in these two sections for which Wittgenstein provides anything approaching a passable argument. A far more sensible conclusion, surely, is that he is critically exploring a powerful philosophical conception and trying to prevent us from falling into a philosophical trap. Few philosophers are less ill-disposed than Wittgenstein to write for the sake of writing, and it is doubtful that he would have devoted so much space to examining what looks like a minor issue if he had not believed it afforded him the opportunity to investigate a serious philosophical worry.

The question of whether the builders' call 'Slab!' counts as a word or a sentence is not very troublesome. As we saw, the answer is that it all depends. The call may be thought of either way and what we say will depend on the nature of our concerns. What bothers Wittgenstein is nothing so trivial as how to classify a call. He is concerned with the question of whether words in languages as different as ours and the builders' can be said to mean the same. For him the crucial issue that needs addressing is: Are philosophers right in thinking that there must be something the meaning of our words 'consist in', something we 'really mean' (§19)? His target – which it would be counterproductive for him to specify too precisely – is the view that communication would be unintelligible were there no 'real meanings' and nothing special 'going on in [us]' (§20). (Compare the suggestion that we really mean – and think – 'afternoon' when we use the abbreviation 'p.m.'. It is tempting to suppose that each time we use 'p.m.' we attach the word 'afternoon' 'in *thought*' (§20).)

In §§19–20 Wittgenstein investigates considerations that might prompt one to think our call 'Slab!' is subordinate to our call 'Bring me a slab' and to treat the longer expression as the 'real meaning' of the shorter one. He concentrates on the relationship between shortened and unshortened sentences and the relationship between sentences and their 'comparisons' because these seem to bolster the idea of real meaning. This, he thinks, is a mistake. If we scrutinize our feeling that our call 'Slab!' really means 'Bring me a slab', we shall come to see that it is fuelled by a confusion about the way language functions. More specifically we shall see that it is not true that we 'must be thinking in some form or another' the sentence 'Bring me a slab' when we shout 'Slab!' to get someone to bring us a slab. Nor is there good reason to think the answer to the question of whether 'Bring me a slab' means four separate words or one long word depends on what is 'going on in [the speaker]'.

Wittgenstein does not claim to have shown that sentences do not have real meaning, still less claim to have established that there is nothing 'in *thought*' accompanying our words. He confines himself to bringing out some of the enormous difficulties that beset the idea of real meaning and the idea of thoughts 'going on in [us]'. It is neither here nor there that there are arguments for these ideas that he has not considered. Wittgenstein's aim is to cast doubt on the philosophical assumption that our words would be unintelligible were it not for the fact that they are associated with real meanings or thoughts that provide them with sense, not to refute this assumption once and for all. He is not unaware of the fact that the relevant 'goings on' are as often as not taken to be subconscious and he would not deny for one moment that this idea also deserves careful consideration.

So I think it cannot be seriously denied that Wittgenstein is challenging our tendency to regard certain ideas as too obvious to require examination and, along with this, taking issue with the all too easy assumption that philosophers' investigations of the nature of language are obviously sound. He is not trying to get us to embrace the idea that there is nothing backing up what we say but rather probing the assumption that there must be something backing it up that gives it its meaning. Thus when discussing the foreigner who 'conceives [a sentence] differently' from a native speaker, he does not contend that 'what we call his wrong conception' cannot lie in 'anything that accompanies the utterance of the command'. He simply notes that it '*need* not lie' in any such thing. His aim is not to answer the question of what is going on in our heads but to challenge the philosophical view that our utterances must be accompanied by meanings.

The discussion in §§19–20 seems to me to illustrate particularly well the tentative exploring of issues I take Wittgenstein to favour. His remarks in these sections are best regarded as belonging to his on-going campaign against the idea that meanings are required to explain the functioning of language. He is not trying to establish a particular thesis about language but trying to get us to do something – think through a common view about how language works. We are supposed to come to appreciate that there are tremendous obstacles to accepting the idea of sentences having real meaning, obstacles that are rarely recognized, let alone seriously investigated. The only difference between §§19–20 and other sections where Wittgenstein exhorts us to reflect on what we are inclined to take for granted is that he spells out more of the details here than he usually does and we are left less of the work to do for ourselves. (Reflecting on what Wittgenstein says in these sections we can, I think, better understand why he would say in the Preface that his 'thoughts were soon crippled if [he] tried to force them on in any single direction against their natural inclination'.)

It should not be thought that Wittgenstein is discussing unimportant issues in §§19–20. He is not merely attempting to turn back the objection that the builders' language is different from our language. This relatively minor worry serves as a pretext for an examination of the important question, which has long exercised philosophers, of how what we mean is related to what we say and how what we say is related to what we think. The issues broached here are among the deepest in philosophy, and if philosophers are, as Wittgenstein thinks, led astray because of misunderstandings about language, we would do well to attend closely to how they think of meaning and thought. Only by examining in detail the all-important twin philosophical ideas of 'real meaning' and 'genuine thoughts' can we reasonably hope to dispel the 'haze [surrounding the working of language] which makes clear vision impossible' (§5).

Sections 21 to 25: Reporting, asking and commanding

The remarks of this instalment centre on the nature of assertions, questions and orders. Wittgenstein takes issue with the suggestion that such forms of speech contain thoughts (or 'assumptions') modified in various ways, discourages us from drawing philosophical conclusions from the fact that questions and commands can be converted into assertions, and reminds us of the enormous variety of ways in which sentences are used. In addition he examines the view that animals do not talk because they do not think.

Section 21

Wittgenstein asks us to imagine builders raising and answering questions about the number, the colour and the shape of building-stones in a pile. There is nothing exceptional about this new language-game. The practice of asking a question and being told the answer is as familiar as the practice of ordering someone to fetch something. What deserves our attention is only how questions, reports and commands are related. For instance, how is the report 'Five slabs' similar to the command 'Five slabs!' and how is it different?

It might seem – especially when one remembers the quotation from Augustine in §1 about how he learnt words – that 'Five slabs' and 'Five slabs!' are the same except for the fact that they are made in different tones of voice and with different facial expressions. On this view reports differ from commands because they are spoken in an ordinary tone of voice rather than urgently.

Wittgenstein thinks this suggestion is confused. He agrees that the report 'Five slabs' and the order 'Five slabs!' are normally made in different tones of voice and with different facial expressions but denies this is what distinguishes them. It is after all perfectly possible to report something is the case and command it be done in exactly the same tone of voice and with exactly the same facial expressions. There need not be anything in how I say the words nor anything that happens in me that makes my words a report rather than a command. What makes 'five slabs' a report may lie 'only in [its] application', in how the phrase is used. The crucial thing is 'the part in which uttering [the words] plays in the language-game'. 'Five slabs' constitute a report in the 'reporting' language-game, a command in the 'commanding' language-game and a question in the 'questioning' language-game.

We could restrict our use of 'statement' and 'command' to apply to different forms of sentences accompanied by different intonations. Nothing prevents our taking sentences to be statements if they have a certain form and are spoken in a certain way regardless of how they are used. This would be comparable to our practice of regarding 'Isn't the weather glorious today?' as a question even though it is often used to say something about the weather – that it is glorious. The point Wittgenstein is making still stands, however. The language-game of reporting is a language-game of reporting however we decide to classify the sentences involved. Using words like 'statement' and 'command' to stand for 'grammatical forms of sentences and intonations' no more changes the facts than using the word 'question' to refer to 'Isn't the weather glorious today?' changes the fact that it is used to say something about the weather. (Compare §3, where Wittgenstein notes that restricting the word 'language' to systems of communication comprising names does not in any way change how people actually operate with words. Also compare §16 and §19.)

As the use of the sentence 'Isn't the weather glorious today?' makes clear, the form of a sentence is no more a dependable guide to its use than the tone of voice or facial expressions of the person who utters it. It is easy to imagine languages in which every statement is expressed as a rhetorical question and languages in which every command is expressed as a question of the form 'Would you like to …?'. A question can function as a command just as the sentence 'You will do this' can despite being in the form of a prophecy. What makes a sentence a question is 'the part which uttering its words plays in the language-game'.

Section 22

Is Wittgenstein right that a report is a report, a command a command and a question a question because they belong to different language-games (see §21)? It might be argued against him that reports, commands and questions differ because they present what they mean differently. In particular, one may be forgiven for thinking that 'every assertion contains an assumption'. On this view – which Wittgenstein attributes to Gottlob Frege, a philosopher he respected – an assertion comprises a content or thought along with something that makes it an assertion rather than a command or other form of sentence. (I shall not consider whether Wittgenstein understands Frege's view correctly; he is not so much concerned with Frege's actual view as with the fact that the conception of assertions as containing assumptions comports poorly with what he said about them in §21.)

Consider 'The door is closed', 'Close the door!' and 'Is the door closed?'. The suggestion is that these three sentences present the same idea, content or thought – the door's being closed – in three different ways. We are to think of the three sentences as differing not because they figure in different language-games but because something different is added to their shared content. (Wittgenstein seems to have initially held such a view since, early on, he wrote: 'Judgment, question and command are all on the same level. What interests logic in them is only the unasserted proposition'.[1])

Wittgenstein objects to what he takes to be the idea on which this view of assertion 'really rests', namely the idea that it is possible 'in our language [to rewrite] every statement in the form: "It is asserted that such-and-such is the case"'. While agreeing that sentences can be rewritten this way, he denies this establishes the point. The fact that 'The door is closed' can be rewritten as 'It is asserted that the door is closed' does not, he insists, show that 'The door is closed' comprises an (unasserted) assumption about the door being closed. In this connection he notes three points.

First 'The door is closed' cannot be read as comprising the assumption 'that the door is closed' and the modifier 'it is asserted' since phrases of the form 'that such and such is the case' do not express thoughts. 'That the door is closed' is not a full sentence; it is a noun phrase, and noun phrases do not function as statements. As Wittgenstein puts it, ' "that such-and-such is the case" is *not* a sentence in our language – so far it is not a *move* in the language-game'.

Secondly it does not help to note that 'It is asserted that such-and-such is the case' can be written as 'It is asserted: such-and-such is the case'. This solves the problem about noun clauses not expressing thoughts since the 'assumption' is now a full sentence ('such-and-such is the case'). But a new problem arises: the phrase 'It is asserted' is 'superfluous'. To say 'It is asserted: the door is closed' is to say no more than 'The door is closed'.

Thirdly it is immaterial that 'The door is closed' can be rewritten as

'It is asserted that the door is closed'. If this shows that the original sentence contains a statement, it also follows by parity of reasoning that it contains a question, it being equally possible to rewrite 'The door is closed' as 'Is the door closed? Yes!' – which is absurd; nobody thinks assertions contain questions.

These observations do not refute the thesis that 'every assertion contains an assumption'. Few philosophers, never mind Frege himself, would concede that it can be dislodged so easily. For one thing the thesis is plausibly regarded as 'really rest[ing]' on very general theoretical considerations about how language works rather than on the possibility of recasting sentences in different forms. And for another it is far from obvious that common usage should be allowed to call the tune, that the phrase 'it is asserted' in 'It is asserted: ...' can safely be discounted, or that all transformations are on a par. None of this, however, means Wittgenstein has missed the boat. It is uncharitable to criticize him for attacking a naive version of the thesis that assertions contain assumptions. Read sympathetically, all he is trying to do is get us to recognize that the thesis is much less clear than usually thought.

We could introduce a sign to distinguish assertions from questions, fictions, suppositions and the like. (Frege used a dash at the beginning of a sentence, as in '–the door is closed', to indicate the assumption or content of a sentence and added a small vertical line, as in '⊢the door is closed', to indicate that the sentence is asserted.) We use question marks to indicate questions, and there is nothing to prevent our using another sort of sign, in addition to a capital letter, to indicate the beginning of a sentence. But equally clearly this is of no philosophical interest. Philosophers who take sentences to contain assumptions are not concerned with how best to punctuate. They are concerned with 'the essence of human language' (§1).

It is one thing to say we might use an 'assertion-mark', quite another to say the assertion 'The door is closed' consists of 'two actions, entertaining and asserting'. Asserting 'The door is closed' is not like first reading a musical score, then singing the notes. When I assert that the door is shut I do one thing, not two – I assert that the door is closed. I am no more entertaining an assumption when I assert this than I am having the thought 'Bring me a slab!' when I call out 'Slab!' (compare §19 and §20). (This is not to deny someone might always first think out what he or she wants to say. Wittgenstein is simply noting that when we assert something, we are doing one thing.)

Finally Wittgenstein observes that 'Frege's assertion sign marks the *beginning of the sentence*' in much the same way as a full stop marks its end. It provides a way of distinguishing between whole sentences and subordinate clauses. (Compare 'It is raining' and 'If he opened his umbrella, it is raining'. In the first sentence 'it is raining' would be preceded by '⊢' but not in the second one.) Such a sign might be useful. For instance it could be used to remove confusions arising as a result of clauses '*within* the period' being taken as 'the whole period'. But this too is irrelevant to the issues concerning philosophers like Frege.

Note at the bottom of page 11

This note clarifies the notion of an assumption introduced in §22. (As the editors remark on p. vi, inserted after the main text had been typed.) Wittgenstein points out that assumptions are comparable to pictures that can be understood in different ways. The assumption regarding the door being closed is like a picture of a boxer, while the 'modifier' is like the manner in which the picture is read – as showing how one should stand to box, showing how one should not stand, showing what standing up involves, etc. In other words assumptions are comparable to 'radicals' in chemistry. They are what is common to various written or spoken sentences in much the same way as the O_2 molecule is common to SO_2, BaO_2 and CO_2.

Section 23

Wittgenstein now ventures the opinion that there are 'countless different kinds of use of what we call "symbols", "words", "sentences"', not just one sort, or just a few sorts. (This should not be taken literally; Wittgenstein's point is simply that there are many kinds of use.) Moreover 'this multiplicity is not something fixed, given once and for all'. Just the reverse, language develops in more or less the same way as mathematics develops. Consider the contemporary practice of using 'he or she' where 'he' would once have been used. This shift in usage is in many respects similar to the shift that occurred in mathematics centuries ago when zero came to be regarded as a genuine number. (Another useful comparison – see §18 – is between language and a city; one obtains a clearer view of how language changes by considering how cities grow and decay.)

Next Wittgenstein re-emphasizes that 'the *speaking* of language is part of an activity, or of a form of life' (compare §7). This is worth noting again since philosophers often treat language as something separate from its application and forget that our use of words is interwoven with other actions. (Elsewhere Wittgenstein says: 'If I had to say what is the main mistake made by philosophers of the present generation ... I would say that it is that when language is looked at, what is looked at is a form of words and not the use made of the form of words'.[2]) It is, Wittgenstein is suggesting, a good antidote to the common philosophical conception of language as a fixed linguistic structure to consider how it functions in everyday life (also compare the comments on §7).

In this connection it is helpful to review 'the multiplicity of language-games' in a series of examples. Giving and obeying orders, describing the appearances of objects, assembling things from descriptions, reporting events, speculating about them, forming and testing hypotheses, and so on, can all be carried out in various ways. Consider reporting. This is not only different from ordering, questioning, hypothesizing, solving a problem and such like; it also comes in a multitude of guises. There are many ways of reporting something, not just one. (This point is developed in the next section.)

Typically philosophers fail to appreciate fully the diversity of language-games. They take language to be a single sort of thing rather than a motley, and it is 'interesting to compare' how they picture it with 'the multiplicity of tools in language and of the ways they are used, the multiplicity of kinds of word and sentence'. How is it, Wittgenstein would like us to ask ourselves, that 'logicians' – including the author of the *Tractatus* – fail to see the multiplicity of language-games and end up thinking that propositions all have the same 'general form'? (When writing the *Tractatus* Wittgenstein focussed his attention on sentences that are used to state how things are. He took propositions to be without exception of the form 'Such and such is the case' and disregarded the fact that even a simple sentence like 'It is raining' can also function as a complaint, a curse, a question, a practical joke, an example of a three-word sentence and an expression of shock.[3])

Section 24

If one forgets the multiplicity of language-games, one is likely to take questions to have a common form and think that 'What is a question?' admits of a general answer. In particular one is likely to think of questions as describing what the speaker does not know, or what he or she wishes to be told, or the character of his or her 'mental state of uncertainty'.

It is not difficult to see that each of these ways of regarding questions is unacceptable. If I ask you 'What are the primary colours?' to determine whether you know them, I am not reporting that I lack knowledge. Nor am I saying what I want to know. Nor am I asserting something about my state of uncertainty. Thinking that questions are disguised descriptions is as implausible as thinking a cry of 'Help!' describes how things are. Normally 'Help!' is a plea. It is not a description of the fact that the person calling out is in difficulty.

Nor are descriptions all of a piece. Describing a ship's position by noting it is located at 20° north latitude and 30° west longitude is different from describing a person as looking exhausted, and different again from describing one's mood as one of exhilaration. (It does not help to say these descriptions are all of the form 'Such and such is the case'. Saying this is like saying they signify; it is – to borrow a phrase from §13 – 'so far [to say] *nothing whatever*'.)

Certainly 'it is possible to substitute the form of a statement for the usual form of question'. The question 'Is N'Djamena the capital of Chad?' can as often as not be replaced by 'I want to know whether N'Djamena is the capital of Chad' or 'I am in doubt whether N'Djamena is the capital of Chad'. Still, questioning and describing are very different activities. The fact that questions can usually be replaced by descriptions does not bring them closer together. (Compare §10, where the value of 'assimilating the descriptions of the uses of words' is queried.)

The possibility of transforming sentences from one form to another can seem important. For instance it seems significant that sentences of the form 'Such and such is the case' can be turned into sentences of the form 'I think such and such is the case' (or 'I believe such and such is the case'). (The philosopher Immanuel Kant put it this way: 'It must be possible for the "I think" to accompany all my representations; for otherwise something would be represented in me which could not be thought at all, and that is equivalent to saying that the representation would be impossible, or at least would be nothing to me'.[4]) Whether we should be impressed by the possibility of such transformations, however, is another matter.

The fact that 'I think' or 'I believe' can be added at the beginning of sentences may make it seem as though we are describing our own inner thoughts whenever we say something. If we are not careful, we can fool ourselves into thinking that even a sentence like 'N'Djamena is the capital of Chad' is about our minds or our thoughts rather than about the world. Worse still, we may end up embracing the philosophical doctrine of solipsism, according to which one – i.e. the speaker or thinker – is the only person there is. It is after all but a small step from the idea that every sentence I utter describes an inner thought of mine to the conclusion that nothing is real besides me. (Wittgenstein returns to the issue of solipsism briefly in §402 and discusses it at greater length elsewhere.[5])

Section 25

The idea that sentences express thoughts and describe our 'inner li[ves]' (§24) fuels the popular conception of animals as being unable to speak because they do not have thoughts. This is misleading since saying 'animals do not talk because they lack the mental capacity' adds nothing to saying they 'do not talk'. We have no independent way of deciding whether an individual has thoughts. To appropriate a sentence from §1: 'Explanations come to an end somewhere'. (There is an echo here of an issue discussed in §§19–20.)

What Wittgenstein is drawing our attention to here is often miscon-strued. He is not suggesting that animals never use language or communicate with one another, even less denying the possibility of biologists or physiologists discovering that some animals have suffi-cient 'mental capacity' to master a language. To the contrary, he speaks of animals as having 'primitive forms of language' and would allow they possess the 'mental capacity' needed to use them. For him the important question is not whether animals possess the wherewithal to use language, primitive or otherwise, but what we are saying when we say they can (or cannot) think.

At the end of the section Wittgenstein observes that using language is 'as much a part of our natural history as walking, eating, drinking, playing'. This is doubly worth noting. First it reminds us that language-games are practices no less than walking and eating and are equally woven into our lives. Secondly it brings out the shaky character of the philosophical thesis that animals are unable to talk because they do not have an appropriate thinking mechanism. We shall be less ready to take speaking to require a thinking mechanism and 'mental capacity' if we compare commanding, questioning, recounting and such like with walking and eating, neither of which is plausibly regarded as backed by a mechanism. Persons, animals, computers or whatever can be said to talk and convey information just to the extent that their forms of life are comparable to ours, 'the *speaking* of language' being – see §23 – 'part of an activity, or of a form of life'. The less animals and machines behave like us, the less reason we have to regard them as saying something rather than as merely making noises.

Interlude (5): 'The multiplicity of language-games'

Whereas philosophers generally take language to be a fixed, unified structure (compare the picture sketched in §1 and the view attributed to Frege in §22), Wittgenstein stresses 'the multiplicity of language-games' (§23). This theme is not new to this instalment. It figures in §11 and §12, the gist of which was that words are as diverse as the tools in a tool-box and the handles in the cabin of a locomotive. What Wittgenstein is doing is extending and reinforcing the point by reminding us of the fact that sentences are similarly diverse. He is trying to get us to recognize that '[t]here are *"countless* kinds [of sentence]: countless different kinds of uses of what we call "symbols", "words", "sentences"' (§23). As he sees it, philosophers are apt to overlook the diverse uses of sentences and would not say some of the things they say if they kept this firmly in mind.

It is easy to misconstrue what Wittgenstein is saying and to read him as suggesting that language essentially comprises a conglomerate of linguistic practices. On this view the essence of human language resides not in the fact that sentences comprise names, the meanings of which are the objects they stand for or anything similar (compare §1). Rather it resides in 'the multiplicity of the tools in language and of the ways they are used, the multiplicity of kinds of word and sentence' (§23). Instead of thinking of assertions as containing assumptions and questions as disguised descriptions (see §22 and §24), we should think of them as having the functions they do by virtue of the language-games to which they belong. The correct view, according to this line of thought, is that our use of language is to be explained in terms of language-games. These, not what our words stand for, are the key to understanding the nature of language.

If we look back over Wittgenstein's discussion, it is, I think, clear that this is not what he is saying. Neither his remarks about assertions in §22, nor his remarks about there being countless kinds of sentence in §23, nor his remarks about questions in §24 imply that it is integral to language that it comprises a multiplicity of language-games. The reason Wittgenstein refers to language-games is not that he thinks language is essentially diverse but that he thinks it is interesting to compare 'what logicians have said about the structure of language' (§23) with how we actually operate with words. Indeed he explicitly says 'the term "language-*game*" is meant to bring into prominence the fact that the *speaking* of language is part of an activity' (same section). Bringing something 'into prominence' is not at all the same as postulating something as a fundamental explanatory category.

The discussion of §21 is somewhat less clear. When Wittgenstein speaks of the report 'Five slabs' and the order 'Five slabs!' differing because the words 'five slabs' are used differently in the two cases, he seems to be putting forward an explanation of the difference between them, one that emphasizes the use of words rather than tones of voice and facial expressions. But this is hardly conclusive. To say 'the difference [is] only in the application' (§21) is to say something of a completely different order from saying the difference lies in the speaker's tone of voice or facial expression. It is not to provide a philosophical explanation of the difference; it is to reject the need for such explanation. Wittgenstein is not saying the phenomenon should be explained in terms of the 'application' of words but that '[e]xplanations come to an end somewhere' (§1). (Also recall what was said in the first and third interludes about philosophical explanation.)

Nor should Wittgenstein be thought as advancing an explanation of the difference between the report 'Five slabs' and the order 'Five slabs!' when he says this lies 'in the part which uttering these words plays in the language-game' (§21). Saying 'Five slabs' is a report because it belongs to the reporting language-game is – in the absence of an independent account of the nature of this language-game – empty; it is totally unlike saying it is a report because it is uttered in a certain tone of voice. Nor is there any reason to believe that Wittgenstein thinks it possible to provide an account of language-games. Actually the opposite. If he thought this were possible, why in §7 did he merely note that he 'will call [certain] games language-games' and why in §23 did he limit himself to reviewing 'the multiplicity of language-games' in a series of examples?

The picture of language as a conglomerate of language-games is not comparable to the 'picture of the essence of human language' sketched in §1. Whereas the conception of language as comprising words that name objects would, if correct, explain the nature of communication (and how we manage to mean what we mean), the observation that there are 'countless different kinds of use of what we call "symbols", "words", "sentences"' explains nothing. It is no more possible to explain how we use words by noting the diverse functions of language than it is possible to explain criminal behaviour by noting that some people are law-abiding, some not. Drawing attention to the diverse forms of a phenomenon is important since it is regularly overlooked. But it cannot by any stretch of the imagination be regarded as explanatory.

Wittgenstein's aims in the sections we have been considering are different from those of Frege and the author of the *Tractatus*, to say nothing of those of the proponent of the picture of language introduced in §1. He emphasizes the diverse functions of words because philosophers tend to ignore them, discount them, or leave them to take care of themselves. Far from defending a new philosophical account of human language, he is trying to get us to appreciate that we are, for one reason or other, disposed to bend the phenomena of language to fit our preconceived ideas about its essential nature. In particular he wants us to appreciate how much philosophers build into their accounts of language, how much they take for granted, how much they gratuitously assume must be true. As before the thrust of his discussion is exploratory rather than explanatory.

§§21–5, then, are mostly concerned to stress the gap between philosophers' theories of language and the linguistic practices in which we actually engage. Wittgenstein is attempting to weaken the grip on our thinking of the picture of language as a unified whole by getting us to reflect on the seemingly anodyne assumption that language is governed by general principles in much the same way as a physical phenomenon. (It is not fortuitous that in the note on page 11 he refers to 'the language of chemistry' when describing Frege's view.) Instead of regarding language as though it were part of the physical world, we should, Wittgenstein thinks, regard it as 'part of our natural history' (§25). If we think of speaking as a practice comparable to the practices of walking, eating, drinking and playing, we are more likely to resist thinking of the study of language as falling in the province of natural science. Is it any more probable, he wants us to ask ourselves, that all forms of speaking and thinking are reducible to a few basic types than all forms of walking are variations on an underlying standard form of walking?

Sections 26 to 32: Defining by pointing

Wittgenstein now reverts to his examination of names and naming. After a few general remarks about learning language, he turns his attention to the process of defining words using phrases like 'This is ...' or 'This is called "..."'. (See §6 for the difference between ostensive definition and ostensive teaching.)

Section 26

We are inclined to think, as Augustine thought (see §1), that 'learning language consists in giving names to objects. Viz, to human beings, to shapes, to colours, to pains, to moods, to numbers, etc.'. But, as we have seen, 'not everything we call language is [a] system [of this sort]' (§3). Naming is not merely a matter of uttering words in the presence of objects; it is more 'like attaching labels to things'. (Recall §15: 'It will often prove useful in philosophy to say to ourselves: naming something is like attaching a label to a thing'.) What is unclear is only the sense in which naming is indeed like labelling.

Naming is certainly a prerequisite for using a name. One cannot significantly use the name 'Mr X' unless it has already been correlated with Mr X. Still the process of correlating names with things is not 'a preparation *for*' just one type of linguistic activity. The fact that a name has to be correlated with its bearer before it can be used tells us nothing about the uses to which it can be put once the correlation has been made.

Section 27

When one considers what naming is 'a preparation *for*' (§26), it is tempting to think that we first 'name things ... then ... talk about them'. The picture that springs to mind is one of our naming things so that we can refer to them (and describe their character, behaviour or whatever). On reflection, however, this is clearly an oversimplification. The process of naming does not fix how names are used. What we do next is not 'given with the mere act of naming'. Naming may be a preparation for talking about something but then again it may not. It may also be a preparation for commanding someone to do something. In the case of language (2), for instance, the builders use the names they introduce to get their assistants to fetch building-stones.

Even when naming is 'a preparation *for*' talking about things, many different things can happen next. There is not 'only one thing called "talking about a thing"'. As we saw in §24 description can take many forms. Describing 'the position of a body by means of its co-ordinates' is different from describing a 'facial expression' and different again from describing a 'sensation of touch'.

To reinforce the point that 'we do the most various things with our sentences', Wittgenstein invites us to consider how sentences like 'Water!', 'Away!', 'Ow!', 'Help!', 'Fine!' and 'No!' are used. While these are all exclamations, they function very differently. Calling out 'Help!' is different from saying 'No!' to a mischievous child, and saying 'No!' to a child is different from saying 'No!' to oneself when one has made a mistake. Certainly it is misleading 'to call [exclamations] "names of objects"', to say nothing of supposing that we are always talking about things.

Wittgenstein next examines the practice of asking for and being given the name of something. He notes that this practice, 'with its correlate, ostensive definition', is a 'language-game on its own'. Imagine asking what something is called and being told 'This is X' or 'This is called "X"'. When we play such a game – it might be called the 'what is this called?' language-game – we are doing something similar to what we do when we define 'X' by pointing to an X and saying 'This is X' or 'This is called "X"'. (The builders described in §2 and §8 cannot play this game since they do not have sufficient words to ask and say what things are called.)

The language-game of asking the name of something is one among many involving names. Another such game involves inventing names for objects and using the names one invents to address and to talk to the objects themselves. Consider the case of children 'giv[ing] names to their dolls and then talk[ing] about them and to them'. A child who has named a doll 'Doll' may use the name to say something about it ('Doll has a hat') and to address it ('Doll, this is a hat'). Actually, the 'calling' language-game is quite distinctive. When I call out 'Jill' to get her attention, I am not saying something about her or about myself or about anything else. I am simply calling her.

Section 28

Having briefly considered the language-game of asking for the name of something, Wittgenstein takes up 'its correlate' (§27), the practice of ostensive definition. (Notice that whereas ostensive training is a process that 'resembl[es] language' (§7), ostensive definition is a full-fledged linguistic process.) To start with Wittgenstein observes that proper names, names of colours, names of fabrics, names of numbers and names of points of the compass can all be defined ostensively. Contrary to what is often supposed, it is not true that names of numbers, directions and the like cannot be defined this way, only the names of people, colours, etc. 'Two' can be defined by saying 'That is called "two"' while pointing to two nuts, and 'west' can be defined by saying 'That is called "west"' while pointing in the direction of the setting sun. These are ostensive definitions no less than 'This is Mr X' (accompanied by a gesture towards Mr X) and 'This is called "sepia"' (accompanied by a gesture towards a reddish-brown patch). Indeed they are 'perfectly exact'.

But how clear is it that 'two' can be defined 'perfectly exact[ly]' by pointing to two nuts? You might think this unlikely since the person being taught 'doesn't know what [the teacher] wants to call "two"'. In this case the person is surely more likely to take the word to apply to the nuts themselves rather than to the number of nuts in the group, the nuts being the only things in full view. As Wittgenstein puts it, a person 'who doesn't know that "two" [names a number] will suppose that "two" is the name given to *this* group of nuts [i.e. the group of nuts being pointed to]'.

In response Wittgenstein limits himself to questioning whether this always occurs. He notes that while it may occur, it need not. The opposite may also happen. I may intend to define the number of nuts in a group and you may take me to be defining the numeral 'two'. Even in the case of a name like 'Mr X' mistakes can happen. I might point to Mr X and say 'This is X' and you might take me to be pointing to a colour (Mr X is white) or to a point of the compass (Mr X is in the direction of the setting sun). There is no guarantee that a definition will always be taken the way it is intended. To the contrary, 'an ostensive definition can be variously interpreted in *every* case'.

Note at the bottom of page 14

This note comments on a different way of learning the meaning of the word 'red'. Wittgenstein observes that it is possible to learn it by being shown something that is not red. This is like learning what modesty is by being told that a certain arrogant person 'is *not* modest'. The existence of 'ambiguity' (and the fact that misunderstanding can occur) is 'no argument against such a method of definition'. As noted in §28 every definition can be 'variously interpreted'.

Still there is a difference between 'such a method of definition' and what we call definition. You may learn what 'red' means by being shown something non-red but it is hard to think of this as 'ostensive definition'. The meaning of 'red' can be conveyed by pointing to a red sample, but not by saying 'no' or gesturing disapprovingly while pointing to a blue sample. (No dictionary writer would put a sample of blue in a dictionary with a line through it to explain the meaning of red.) It is irrelevant that the 'practical consequences' are the same and one goes on to use the word 'red' as everyone else does. Roundabout definition of the sort described is very different 'from what we ordinarily call "ostensive definition"'.

Section 29

Is it true that 'an ostensive definition can be variously interpreted in *every* case' (§28)? You might think that Wittgenstein's characterization of ostensive definition falls short because he fails to note that alternative interpretations can be excluded by specifying more exactly what is being defined. After all, misunderstanding about what 'two' applies to can be excluded by saying 'This *number* is called "two"' (instead of 'This is called "two"'). If I tell a child that the word 'two' applies to a number, he or she will – given sufficient knowledge of the language – take it to apply to the number rather than to '*this* group of nuts'. And likewise for colours and lengths. Confusion about them can be averted by saying 'The *colour* is called so-and-so' and 'The *length* is called so-and-so'. Misunderstanding may indeed be forestalled by indicating 'the post at which we station the word', i.e. 'what place in language, in grammar, we assign to [it]'.

But while misunderstanding can often be avoided this way, Wittgenstein's point still stands. It remains true that 'ostensive definition[s] can be variously interpreted in *every* case'. The problem has simply been deflected onto the words 'number', 'colour', 'length', etc. 'This *number* is called "two"' can be 'variously interpreted' no less than 'This is called "two" '. Nothing precludes the word 'number' being construed as referring to a number or to a position in a sequence or to something else. And similarly for the word 'colour'; this can be interpreted as referring to the colour's saturation or to its hue. To prevent such misunderstandings, the word used to indicate the post at which the new word is to be stationed – 'number', 'colour' and so on – would also have to be explained.

This may seem like a minor problem since the words indicating how the original word is to be understood can also be defined. But then how are we to think of the ' "last" definition'? Is not this also open to being variously interpreted? It is no answer to say there is no such thing as a last definition. That is like saying there is no last house in a road because an additional one can always be built. If my house is the last in the road, it is the last one regardless of what might be built there in the future.

The possibility of misunderstanding depends on 'the circumstances under which [the definition] is given, and on the person [to whom it is given]'. What matters is not whether further misunderstanding can arise (this can always happen) but whether it occurs in practice. As often as not, the pupil will grasp that 'two' is meant when told 'That is called "two" ', or 'This *number* is called "two" ' or something more complicated. Still there is no guarantee that such definitions will always work. A pupil may fail to cotton on despite our best efforts.

Whether one 'takes' a definition of 'two' to define a number, a colour or something else can be discerned in how one goes on to use the word. What matters is how one proceeds, not anything that goes on in one. If I take 'two' to define a number, I shall use it to count objects; if I take it to define a colour, I shall use it to refer to things of such-and-such a colour. (Recall that in §6 Wittgenstein stresses that the builders' understanding of their four words manifests itself in the use they make of them. Also notice that whereas in §28 Wittgenstein focusses on the interpretation of ostensive definitions, in this one he focusses on how they are 'take[n]'.)

Section 30

Wittgenstein has been saying that ostensive definition can be deployed to explain 'the use – the meaning – of [a] word when the overall role of the word in language is clear'. You will understand me when I say 'This is called "sepia" ' if you know that I am talking about a colour. (Here Wittgenstein is reminding us that the circumstances have to be right for explanations of the uses and meanings of words to work; he is not equating the meaning of a word with its use.) This is obvious enough, and we shall not go wrong as long as we remember that 'all sorts of problems attach to the words "to know" and "to be clear"'. (The reason that difficulties arise is that these phrases are often construed in odd ways. Philosophical preconceptions about genuine knowledge being unavailable and true clarity being unattainable seem to throw into question the possibility of ostensive definition.)

Nobody can deny that we need to know something (and need to be able to do something) to ask the name of a thing. We would not latch on to what is being defined – except by chance – if we did not have the right background knowledge and special abilities. But precisely 'what does one have to know?' What sort of background knowledge does one need to possess to be able to ask for the name of a thing? (This question is taken up in the next section.)

Section 31

To clarify the question raised in the last section about what we need to know to learn the name of something Wittgenstein describes three ways a person might learn that a certain piece in chess is called 'the king'. (Presumably the reason he shifts from talking about the names of numbers and colours to talking about the names of chess pieces is that he can make the points he wants to make more easily using this example.)

In the first scenario a person already knows the rules of chess. The person understands the role of the king and only has to be told which sort of piece functions as a king. Everything has been prepared and all he or she needs to know is how to identify pieces as kings. In this case saying 'This is the king' while pointing to the piece seals the matter. The person will – all things being equal – come to appreciate that 'king' is the name of what is being pointed to.

In the second scenario a person who has mastered the game without explicitly learning the rules is shown pieces of unfamiliar shapes. In this case saying 'This is the king' will suffice to convey which pieces are kings. As before, the person will normally come to understand 'the use of the piece because … the place for [the word] was already prepared'. People in this sort of situation do not know the rules in the sense of being able to recite them. But they know them 'in another sense' since they know how to proceed. It is like knowing one's native language. While most of us know when sentences are grammatical, few of us can specify the grammar of our language in any detail.

In the third scenario a person is told 'This is the king; it can move like this, ... and so on'. If the person ' "knows what a piece in a game is" ' having 'already played other games, or [having] watched other people playing "and understood" – *and similar things*', this will suffice to fix the meaning of 'king'. As in the first two scenarios, the place for the word has been prepared. The person knows enough for the new information to fix the use of the word. Moreover, as Wittgenstein goes on to remind us, 'only under these conditions will [a person] be able to ask relevantly in the course of learning a game "What do you call this?" ' regarding one of its pieces. The person who lacks such information is in much the same situation as the child who knows nothing about chess. He or she will take the word 'king' to mean 'thing of a certain shape' or something similar, not 'chess piece governed by such-and-such rules'.

At the end of the section Wittgenstein emphasizes two other points. First he notes that only those who 'know how to do something with it can significantly ask a name'. Unless you know at least some of the ways names function, it makes no sense to ask the name of something. Secondly he reminds us that the person being asked what we call something may – for one reason or another – reply 'Settle the name yourself'. In this event 'the one who asked would have to manage everything for himself'. He would have to try to figure out what the word means on his own (or else remain ignorant).

Section 32

When we arrive in a strange country, we may have to shift for ourselves just as I would have to shift for myself if someone were to tell me to '[s]ettle the name [myself]' (§31). We may learn the language being spoken by being shown what words name but we may have to guess what is being referred to. For instance if it were unclear whether a word of the new language corresponds to our word for 'sepia' or to our word for 'shape', we would have to choose one of them and hope for the best. In such cases the place for the word is not fully prepared for us, and we are thrown back on our own resources. This is not a serious problem, however. The odd wrong guess is rarely an impediment to learning a language. (Significantly, Wittgenstein underlines the word 'guess'. Guessing involves formulating hypotheses, something children learning their first language cannot do until quite far along. As Wittgenstein noted in §5, language learning is initially a matter of training, not explanation.)

Wittgenstein adds that Augustine describes the way he learnt a language as though he were learning a second language (compare the quotation from Augustine given in §1). Reading Augustine one has the impression that he believed he had a set of 'posts' at which to station words before he learnt to speak. He does, it is true, speak of himself as having 'grasped' what was being named. But when he speaks of using the signs he was taught 'to express his desires', it sounds as though he believes he is already able to think (where this means 'something like "talk to [himself]"'). Indeed learning a first language, as Augustine describes it, is comparable to entering a country and trying to figure out what the inhabitants are saying.

This is not to suggest there is nothing to be said for thinking of learning a first language on the model of learning a second one. Much can be said – and much has been said by philosophers and cognitive scientists – in support of the idea that we are born with the relevant 'posts' in place. Once again, however, we should hesitate before discounting Wittgenstein's remarks. He is inviting discussion rather than closing it down. Far from dismissing the idea of an innate language of thought out of hand, he would encourage us to consider carefully what it amounts to.

Interlude (6): The demand for perfect exactness

What is Wittgenstein trying to get over in his discussion of ostensive definition? I think it clear that he is not, as often supposed, disparaging such definition. He allows, even insists, that many words can be defined by pointing and saying 'This is ...' or 'This is called "..."'. As he sees it, the idea of children asking and being told the names of things is no more outlandish than the idea of their being trained to name things. In fact he accords a wider role to ostensive definition than most philosophers. (§28 leaves little doubt that he thinks ostensive definitions can be provided not only for words that apply to things that can be seen, touched or smelled but also for words that apply to things that cannot.) He is trying to do what he was trying to do when discussing ostensive training in §6 – clarify something about language that is often misunderstood. His aim is to disabuse us of a widespread philosophical misconception about what ostensive definition involves and what it manages to achieve.

We can appreciate better what Wittgenstein is driving at by briefly considering the most common picture of how the meanings of words are explained. On this view the meaning of a word can be explained either in terms of other words or by pointing to something to which the word applies. For obvious reasons, the first sort of explanation is frequently called 'verbal definition', while the second sort is called 'ostensive definition'. Thus I might explain the meaning of 'sepia' verbally as 'dark, reddish-brown' or ostensively as this colour (here I point to a sepia object). When verbally defining a word I relate one bit of language to other bits of language. When ostensively defining a word I relate a bit of language to a bit of the world (this is done in some dictionaries by exhibiting an appropriate example or sample). Verbal definition remains within language, and it is, we are told, only by means of ostensive definition (or ostensive training) that we are able to break out of the circle of words.

If we accept this picture of meanings, it is but a short step to the conclusion that the meanings of some words must be fixed by ostensive definition (or ostensive training) in a way that precludes every chance of misunderstanding. Once we agree that ostensive definition provides our sole way into language – verbal definitions being in terms of other words – we are practically forced to think of this sort of definition as pinning down the meanings of the words it defines. Were ostensive definition never 'perfectly exact', every word could, we think, be 'variously interpreted' (§28). Everything we say would be vague, indefinite or equivocal, and we could never be sure we are making sense. Thus since we normally make sense and our words are only rarely open to misunderstanding, it must – according to the present line of thought – be possible to link words with things by means of ostensive definition in a direct, unmediated, presuppositionless manner. (Nobody should be surprised that philosophers mostly hold that only words for things that can be touched, tasted, smelt, seen or heard can be defined ostensively. Since it is impossible to touch, taste, smell, see or hear numbers, directions and the like, these cannot, they conclude, be named. In such cases direct, unmediated, presupposition-less links are out of the question.)

The burden of Wittgenstein's remarks in the present instalment is that this conception of ostensive definition crumbles between our fingers when pressed. He points out that ostensive definition does not and cannot connect words with things in the direct and unmediated way philosophers are inclined to suppose. The idea of a pinpoint connection between a word and a thing is deeply problematic since it runs foul of the fact that 'the place for a word [must be] already prepared' (§31). It is no more possible to associate words with things in the absence of such preparation than it is possible to set up a brake 'by connecting up rod and lever' in the absence of 'the whole of the rest of the mechanism' (§6). There is a gap between language and the world, a gap that not even the most careful ostensive definition can bridge.

Words cannot be brought right up to things. Some sort of additional support is always necessary.

This is not to say there is no connection between words and things, even less to suggest our words are always indeterminate. It does not follow from the fact that 'ostensive definition can be variously interpreted in *every* case' (§28) that words cannot be correlated with things. This follows only if knowing the meanings of words requires at least some of them to be associated with the objects they stand for in a direct, unmediated fashion (and 'perfectly exact' definitions are always necessary for intelligible thought). Once this dubious philosophical view is set aside, the problem of how the meanings of words can be known evaporates. We do not have to invoke the idea of pinpoint connections between words and things (and commit ourselves to the philosopher's conception of perfect exactness) since we can observe that 'the post at which we station the word' is usually settled in advance (§29) and 'the overall role of the word' is hardly ever unclear (§30).

It helps to recall Wittgenstein's point about 'commanding, questioning, recounting, chatting, [being] as much a part of our natural history as walking, eating, drinking, playing' (§25). Ostensive definition does not rest on our being able to hook up words directly with things by an extraordinary feat of mental wizardry. It rests on the fact that people like us – given the sort of world we live in – can be taught to use words like 'two', 'sepia' and 'west' by pointing. If children naturally came towards a pointing finger (as cats do) rather than looked in the direction being pointed to, it would be harder, perhaps impossible, to teach them words by means of ostensive definition. Learning a language, like walking and eating, is something we do. It too depends on our having certain natural abilities. (Some of what is involved here becomes clear when one considers the difficulty of teaching language to autistic children, who do not react instinctively the way most of us do. It is hard to teach them words because they do not naturally grasp that words stand for the objects being pointed to.)

In short, Wittgenstein is mainly urging two points in this instalment. First the philosophical idea of ostensive definition as connecting words with things in a direct, unmediated, presuppositionless way is open to the criticism that it is impossible to forge connections between language and the world in the absence of appropriate linguistic 'supports'. Secondly language learning does not rest on the possibility of words being connected with things in such a fashion. The fact that what is meant cannot be pinned down once and for all and misunderstanding is always possible is no reason to think that our words lack meaning. Fortunately human beings are for the most part able to grasp what is being defined and there is no need to assume that words for colours, numbers, shapes and the like must be explicable by pointing to things in a sure-fire way.

Sections 33 to 38: Characteristic experiences and genuine names

In this instalment Wittgenstein continues his examination of common misconceptions regarding ostensive definition. He criticizes the idea that grasping what a word means is a matter of having appropriate experiences, notes how philosophers typically respond to this sort of criticism, questions whether names are related in just one way to their bearers, and scrutinizes the philosophical view that 'this' is the only genuine name.

Section 33

Is Wittgenstein right in thinking that the use of a word can be explained by means of an ostensive definition only when its 'overall role ... in language is clear' (§30) and its 'place ... has already been prepared' (§31)? It is tempting to deny this on the grounds that 'all you need – of course! – is to know or guess what the person giving the explanation is pointing to'. In fact this seems almost too obvious to debate. If I point to the shape of a thing, surely the person I am addressing can 'know or guess' what I am pointing to – the shape rather than the colour or number.

Doubts creep in, however, when we consider what pointing to the shape and pointing to the colour consist in. The question is not whether you can know or guess what I am pointing to but whether this shows you can understand my definition straight off. Were there some-thing to be known or guessed, something I do differently when I point to the shape as opposed to the colour, you would not have to know 'the overall role of the word in language' (§30). No initial preparation would be required. You could grasp my meaning without knowing anything. The only trouble is that it is far from evident that we do something different when we point to the shape from when we point to the colour, and do something different again when we point to the number of something. (Presumably Wittgenstein says it is 'queer' to speak of the number of something because we do not usually speak of pointing to the 'oneness' of an object.)

Consider pointing to the shape of an object, then to its colour, then to its number. Do you do something different each time, something someone else could see or guess you are doing? Certainly you mean something different. But how is this possible? Is it that you concentrate your attention on the shape in the first case, on the colour in the second and on the number in the third? Perhaps you do. But then the question arises 'how is *that* done?' – how do you manage to direct your attention to the colour or the shape? Is there one thing you always do when you concentrate on the colour of an object? Is there anything that makes your action one of directing your attention to the colour?

Wittgenstein agrees that you do something different when you obey an order to concentrate on the colour of a vase from when you obey an order to concentrate on its shape. But he questions whether 'you always do the *same* thing when you direct your attention to the colour'. This is improbable. There does not seem to be one thing you do, one thing that counts as directing your attention to the colour of an object. Just the reverse, the rubric of 'attending to the colour' applies to a multitude of activities (and likewise for 'pointing to the colour').

Consider attending to the colour blue. (Recall Wittgenstein's strategy in §24. There he reminds us of the variety of things 'description' covers; here he reminds us of some of the many ways we use the phrase 'attending to colour'.) One can attend to a blue patch to see whether it is the same shade of blue as another patch, attend to the colour of paint to determine whether it matches the colour of the sky, attend to the colour of the sky to see if the weather is improving, and attend to two shades of blue with an eye to their effects (e.g. whether they seem warm or cool). Furthermore one can attend to the blue colour of a book, attend to the colour of a blue-light signal because of some special significance it has, and attend to a blue patch when one wants to know whether it counts as 'indigo'. Nor should it be forgotten that when attending to a colour, we sometimes put our hands in front of our eyes to shield the outline from view, sometimes avert our eyes from the outline, sometimes focus on the colour, trying to remember when we had seen it before.

And similarly for attending to a shape. When one attends to the shape of something, one sometimes traces its outline, perhaps screws up one's eyes so that its colour becomes less prominent, and such like. Nobody can deny one does such things '*while* one "directs one's attention to this or that"'. But attending to the shape of a thing is not the same as tracing its outline, screwing up one's eyes and the like. These activities are mere accompaniments of attending to the shape. My tracing the outline of an object no more characterizes my attending to the shape than my having an image constitutes the meaning of the word I am uttering (compare §6).

To attend to the colour or the shape of a thing is not to do something while one attends to it, 'nor yet [is it for something to occur] in one's thoughts and feelings'. (Compare §20, where Wittgenstein explores the idea that what we mean is fixed by what 'go[es] on' in us.) Directing one's attention to something is more like making a move in chess than like tracing the outline of an object with one's eyes or experiencing a headache. It is the context – you might say the language-game being played – that makes one's action an instance of attending to the colour just as it is 'the circumstances that we call "playing a game of chess", "solving a chess problem", and so on' that makes the chess player's action a move in chess. (Wittgenstein is noting how phrases like 'attending to the shape' are normally used; he is not putting forward a philosophical theory of attending to something or of meaning or understanding. The points he makes are worth making because they are often overlooked.)

Section 34

Wittgenstein has been suggesting that attending to something is not a matter of experiencing this or that. Now he adds that this holds even for people who invariably do the same thing and have the same feelings when attending to the shape of an object. (In §6 Wittgenstein imagined ostensive teaching always having the effect of evoking images; here he imagines attending to something always being accompanied by a certain sort of experience.) There is no guarantee that the rest of us will know what such a person is pointing to. If he or she were to define 'circle' ostensively – by pointing to a circle and saying 'That is called a "circle"' – a child might still fail to catch what is being taught. The child may see the person's eyes following the outline and have exactly the same feelings yet take 'circle' to mean what is normally meant by 'not a square' and later point to an oblong shape when told to point to a circle.

Intending a definition to be understood a particular way is not a matter of doing something and of having certain feelings. Nor is interpreting a definition a matter of noticing what the person giving the definition does and of feeling what he or she feels. Neither intending nor interpreting something is a 'process which accompanies the giving and hearing of the definition'. When I intend a definition of a circle to be understood a particular way, I mean 'circle' to be applied in the usual fashion to circles. And when I interpret a word a particular way, my ' "interpretation" may also consist in how [I now make] use of the word'.

Section 35

Wittgenstein now wards off a possible misunderstanding of what he has been saying about pointing to things and having experiences. He notes that he is not denying that there are 'what can be called "characteristic experiences" of pointing to (e.g.) the shape', experiences that may be present whenever we define shapes ostensively. To the contrary, there are, he tells us, experiences of 'following the outline [of an object] with one's finger or with one's eyes as one points'. What he is disputing is not the existence of such experiences, only the view that having them is sufficient for understanding ostensive definitions and the contention that knowledge of the sort mentioned in §31 is unnecessary.

To reinforce this point, and to underline that the existence of characteristic experiences does not in any way contradict what he has been saying, Wittgenstein stresses that the characteristic experiences that accompany 'mean[ing] the shape' are merely typical, common, representative. We can 'mean the shape' – that it is a circle – without having any 'characteristic experiences' or indeed any experiences at all. And even were we always to have a particular sort of experience whenever we point to the shape, what is meant would still depend on the 'circumstances'. That it is the shape rather than the colour is a function of 'what happen[s] before and after the pointing'. What the person doing the pointing is pointing at depends on what it makes sense to speak of him or her as pointing at, no more and no less.

This becomes clearer when we reflect on the difference between how we use 'to point to the shape' and 'to mean the shape' and how we use 'to point to this book (not that one)' and 'to point to the chair, not the table'. What makes my pointing a case of pointing to the shape rather than a case of pointing to the book is not a matter of my having different experiences. It is a matter of the context in which I do the pointing – of whether, say, geometry or furniture is being discussed and whether there is another book near at hand. It is not by chance that we learn phrases like 'to point to this thing' and 'to point to that thing' differently from how we learn phrases like 'to point to the colour, not the shape' and 'to mean the colour'. The latter phrases are more complicated and children have to know more to learn them than they have to know to learn phrases like 'to point to this thing'.

The experiences accompanying the practices of pointing to the shape or to the number of something are inessential for ostensive definition to work. They are 'characteristic experiences', experiences which 'recur often (not always) when shape or number are "meant"'. Moreover in some cases – for instance, the case of pointing to 'a piece in a game *as a piece in a game*' – the idea of an accompanying characteristic experience is hard to credit. When I consider what happens when I point to a chess piece, say a king, I do not find myself having a 'characteristic experience' of meaning it as a piece that can move in certain prescribed ways as opposed, say, to a piece of wood of a certain shape. Yet it may still be true of me that 'I mean that this *piece* is called the "king"'. And likewise for recognizing, wishing, remembering and the like. It is equally implausible to regard these as a matter of having 'characteristic experiences'.

Note at the bottom of page 18

The miscellaneous points about meaning in this note are loosely connected to the discussion of the last few sections. First Wittgenstein briefly considers a confusion that can arise because '*That* is blue' is used both to provide information about the colour of an object and to explain the word 'blue'. It is, he notes, a mistake to think that '*That* is blue' in the second case 'really means "That is called 'blue'"'. We do not mean 'is' sometimes as 'is', sometimes as 'is called', nor do we mean 'blue' sometimes as 'blue', sometimes as '[the word] "blue"'. (Also compare §19 on really meaning something.)

Secondly Wittgenstein observes that the meaning of a word can on occasion be learnt from a piece of information. For instance I might learn the meaning of 'sepia' from the information that an old photograph is sepia-toned. In this event I would come to understand the word without being shown anything. But while this is clear enough, there is 'a crucial superstition' lurking here – presumably the idea that explanations of words describe the essence of things. (It is unsurprising that Wittgenstein uses the word 'superstition' given that he takes philosophical views of meaning to be primitive beliefs that have grown up around our thinking about language over the years.)

Thirdly Wittgenstein reminds us that words have meaning only when they have a place 'in language'. 'Bububu' could come to mean 'If it doesn't rain I shall go for a walk', but at the moment it means nothing. My wanting a word to mean something does not make it mean it, nor does my having certain experiences when I hear the word. The 'grammar' of 'to mean', i.e. how we use it, is different from the grammar of 'to imagine'. When I imagine something, I have an experience, but not when I mean something. In contrast to imagining something, which happens in us, 'it is only in a language that [we] can mean something by something'. (Here Wittgenstein emphasizes the difference between meaning and imagining by noting trivialities about the use of the phrase 'to mean'. He is not surreptitiously invoking a philosophical theory of 'grammar', still less advancing a philosophical thesis about meaning.)

Section 36

In the last few sections Wittgenstein has been taking issue with the idea that the phrases 'pointing' and 'attending to' (and – see §35 – 'meaning', 'recognizing', 'wishing' and 'remembering') do not correspond to single actions or single experiences. Now he considers how philosophers tend to respond to this sort of situation. When we cannot find 'any *one* bodily action' (or characteristic experience) to which 'pointing' corresponds, he declares, 'we do what we do in a host of similar cases'. We assume the activity corresponds to 'a *spiritual* [mental, intellectual] activity'. We postulate something in our minds or in some kind of abstract realm.

This is unnecessary. There is no need to postulate a '*spirit*' whenever 'language suggests a body and there is none'. It is not true that there has to be something behind or above our words for us to be able to think and communicate intelligibly with one another. Saying there must be something supporting what we say is like saying there must be something supporting the individual links of a chain, something that holds them together. Our linguistic practices are 'as much a part of our natural history as 'walking, eating, drinking, playing' (§25) and as little in need of external support. (It is important to notice that Wittgenstein does not say that there is nothing to our mental life save for behaviour and nothing to language except words for concrete objects. It is one thing to disparage the search for '*spirit[s]*', quite another to defend an alternative philosophical view.)

Section 37

If we discount the importance of 'characteristic experiences', we shall want to know what 'the relation between name and thing named' is. But this too is to take a wrong step. If we look at how names and things are related in the case of language-game (2) or other simple language-game, we shall see that the relation can consist in various things. For instance it can consist – partly at least – in the fact that we conjure up an image when we hear a word or in the fact that a name is written on the thing it names or is pronounced whenever someone points at the thing. (Compare §15, where Wittgenstein notes that words can signify in many ways.) There is no one answer to the question of what the relation between name and thing named is. What counts as an answer depends on the language-game that is being played.

Section 38

But even granting there is no one thing 'the relation between name and thing named ... consists in' (§37), you may still wonder how 'this' and 'that' are connected with the things they signify. Surely we still require an answer to the question of what 'the word "this" [is] the name of in language (8)' and what 'the word "that" in ostensive definitions [is the name of]'. In response Wittgenstein suggests these questions are misposed since 'this' and 'that' are not names. (Compare §9, where he notes that names are taught and used differently from demonstratives.)

The reason some philosophers take 'this' to be 'the only *genuine* name' is that they 'sublime the logic of our language' and regard it as an abstract structure rather than as 'part of our natural history' (§23). They are drawn to this unusual conception of what is after all a very ordinary English word because they regard language as standing outside our everyday practices rather than as 'woven' into them (§7). Discounting or forgetting how we use the word 'this' in daily life, they take it to be a special sort of name and deem ordinary names like 'Napoleon' and 'Paris' to be names 'only in an inexact, approximate sense'.

The 'proper answer' to our tendency to regard language as sublime is that 'we call very different things "names"' and employ 'the word "name" ... to characterize many different kinds of use of a word'. Thinking that there is just one genuine name is as much a mistake as thinking there is just one sort of description (compare §24). Names may, it is true, be used in various ways – to identify people, to ridicule them, to praise them and so on (compare 'Joseph Haydn', 'Mr Fancy Pants' and 'The Sun King'). Still 'the kind of use that "this" has is not among [such uses]'. In the normal course of events we do not use 'this' to identify people, to ridicule them or to praise them.

When ostensively defining words we sometimes say the word 'this', sometimes say the name of the object we are pointing to. Moreover we frequently use demonstratives in sentences instead of names (compare 'This is black' with 'Spot is black'). But for all that, demonstratives are not names. While the name 'N' can be 'defined by means of the demonstrative expression "That is N"', the demonstrative 'this' cannot be defined by saying 'This is this' or 'This is called "this"'. (Wittgenstein is not denying that language-games can be imagined in which 'this' functions as a name. He is not precluding the possibility of a person naming a pet 'This'.)

If you try to figure out how names are correlated with objects by staring at something and saying 'N' or 'this', naming will seem to involve 'a *queer* connexion'. Worse, it will appear to be an 'occult process' in which the name somehow reaches out to the thing named, one that establishes a connection between word and world by a 'remarkable act of mind'. When one considers how names and things are related in a simple language like language (2), by contrast, the mystery vanishes. What initially looks like a '*queer* connexion' now looks very much less odd. The idea of naming as an extraordinary form of baptism gives way to the anodyne view that 'naming something is like attaching a label to a thing' (§15).

Once we have convinced ourselves that the word 'this' is used in much the same way as a name, it is a small step to the conclusion that it enjoys a special kind of relationship to the thing it names. But far from having made an important discovery about language, all we have really done is detach the word 'this' from the language-game to which it ordinarily belongs. The idea that 'this' is a genuine name is a spurious solution to a spurious problem. We think there is a significant philosophical issue here only because 'our language *[has gone] on holiday*'. (This is a major theme in Wittgenstein's philosophy. In the *Tractatus* he says 'the method of formulating [the problems of philosophy] rests on the misunderstanding of the logic of our language'.[1])

Interlude (7): Naming as an occult process

What Wittgenstein is driving at in this instalment is for the most part easy to fathom. Though the details of §§33–5 (and the accompanying note on page 18) are complicated, the main thrust of them is clear enough. Wittgenstein is trying to get us to see that a person's pointing to something counts as an instance of pointing to its shape rather than of pointing to its number or its colour because of the surrounding circumstances, not because of some supposedly distinctive feature of the action of the person doing the pointing or because of the experiences he or she happens to be having. Similarly the discussion of §36 and §37 is relatively straightforward. In §36 Wittgenstein notes that we tend to postulate a spirit when we cannot find any bodily action that pointing corresponds to, while in §37 he broaches the allied issue of how names are related to things and declares, not unexpectedly, that they may be related in many ways. Where difficulties mostly arise is in connection with §38. Why would anyone think 'this' is 'the only *genuine* name'?

To see why, it helps to recall what was said about definitions in the last interlude, focussing now on names like 'Napoleon' rather than on nouns like 'sepia'. Transposed to the case of the name 'Napoleon', the idea is that the meaning of the word can be explained using other words, words that can in turn be explained either in terms of other words or directly by means of ostensive definitions. This leads on to the idea that the meanings of ordinary names like 'Napoleon' are always definable in the final analysis in terms of 'genuine names', i.e. names that connect up with things in an unmediated, presupposition-less way. On this view a 'genuine name' differs from an ordinary name in that it can only be defined ostensively. Whereas 'Napoleon' can be defined in terms of other words (e.g. as 'the emperor of France between 1804 and 1815'), 'genuine names' cannot be. If a name is verbally definable, it is not primitive; it does not stand at the end of the road.

Once we have come this far, there is not much more distance to travel. The conclusion that 'this' is 'the only *genuine* name' now follows almost immediately. If a name can only be defined ostensively, there is nothing that can be said about it. It must be directly linked with the thing it names. It cannot describe the thing it names, only indicate, exhibit, point to it. The connection has to be a pinpoint connection; the name must reach out to the world without the help of any interme-diary. In other words it must function as though it were a demonstrative, i.e. it must demonstrate in the way 'this' demonstrates. Whence we are led to the thesis that 'this' is, strictly speaking, 'the only *genuine* name'. No other word is plausibly taken to be purely demon-strative – apart from another demonstrative such as 'that'. Only words like 'this' seem capable of directly picking out things.

It should now also be clear why naming can seem to involve 'a *queer* connexion of a word with an object' (§38). If you think 'this' is the 'only *genuine* name', you can hardly avoid treating 'the conception of naming as, so to speak, an occult process', one that requires a 'remark-able act of mind, as it were a baptism of an object'. While there is nothing mysterious about baptising a child 'Charles Henry William', the possibility of effecting a pinpoint connection between a word and a thing seems extraordinary, even miraculous. Insofar as genuine naming – construed as something that is not in the least 'inexact, approximate' – is possible, it would seem that we must be able to get our minds en rapport with things just as they are. We must be able to get right up to the world. Small wonder, then, that philosophers are prone to 'staring at an object in front of [them] and repeating a name or even the word "this" innumerable times'.

I hope it will be agreed that, however odd, this line of thought is not unattractive. While the conception of genuine naming is, as Wittgenstein says, 'queer', it is easy to see why it has often been defended. When we reflect on language and the world in a philosophical spirit, it seems that names must have some direct connection with the world and that it must be possible to break out of language and grasp the things named in and of themselves. Indeed this is one of the more important impetuses to philosophical thinking. The idea that we must be able to seize objects in a pure and unadulterated form if we put our minds to it is not easily resisted. As Wittgenstein notes, there does not seem to be any difficulty about 'say[ing] the word "this" *to* [an] object, as it were *address* the object as "this"' (§38). The fact that this is 'a queer use' of 'this', one that 'only occurs in doing philosophy', pales by comparison. (The tremendous grip of the idea that we can address objects directly is amusingly illustrated in a response Russell made to a question following a lecture he gave in 1918. When asked: 'If the proper name of a thing, a "this", varies from instant to instant, how is it possible to make any argument?', Russell answered: 'You can keep "this" going for about a minute or two. I made that dot and talked about it for some little time. I mean it varies often. If you argue quickly, you can get some little way before it is finished'.[2])

Contrary to how it may seem at first sight, then, the discussion of §38 is far from tangential to the main thrust of Wittgenstein's concerns in the *Investigations*. It is closely linked with what he has been saying about ostensive definition, and it introduces an important new issue for consideration. If ostensive definition is regarded as a matter of connecting words to things in the way we are inclined to think – i.e. as providing what in §28 Wittgenstein referred to as 'perfectly exact' explanations of their meanings – it is hard to see what else could serve as a 'genuine name' besides 'this'. And once 'this' is reckoned the only name that names precisely instead of 'inexact[ly]' and 'approximate[ly]', it is clearly of the utmost importance that we get straight about how it does the trick. It is not fortuitous that having criticized the idea that 'to point' and 'to mean' are names of bodily or mental actions in §§33–6, Wittgenstein turns his attention in §37 to 'the relation between name and thing named' and goes on in §38 to decry 'the conception of naming as, so to speak, an occult process'.

Sections 39 to 47: Names and their bearers

In §38 Wittgenstein notes that 'strange to say, the word "this" has been called the only *genuine* name'. In the next nine sections, he focusses on the allied idea that a genuine name designates something absolutely simple. He takes issue with two important assumptions underlying this idea: the assumption that names mean what they stand for and the assumption that things are properly spoken of as absolutely simple or absolutely complex.

Section 39

Why is 'this' sometimes taken to be a name 'when it is evidently *not* a name' (compare §38)? Wittgenstein notes that this idea is fuelled by the philosophical supposition that '*a name really ought to signify a simple*'. Taking names properly so called to denote things that are not composed of anything else, many philosophers have disparaged ordinary names like 'Napoleon' and 'Paris' as names 'only in an inexact, approximate sense' and taken 'this' to be 'the only genuine name', i.e. to be the only word that names things with no component parts (§38). In their view it is characteristic of a genuine name – in contrast to an ordinary name, which always signifies a composite – that it signify a simple.

But why think '*a name really ought to signify a simple*'? One argument runs as follows. (Here Wittgenstein considers a somewhat different line of reasoning from the one mentioned in the last interlude.) We begin by noting that a sentence containing an ordinary name, say, 'Excalibur has a sharp blade', is meaningful whether or not the word 'Excalibur' names something. (It does not matter whether one thinks of Excalibur as a real sword or as King Arthur's magic sword. In the German text Wittgenstein uses the example of 'Nothung', the mythical sword of Siegfried in the *Nibelungenlied*. He inserted 'Excalibur' for 'Nothung' when correcting an earlier translation of §39.) Next we note that 'Excalibur has a sharp blade' would not be meaningful were 'Excalibur' a meaningless word. Then – assuming that names are meaningful only if they name – we note that 'Excalibur' would be a meaningless word if it did not have a bearer. Whence since 'the sentence "Excalibur has a sharp blade" makes *sense* whether Excalibur is still whole or is broken up', we conclude finally that 'Excalibur' cannot be a 'genuine name'. (In brief: since genuine names always have bearers 'Excalibur' cannot be a genuine name, it being possible for Excalibur to be broken up.) Moreover, since the same goes for any name that names something that can be destroyed, we are forced to conclude that to be 'genuine' a name must name a simple, i.e. must name something that has no component parts and cannot go out of existence.

How then should 'Excalibur has a sharp blade' be understood? Since the sentence makes sense whether Excalibur is intact or broken, it cannot – according to the present line of thought – be about Excalibur. It must be about something else. As Wittgenstein puts it: 'the word "Excalibur" must disappear when [its] sense is analysed and its place [in the original sentence must] be taken by words which name simples'. The upshot of the whole argument, the cogency of which still remains to be considered, is thus that meaningful sentences can always be transformed into sentences the names of which are 'real names', i.e. names that name things that cannot be 'broken up'.

Section 40

Wittgenstein begins his discussion of the argument sketched in §39 by examining its crucial premise, namely that names are meaningless when they do not have bearers. (Compare the philosophical picture introduced in §1. If a name means what it stands for, it is meaningful only if it stands for something.) This line of thought, Wittgenstein notes, is problematic if only because 'the word "meaning" is being used illicitly if it is used to signify the thing that "corresponds" to the word'. To hold that names mean what they stand for is 'to confound the meaning of a name with the *bearer* of the name'. 'Excalibur' does not become meaningless when the sword is broken up any more than 'Mr N.N.' becomes meaningless when Mr N.N. dies. What dies when Mr N.N. dies is a person, not the meaning of a name, and what is broken up when Excalibur is broken up is the sword, not a meaning. 'Excalibur has a sharp blade' and 'Mr. N.N. is dead' make sense whether or not their subjects exist. Saying the meaning of 'Mr N.N.'

dies when Mr N.N. dies is 'nonsensical' for the simple reason that 'if the name ceased to have meaning it would make no sense to say "Mr. N.N. is dead"'.

This hardly shows that philosophers who accept the idea of analysis are wrong. Wittgenstein knows it is no part of their view that sentences like 'Excalibur has a sharp blade' and 'Mr. N.N. is dead' are meaningless if their names have no bearers. He has not forgotten what he said about 'Excalibur' disappearing 'when the sense [of the sentences in which it occurs] is analysed' (§39). What Wittgenstein is trying to do is get us to recognize that the argument is less obviously correct than often supposed. He is reminding us that we do not normally take the meaning of a name to be its bearer; we take names to be meaningful irrespective of the fate of their bearers. Actually the discussion of naming and analysis will continue for another twenty-four sections.

Section 41

Wittgenstein is trying to get us to appreciate the oddness of the philosophical idea that the meaning of a name is the thing it names. In §40 he reminds us that 'Mr N.N.' does not cease to have a meaning when its bearer, Mr N.N., ceases to exist. In this one he considers the case – first discussed in §15 – of builders using marks to signify tools. What would happen, he asks, if a builder gave his assistant a sign for a tool, say 'N', when the tool bearing this name has been destroyed? Since '[w]e have not settled anything about this' we cannot at the moment say whether it would become meaningless or not.

If the builder's assistant were to 'stand there at a loss, or shew [the builder] the pieces', one '*might*' say the sign 'N' has ceased to have a meaning. And one might say the same thing if the tool had been given a new name, say 'M'. On the other hand it is easy to imagine situations in which 'N' remains meaningful when the tool it names is broken. If the builders were in the habit of shaking their heads when giving the sign to convey that the tool that had carried the sign is broken, the sign would still be meaningful. 'N' would have a place in the language-game whether it had a bearer or not.

By reflecting on such scenarios Wittgenstein hopes we shall agree that philosophers who take names to be meaningful only if they have bearers are – to use a phrase from §38 – 'sublim[ing] the logic of our language' and treating it as a structure apart from its application. His aim is to get us to see that philosophical thinking about names is radically at variance with how we actually operate with them. He wants us to appreciate that a name has a use and is meaningful when it has 'a place in [a] language-game'. It does not have to have a bearer.

Section 42

But what about the case of a name, say 'X', that has '*never* been used for a tool'? Can such a name be said to have a meaning in the language-game described in §15? One might think not since 'X' does not stand for a tool. But even here matters are not clear-cut. There does not have to have been something corresponding to 'X'. 'X' could still have a place in the builders' language-game just as 'N' could have when the tool that the word names is broken (see §41). When a builder calls out 'X', the assistant may, for instance, be expected to shake his head as a joke. This is not an incoherent scenario.

Section 43

Wittgenstein next interpolates an observation about how we use the word 'meaning'. He says that 'for a *large* class of cases' in which we employ the word (including, presumably, his uses of it in the last few sections) 'the meaning of a word is its use in the language'. But not always. As Wittgenstein goes on to remind us 'the *meaning* of a name is sometimes explained by pointing to its *bearer*'. (The English translation is slightly misleading. Wittgenstein does not say that the word 'meaning' can be 'defined' as its use in the language. He uses the word 'erklären' and apparently preferred 'explain' in an earlier translation. While 'defined' is not a bad translation, 'explained' has a different tone and would perhaps be preferable, especially given that 'erklärt' is rendered as 'explained' in the second paragraph.)

This section is widely misunderstood. Contrary to what is often supposed, Wittgenstein does not identify the meaning of a word with its use. Actually the reverse, he explicitly states that the meaning of a word is its use 'for a *large* class of cases – though not for all' and immediately notes an exception. He says that while in many cases you can come to know the meaning of a word by coming to understand how it is used, in certain cases – e.g. the case in which a person is near at hand – the meaning can be explained by the simple expedient of pointing and saying 'That is ...'. To say that the meaning of a word can sometimes be explained by describing how the word is used, sometimes by pointing to an object, hardly adds up to a philosophical view, let alone a theory of meaning.

Section 44

How are we to explain the fact that 'Excalibur has a sharp blade' is meaningful 'even when Excalibur was broken into pieces'? Wittgenstein has been criticizing what he takes to be an unacceptable answer, the gist of which is that such sentences count as meaningful because they can be analysed into sentences all the names of which stand for simple objects. Now he points out that 'Excalibur has a sharp blade' makes good sense because it has a use. In our language-game 'a name is also used in the absence of its bearer' and sentences are meaningful whether or not all their names have bearers.

This is not to deny it is possible to imagine language-games in which names are used only in the presence of their bearers and can always be replaced by 'this' and a pointing gesture. Consider the name 'Queen Z'. In the country Queen Z rules over, it could be a law that her name is to be used only when she is in full view. Then, assuming the law were always obeyed, the name 'Queen Z' could be replaced by 'this' and a pointing gesture, and 'Queen Z is rich' would be equivalent to 'She – or this – is rich' accompanied by a gesture towards the person herself. This is another example of 'a narrowly circumscribed region' where a philosophical conception applies (see §3). It is not one of our language-games but it could have been.

Section 45

Wittgenstein grants that 'the demonstrative "this" can never be used without a bearer'. (This overstates the point somewhat. In some sentences – e.g. 'King Arthur picked up Excalibur; this was his sword' – the word 'this' need not have a bearer. Generally, however, 'this' is used, as Wittgenstein says, in the presence of a bearer. It is used in much the same way as 'Queen Z' in the example just given.) Indeed Wittgenstein even allows that 'so long as there is a *this*, the word "this" has a meaning too, whether *this* [the thing referred to] is simple or complex'. Still he is adamant that 'this' does not count as a 'genuine name' (§38). It is, he insists, a mistake to take the fact that 'this' cannot be used without a bearer to show it is a name. The word 'this' is altogether different from a name, which 'is not used with, but only explained by means of, the gesture of pointing' (see also the remarks about 'this' in §9 and §38).

Section 46

Wittgenstein now cites a passage from Plato's *Theaetetus*, which he takes to reveal 'what lies behind the idea that names really signify simples'. (The quotation is from *Theaetetus*, 201e–202b.) In this passage Socrates says he has heard it stated that 'there is no definition of the primary elements' – i.e. simples – because 'everything that exists in its own right can only be *named*, no other determination is possible, neither that it *is* nor that it *is not*'. On this view 'we and everything else are composed [of primary elements]'. Sentences are ultimately about things that cannot be described, only named, and it follows as night follows day that 'a *name really ought to name a simple*' (§39).

The idea that the 'primary elements' cannot be described, only named, can be bolstered by various considerations. If each describable thing has a differentiating characteristic (other than a name) and each thing with a differentiating characteristic is complex, nothing describable can be a primary element and exist in its own right. What is describable must comprise more basic elements and be ultimately decomposable into simples. In other words, we are always talking in a roundabout way about the primary elements. As Plato put it, 'the essence of speech is the composition of names [i.e. words that signify simples]'.

The idea that the ultimate constituents of the world are simples is one that Russell and Wittgenstein had earlier canvassed. As Wittgenstein notes, the 'objects' referred to in the *Tractatus* and Russell's 'individuals' are primary elements. (In the *Tractatus* Wittgenstein declares that 'I can only *name* [objects]' and 'Objects ... cannot be compound', while in a somewhat later work he notes that Plato takes 'object' to mean 'reference of a not further definable word' and takes 'description' to mean 'definition'.[1]) Clearly there is an important connection between Plato's conception of language and the conception Wittgenstein sketches in §1. The main difference is that for Plato the names in question are 'bare name[s]', i.e. names of 'primary elements'.

Section 47

In opposition to the idea that names name simples, Wittgenstein invites us to consider what it means to speak of the 'simple constituent parts of which reality is composed'. Does it make sense to speak of the world as comprising 'primary elements', which can only be named? In particular, is it really possible to debate whether the 'simple constituent parts of a chair', say, are 'the bits of wood of which it is made [or] the molecules or the atoms'?

Wittgenstein hopes we shall agree that what counts as a simple constituent part of a chair depends on our interests. While a chair can be sensibly said to comprise parts that are simple in this or that respect, 'it makes no sense at all to speak absolutely of the "simple parts of a chair"'. In a carpenter's workshop, a piece of wood might count as simple while in a physicist's laboratory the molecules or atoms might. True, 'simple' means 'not composite'. But judgements of compositeness are just as relative to our concerns and interests as judgements of simplicity. (This is not a form of relativism. Wittgenstein is not saying that the facts are constituted by language-games or that the world depends on how we choose to speak about it. A chair consists of a seat, a back, arms and legs and of molecules and atoms however we describe it. Nor is it an argument against Wittgenstein that physicists take elementary particles to be simples. Such particles are not 'absolutely simple' in the philosopher's sense. They are simple as a matter of fact, not as a matter of necessity, and 'other determination[s]' are possible.)

When Wittgenstein says 'it makes no sense at all to speak absolutely of the "simple parts of a chair"', he is noting something he thinks we shall end up agreeing with if we try to figure out what its absolutely simple parts are. He is not dogmatically asserting anything, just questioning whether we have as clear an idea of what it is for something to exist 'in its own right' as we think we have. His point is that ordinarily when we speak of the bits of wood of which the chair is fabricated – or of its molecules or atoms – as its simple constituents, we do so relative to a standard rather than 'absolutely'.

Wittgenstein next reiterates that it is senseless to speak absolutely of the 'simple parts' of something as opposed to parts of it that are simple in such-and-such respects. He stresses that a visual image of a tree or a chair may be said to be composite in various ways and probes the assumption that there is a single answer to the question 'What are its simple component parts?'. After all, visual images may properly be said to be complex because they are multi-coloured, because their outlines are not uniform, or because of some other feature they have. Even a curve may be regarded as composed of ascending and descending parts.

The question 'Is what you see composite?' makes sense only with respect to a specific conception of compositeness. If a visual image of a tree is understood to be composite just if it is an image of its branches and its trunk, one can sensibly ask whether a given image of a tree is simple or composite – it will count as composite if it is an image of the branches and trunk of a tree. And likewise for the question 'What are its simple component parts?'. This can be answered by describing the individual branches. (The reason why 'the branches' is the wrong answer is that visual images comprise smaller images, not things. 'The branches' is an answer to the '*grammatical* question' of what the components of the image are called, not an answer to the question of what its components are.)

It would be wrong to insist that some things, chessboards for instance, are 'obviously, and absolutely composite'. A chessboard cannot be said to be 'absolutely composite' since there are 'quite different ways of looking at it'. To count as 'absolutely "composite"', there would have to be a single essential respect in which the board is composite whereas in fact it counts as complex in many regards – in the sense that it comprises sixty-four squares, the sense that it comprises a schema of squares and the colours white and black, and so on.

It is senseless to ask whether things are simple or composite '*outside* a particular language-game'. Puzzling over the question of whether something is truly simple or complex is as silly as puzzling over the question of whether 'to sleep' means something active or passive. An object can be simple in one language-game and complex in another no less than 'to sleep' can count as a verb in the active voice and denote a passive activity. (It should not be thought Wittgenstein can be answered by noting that metaphysics is itself a language-game and the elements are whatever count as simple in this game. It is far from obvious that there is any such language-game, and Wittgenstein deprecates metaphysical speculation.)

While 'simple' and 'complex' are often regarded as applying or not applying absolutely, they are actually used in a multitude of ways. There is no one answer to the question of whether the colour of the white squares of a chessboard is simple or a mixture of pure white and pure yellow. Nor is there a single answer to the question of whether the colour white is simple or a combination of all the colours of the rainbow. Nor even a single answer to the question of whether a 2 cm length is simple or a combination of two 1 cm lengths (or combination of a 3 cm length and a 1 cm length in the opposite direction).

If questions about simplicity and compositeness are decidable only given specific standards of simplicity and compositeness, objects cannot be spoken of as absolutely simple or absolutely complex. It is no answer to the '*philosophical* question' of whether the visual image of a tree is composite to say it 'depends on what you understand by "composite" '. To the contrary, this amounts to 'a rejection of the question'. It is tantamount to saying it makes no sense to speak of images as simple or composite '*outside* a particular language-game'.

Interlude (8): Rejecting the question

§39 introduces a powerful argument, one that Wittgenstein took seriously when he was writing the *Tractatus*. The basic idea of the argument can be expressed as follows. We start by noting that a sentence may make good sense despite the fact that what it seems to be about does not exist. From this we infer that what sentences mean becomes clear only when they are analysed. Next we reason that in the course of analysis ordinary names are replaced by names of simple objects, that is objects that cannot but exist. (This is because objects other than simple objects can be broken up or otherwise go out of existence and their names lose their bearers.) Whence we conclude that all meaningful sentences must be analysable into sentences, the names of which are 'real names'. If names are meaningful only if they name, sentences involving names are meaningful only if they are really about simple objects.

The importance of this line of thought from the standpoint of traditional philosophy can hardly be overstated. If we are not to be misled in our thinking about the nature of the world, analysis would seem to be essential. We must figure out what exactly we are thinking. Consider 'Excalibur has a sharp blade'. If we take this sentence at face value – and assume the meaning of a name is what it names – we become committed to the implausible view that something must correspond to Excalibur, something that has a sharp blade, whether there is such a sword or not. (It is hard to credit the suggestion – compare §36 – that 'Excalibur' must pick out a '*spirit*'; ideas and abstract objects do not have blades, let alone sharp ones.) To avoid this difficulty, we must, it would seem, engage in analysis and attempt to figure out what the sentence really means, what it is really about.

Not surprisingly, Wittgenstein challenges this line of argument. As we have seen, he assails the assumption on which it centrally turns, the idea that to be meaningful, names must have bearers. Since the problem regarding 'Excalibur' arises only if its meaningfulness depends on its naming something, the argument fails if this assumption fails. If we agree that 'Excalibur' can count as a meaningful name regardless of whether it has a bearer or not, we can take 'Excalibur has a sharp blade' to be meaningful just as it stands. Moreover, as Wittgenstein emphasizes, ordinary names like 'Excalibur' are normally taken to be meaningful regardless of whether their bearers are complex (and can go out of existence). To be meaningful it is enough for a name to have a 'use in the language' (§43). It is not true that 'Excalibur' has to be analysed away since in our language 'a name is also used in the absence of its bearer' (§44).

These considerations cast doubt on the argument sketched in §39. But there are other problems as well. In §46 Wittgenstein directs our attention to a second questionable assumption, specifically the assumption that 'real names' – i.e. names that take the place of ordinary names when sentences are analysed – 'name simples' (§39). This too, Wittgenstein would like us to agree, is deeply confused. It is senseless to talk of the existence of objects that are absolutely simple, i.e. simple in and of themselves. While it is tempting to regard the world as comprising primary elements, '[i]t makes no sense at all to speak absolutely of the "simple parts of [an object]" ' (§47). There is no such thing as absolute simplicity.

When Wittgenstein says this, he is alluding to the conception of simplicity that philosophers work with. What concerns him is the philosophical thesis that certain sorts of things – sensations, material points, qualities like redness, perhaps the self, perhaps logical forms – are simple in an absolute, unqualified, sense. He is questioning the coherence of a question he spoke of early on as a 'real philosophical' question.[2] In the *Investigations*, he expresses the same doubts as he expressed in 1914 regarding the cogency of the question 'Is a point in our visual field a *simple object*, a *thing*?' (*ibid*). Here too he thinks there is 'a mistake in formulation' since 'it looks as if I could say definitely that these questions could never be settled at all' (*ibid*). What is new in the *Investigations* is the suggestion that the mistake derives from the fact that it makes no sense to speak of the simplicity and complexity of objects '*outside* a particular language-game' (§47). The trouble with the 'real philosophical [question]' is that it fails to recognize that it only makes sense to classify things as simple or complex from a point of view. (Compare §17 where Wittgenstein stresses the 'different points of view from which one can classify tools or chessmen'.)

I hope it will not be thought that Wittgenstein is saying that questions about the simplicity of objects are always nonsensical. His contention is not that questions about simplicity never make sense, only that it is senseless to ask whether something is absolutely simple. He does not deny a person can ask 'Does my visual image of this tree, of this chair, consist of parts?' (§47, paragraph 2). Indeed far from denying the obvious, he emphasizes that such questions are perfectly intelligible given appropriate standards of what counts as simple and complex. There can be no denying that clear criteria of simplicity and complexity are normally available, and if unavailable can readily be fashioned. Wittgenstein would only emphasize that we change the subject when we reformulate the philosophical question so that it makes sense. From a philosophical standpoint, questions about simplicity that have 'a clear sense – a clear use' fail to address the issue at hand.

So far then Wittgenstein has launched two attacks on the idea that every ordinary name 'must disappear when the sense [of the sentences in which it occurs] is analysed and its place be taken by words that name simples' (§39). He has taken issue with the suggestion that such names 'must disappear' on the grounds that the way we use language allows for the possibility of meaningful sentences involving names without bearers. And he has suggested that the idea of a 'simple object' that exists in its own right 'makes no sense at all' (§47). What we see when we examine language closely, he would like us to agree, is that names are used very differently from how philosophers are inclined to suppose. The criteria of simplicity and complexity that we use in our everyday affairs depend on the language-game with which they are associated, and the idea of absolute simplicity, which is frequently taken to be perfectly intelligible, lacks application.

Sections 48 to 54: 'But are these simple?'

Having criticized the philosophical conception of 'absolute simplicity' in §47, Wittgenstein introduces a language-game, the names of which are plausibly taken to signify simples. This sets the stage for an examination of the idea of a thing existing in its own right and the conception of a name corresponding to an object. At the end of the instalment Wittgenstein briefly examines the notion of playing a game according to rules.

Section 48

Wittgenstein asks us to imagine a language for which the account of language in the quotation from the *Theaetetus* in §46 is 'really valid'. In this language 'R', 'G', 'W' and 'B' correspond to red, green, white and black squares while sequences of letters – e.g. 'RRBGGGRWW' – describe arrangements of squares. We are to think of the coloured squares as 'the simples' and to think of 'R', 'G', 'W' and 'B' as 'genuine names'. (Recall that in the passage quoted Socrates says 'the names of the elements become descriptive language by being compounded together'. Presumably Wittgenstein shifts to a discussion of coloured squares because these are more reasonably thought of as simples than building blocks.)

You might complain that coloured squares are not simple since they can be regarded as combinations of squares and colours, as composed of two rectangles, as mixtures of different colours, etc. But if coloured squares are not simples in the present language-game, it is hard to know 'what else [could count as] "the simples"'. Indeed there would seem to be no 'more natural' example of a language-game for which the account in *Theaetetus* is 'really valid'.

In other circumstances – in other language-games – a square might be more naturally thought of as composite, as made up of two rectangles, for instance. One can even imagine language-games in which 'a smaller area [is] said to be "composed" of a greater area and one subtracted from it'. As Wittgenstein notes, something like this occurs in the case of the composition of forces. When two forces are compounded, the resulting force may be 'simpler' than either of the original forces. In a tug-of-war, for example, when the teams are balanced, the forces cancel one another.

Nor is it a problem that the figure described as 'RRBGGGRWW' may be taken to comprise four colours or nine elements. This does not show that the squares should not be counted as simple. The same ambiguity arises in the case of the description 'RRBGGGRWW' itself. We can say this sequence of letters comprises four types of sign or nine individual signs. It does not matter which we take it to be as long as 'we avoid misunderstandings in any particular case'.

Section 49

If we ask what it means to refer to an element as being nameable but not describable (see §46), one possible answer is that 'its description is simply the name of the coloured square'. (Notice that Wittgenstein says we 'might' think of elements that cannot be described this way; he does not say that we must do so.) The thought is that 'R' counts as 'a limiting case'. It is a sequence of symbols corresponding to 'a complex consist[ing] of only *one* square', specifically an arrangement comprising a single red square.

The sign 'R' may be 'sometimes a word and sometimes a proposition'. Which it is 'depends on the situation in which the word is uttered or written'. The question of how 'R' should be understood no more has a single answer than the question of whether 'Slab!' is a word or a sentence (compare §19). If I describe the colours of the elements in an arrangement of squares and use 'R' to inform you that a particular complex comprises a single red square, I am using it as a description. But if I am trying to memorize the word 'R' and what it means or trying to teach it to you, I am using it as a name.

There is an important trap to be avoided here. The fact that 'R' can be a word or a proposition can lead to 'all kinds of philosophical superstition'. For instance it might lead one to think that propositions name – or are – abstract objects existing alongside ordinary objects. (I interpolate an example of the sort of thing Wittgenstein may have in mind.) Starting from the triviality that signs can function both as names and sentences, many philosophers have ended up embracing the far from trivial conclusion that sentences are names, the bearers of which reside in a parallel universe of mental representations or objective thoughts. (Recall §36: 'Where our language suggests a body and there is none: there, we should like to say, is a *spirit*'.)

The fact that 'R' functions as a name when we are memorizing words or trying to teach words to someone else hardly means the element it names 'can *only* be named'. It is one thing to say 'R' is introduced as a name for squares of a particular colour, quite another to say it can only be used as a name. As Wittgenstein noted in §27, what we do with a name is not 'given with the mere act of naming'. While 'R' may be introduced as a name for red squares, it may subsequently be used to inform someone of the colour of a square.

Naming does not 'stand on the same level' as describing but is a 'preparation' for it. It is no more a 'move in a language-game' than setting out chess pieces on a chessboard is 'a move in chess'. One can speak of 'R' as having a function only in the context of a language-game. It is not even possible for a thing to have a name apart from a language-game. (Compare §6 where Wittgenstein notes that a word may mean 'anything, or nothing' in the absence of 'the rest of the mechanism' and §31 where he stresses that 'only someone who knows how to do something with it can significantly ask a name'.)

Wittgenstein's point is similar to a point Frege made about the meanings of words depending on the sentences in which they occur. (Consider the word 'Paris' in 'Paris is a beautiful city' and 'Paris abducted Helen'.) Where Wittgenstein mainly differs from Frege is over the question of what counts as the relevant context. For Frege this is the sentence in which the word occurs; for Wittgenstein it is the language-game to which it belongs. Wittgenstein would say Frege had the right idea but yielded to what in §38 he calls the 'tendency to sublime the logic of our language'.

Section 50

Wittgenstein now takes up another idea mentioned in the passage quoted in §46, the idea that primary elements cannot significantly be said to be or not to be. He agrees that this sort of element cannot be spoken of intelligibly as being or as not being if 'everything we call "being" and "non-being" consists in the existence and non-existence of connexions between elements'. Obviously it makes no sense to speak of things that have no constituents as having or as lacking connections between their constituents. (Compare 'destruction'; if this is understood in terms of 'the separation of elements, it makes no sense to speak of the destruction of an element'.) But, while true, this does not make the view Socrates entertains any more believable. The notion of 'being' as a matter of 'the existence or non-existence of connexions between elements' is totally different from the traditional philosophical notion of 'being'. Saying a thing can exist because there are appropriate 'connexions between [its] elements' is not comparable to saying it 'exists in its own right' (§46).

Still you might try to defend the idea that 'existence cannot be attributed to an element' by noting that primary elements (or simples) cannot meaningfully be said not to exist. A primary element, you might argue, differs crucially from an ordinary object such as King Arthur's sword, Excalibur. For while it makes good sense to say 'Excalibur does not exist', it makes no sense to say 'A does not exist' where 'A' names a primary element. As Wittgenstein puts it, 'if [an element] did not *exist*, one could not even name it'. Thus, if sentences are meaningful only if their negations are meaningful, it seems undeniable that 'A exists' is meaningless and hence undeniable that 'existence cannot be attributed to an element'. (Russell once stated the point this way: 'The proposition "the so-and-so exists" is significant whether true or false; but if *a* is the so-and-so (where "*a*" is a name), the words "*a* exists" are meaningless'.[1])

To explore this line of thinking Wittgenstein introduces an analogy. He asks us to consider the case of the metre-rule, located in Paris, which serves as a standard of a metre length. (It is irrelevant that the metre in Paris is no longer our standard; it is enough for Wittgenstein's purposes that it could be.) Since this object determines what counts as a metre, it is senseless to speak of it as being a metre or as not being one. And similarly for samples of colours kept in hermetically sealed containers in Paris as standards. It does not make sense to speak of the colour of the sepia sample as sepia or as not sepia.

How does this bear on the issue of the being and non-being of primary elements? Wittgenstein wants us to agree that primary elements are no more plausibly regarded as metaphysically special than the standard metre in Paris. The fact that we cannot speak of the standard metre as a metre (or as not a metre) hardly shows it has an 'extraordinary property'. So why take the fact that we cannot speak of a primary element as 'being' or 'not-being' to show it 'exists in its own right' (§46)? The primary elements in language-game (48) are surely no more remarkable than the standard metre in the language-game of measuring.

What is special about the standard metre is not that it has an extraordinary property but how it functions in the language-game to which it belongs. We cannot meaningfully say it is one metre long for the simple reason that it serves as a sample and is used to define a metre. And likewise for the coloured squares in language-game (48). Taking them to be primary elements is like taking the standard metre to be our standard for measurement. The impossibility of meaning-fully saying that the squares exist or do not exist marks their peculiar role in language-game (48) just as the impossibility of meaningfully saying that the standard metre is a metre or not a metre 'mark[s] its peculiar role in the language-game of measuring with a metre-rule'.

Wittgenstein next clarifies the point that samples function in a special way in the language-games of judging lengths and colours. He observes that a sample of sepia is 'an instrument of language used in ascriptions of colour'. (Recall that in §16 Wittgenstein said 'It is most natural, and causes least confusion, to reckon the samples among the instruments of the language'.) In the language-game of ascribing colours to objects, a hermetically sealed sample in Paris would func-tion as a 'means of representation'. It would no more be 'something that is represented' than the standard-metre is. (The metre-rule is what we use to measure length; it is not something that can be measured.) And likewise for the element we refer to when explaining the symbol 'R' in language-game (48). Taken as a sample it is 'a *means* of repre-sentation' comparable to the standard metre or the standard sepia.

To say of the samples in language-game (48) that they could not have names if they did not exist is to say they can be a 'means of repre-sentation' only if they exist. They must exist if they are to serve this function; 'we could not use [them] in our language-game' otherwise. A sample red square in language-game (48) functions as 'a paradigm in [the] language-game' – it is an instrument of language, 'something with which comparison is made'. We cannot attribute existence to it but not because of the essential nature of the world. As Wittgenstein says: 'What looks as if it *had* to exist is a part of language'. (The reason he says this may be an 'important observation' is that it alerts us to the error, common in philosophy, of taking what is used to do the repre-senting to be itself a representation.)

Section 51

Wittgenstein has been questioning the cogency of the idea of a primary element as absolutely simple. When describing the language-game with coloured squares in §48, he did not say anything about the nature of the correspondence between 'R' and red squares, 'G' and green ones, 'W' and white ones, and 'B' and black ones. He only stated that there is a correspondence between them. The question of what 'this correspondence consist[s] in' thus still remains to be considered. If we are to understand the nature of language, it would seem that we need to get clear about the sense in which the signs of the language correspond to different coloured squares. (Compare §37 where Wittgenstein asks 'What is the relation between name and thing named?'; here he asks 'What does this correspondence consist in?'.)

Wittgenstein first observes that it was 'presupposed [in §46] that the four signs were differently taught – that 'R' was taught by pointing to a red sample, 'G' by pointing to a green sample, and so on. (Here the coloured squares function as paradigms.) This is certainly right but one still wants to know what it means to say that 'in the *technique of using the language* certain elements correspond to the signs'. How, for instance, is 'R' in 'RRBGGGGRWW' connected to the red squares in the arrangement of squares in §46?

Two possible answers immediately suggest themselves. One is that the correspondence consists in the fact that people use 'R' when describing red squares, the other that it consists in the fact that people have images of red squares when they use 'R'. (Notice that neither answer refers to the language-games in which the connections are set up; each treats the correspondence relation as an objective relation in the world, one that is – compare §47 – '*outside* a particular language-game'.)

Both suggestions are questionable. The first suggestion – that the relationship consists in people using 'R' to describe red squares – falls short because we make mistakes when describing things. (In a characteristic touch Wittgenstein asks us to consider how we decide that such a mistake has been made; this too needs careful examination.) The second suggestion – that people who use 'R' have an image of a red square – is unsatisfactory because one can use a sign correctly without having the right image. (Here Wittgenstein expects us to recall what he said about using language and having images in §6.)

When considering the question of how words are connected with things 'we must focus on the details of what goes on; must look at [the matter] *from close to*'. To see how 'R' corresponds to red squares we need to consider how the sign is used in practice.

Section 52

'[T]o see more clearly' how signs correspond to things, we must look at 'the *technique of using the language*' (§51). The question of how 'R' is connected with the colour of a red square has to be considered as carefully as the question of how a mouse that seems to have been generated out of rags came to be there. If I think the mouse just mate-rialized, I would 'do well to examine those rags very closely to see how a mouse may have hidden in them, how it may have got there and so on'. And if I think 'R' is connected with red squares I would do well to examine how it came to be connected with them. In neither case should the idea of 'spontaneous generation' be invoked straight off. ('Spontaneous generation' is the translator's rendering of 'Urzeugung'; a more literal though less elegant translation would be 'primitive fathering'.) Of course if one is already convinced that mice do not just materialize, such an investigation will 'perhaps be superfluous'. And likewise for those already convinced that correspondences do not come about spontaneously. Considering how words could be correlated with things will be as unnecessary as considering how the mouse could appear in the rags.

Why is it that those of us who take an investigation to be necessary rather than 'superfluous' fail to examine 'the details of what goes on ... *from close to*' (§51)? Why do we resist looking at matters closely? What is it 'in philosophy' that opposes the careful examination of details? This, says Wittgenstein, is something 'we must learn to under-stand'. (When writing this, Wittgenstein may have had in mind his own earlier failure to consider closely the correspondence of words with things. In the *Tractatus* he did not examine how signs correspond to things but took it for granted that they do. In this work he averred that '[t]o the configuration of simple signs in the propositional sign corre-sponds the configuration of the objects in the state of affairs'.[2])

Section 53

In §51 Wittgenstein criticized two general explanations of how words correspond to things. In this section, which originally came immedi-ately after §51, he mentions two ways in which words can properly be said to correspond to things. He points out that in language (48) the correspondence might consist in the fact that people were taught to use 'R' in a certain way, and adds that it might also consist in the fact that 'R' is correlated with a red square in a table. In the latter case a table is first used to teach what 'R' corresponds to, then used to settle disputes over the colours of things.

These suggestions are very different from those canvassed in §51. Unlike the earlier suggestions, which purport to provide a general account of the correspondence between signs and things, the new ones spell out specific ways in which words or names can be said to corre-spond to things. Wittgenstein does not claim to provide a general philosophical answer to the question of what the correspondence between occurrences of 'R' and red squares consists in but directs our attention to 'the details of what goes on' (§51). Philosophical worries about the nature of the correspondence between words and things are, he observes, misplaced. (It is no objection to what Wittgenstein says that he is changing the subject. This is exactly what he intends to do. Compare §47, where he rejected rather than answered the 'philosophical question' of whether the visual image of a tree is composite or simple. The question about the correspondence between words and colours he answers in this section is like the reformulated question in §47. It admits of an answer but is of no philosophical interest.)

Wittgenstein reinforces the point that there are '*various* possibilities', i.e. various ways in which words can correspond to things, by noting that a table specifying such a correspondence can function as 'a tool in the use of the language'. He notes the possibility of a person using a table specifying the correspondence between the words of language (48) and coloured squares to determine what 'R', 'G', 'W' and 'B' are correlated with. (Imagine a person determining what 'RRBGGGRWW' says in the manner of the shopkeeper of §1 by checking what 'R' corresponds to, what 'R' corresponds to a second time, what 'B' corresponds to, and so on.) This use of a table is uncommon but perfectly intelligible; if we had awful memories we might be forced to use tables this way. Moreover in certain situations – for instance when choosing or mixing paint – it is normal to use colour charts.

A table or chart that functions as 'a tool in the use of the language' may be regarded as 'the expression of a rule of the language-game'. But if we regard it this way, we must not forget that 'what we call a rule of a language-game may have very different roles'. Rules function in various ways, and tables and charts likewise.

Section 54

Having noted that 'what we call a rule of a language-game may have very different roles in the game' (§53), Wittgenstein reminds us of some of 'the kinds of case where we say that a game is played according to a definite rule'. A rule may figure as an aid in teaching the game or as an 'instrument of the game'. Moreover a principle discernible in the behaviour of the players is spoken of as a rule. An example of an aid in teaching is the directive 'You must first deal three cards to each player'; an example of an instrument is a list of instructions used in a treasure hunt; an example of a principle discernible in the players' behaviour is the rule manifest in chess players' moving bishops diagonally.

Rules displayed in the playing of games are analogous to natural laws in that they can be read off 'from the practice of the game'. For instance the rules of chess can be gleaned from how chess players proceed in much the same fashion as the law of motion of a planet can be gleaned from its movements. But rules also differ from natural laws since they can be violated as well as obeyed. Whereas the planets cannot but proceed in accordance with laws of nature and it makes no sense to praise or blame them for going around the Sun, chess players may or may not proceed in accordance with the 'law' governing the movement of bishops and it makes sense to praise and criticize them for the moves they make.

It should not be thought it is impossible to 'read the rules [of a game] off from the practice of the game' because games can be played incorrectly as well as correctly. Even when we do not know the game being played, we can usually distinguish 'between players' mistakes and correct play'. For the most part it is clear from the behaviour of chess players and their reactions to their opponents' play that moving a bishop diagonally is permissible while moving it horizontally is not. Just as there are tell-tale indications in our behaviour when we correct slips of the tongue (indications that are discernible even to those ignorant of the language), so too there are tell-tale indications in the behaviour of the players when they proceed incorrectly (indications that are discernible even to those unfamiliar with the rules of the game).

Interlude (9): 'We must focus on the details'

In §48 Wittgenstein 'appl[ies] the method of §2' to the conception of genuine names referred to in §46. Just as in §2 he provided an example of 'a language for which the description given by Augustine is right', so in §48 he provides an example of a language for which 'the account in the *Theaetetus* ... is really valid', i.e. an example of a language-game in which sentences are complexes of names corresponding to complexes of primary elements. Actually he proceeds almost exactly as he did in §§1–2. In §§46–8 he first introduces a picture of the essence of language, then reminds us – as he puts it in §1 – of how 'one operates with words', then introduces an example to which the picture applies. If we bear in mind the strategy he adopts in the earlier sections of the book, his discussion of the conception Socrates refers to becomes clearer. And conversely.

The purpose of §48, like that of §2, is to show that a particular philosophical conception of language has application. In the example

Wittgenstein provides it is 'natural' to regard the coloured squares as 'the simples' (§48) and to suppose that 'the names of the elements [or simples] become descriptive language by being compounded together' (§46). In fact it is reasonable to view the concept of meaning Socrates adumbrates as 'a philosophical concept of meaning [that] has its place in a primitive idea of the way language functions' or as 'the idea of a language more primitive than ours' (see §2). Language (48) may even be regarded as a 'complete primitive language' (§2), one that could be 'the whole language of a tribe' (§6). Like the description of the builders' language in §2, Socrates's description is 'appropriate', albeit 'only for [a] narrowly circumscribed region' (§3).

In §§49–54 Wittgenstein scrutinizes the account of language in the *Theaetetus*, i.e. the philosophical view that 'the essence of speech is the composition of names [corresponding to simples]' (§46). While granting that the account has application, he questions whether it applies across the board (and whether it captures what is fundamental to language). On the one hand he challenges the conception of primary elements as objects that can only be named and disparages the assumption that the correspondence between signs and elements somehow transcends the exigencies of particular language-games. On the other hand he points out that the arguments advanced by philosophers for these conclusions seem plausible only when important facts about language are overlooked or misconstrued. His aim is to get us to see that the account of language in the *Theaetetus* is unavailing and unnecessary – unavailing because it rests on dubious assumptions and unnecessary because the phenomena do not require an explanation of the sort it purports to provide.

In this connection Wittgenstein argues that the conception of naming adumbrated in the *Theaetetus* falls short in various ways. First it is not true that 'naming and description ... stand on the same level'; the fact a sign names an element is no reason to think that the 'element can *only* be named' (§49). Secondly the conception of elements as things that cannot be described, which exist in their own right, cannot be established by noting that 'existence cannot be attributed to an element'. This no more shows elements are special than the fact that the standard metre cannot be significantly said to be a metre long shows it has an 'extraordinary property' (§50). Thirdly there is the difficulty that common views about the correspondence of signs with things are open to the objection that people do not always use signs in the presence of appropriate colours and do not always have colours before their minds.

The truth of the matter is rather that objects count as 'primary elements' because of their role in a particular language-game, and the correspondence between signs and objects is achieved in various ways in the context of particular games. Far from being 'only' nameable – i.e. nameable in the direct fashion philosophers envision – a thing 'has not even *got* a name except in [a] language-game' (§49). Nor is it relevant that we cannot meaningfully speak of this or that as existing or as having length or whatever. This merely reflects the 'peculiar role [of the thing] in our language-game' (§50). That one sign corresponds to one object, another sign to another object, is not in the least mysterious. We are taught that they go together or that there are tables correlating them or something similar (§53). What seems necessary is merely an artifact; "[w]hat looks as if it *had* to exist, is part of language" (§50).

In making these points Wittgenstein is not claiming to have refuted the idea that 'the essence of speech is the composition of names' (§46). He knows that his observations about the use of language do not settle the matter and that his critical remarks may be challenged. He does not purport to have shown there is no satisfactory account of the correspondence between signs and things, just that two simple accounts of it fall short. (He would agree that the idea that 'R' corresponds to an internal representation of red at a subconscious level also deserves an airing.) Nor would he be surprised to learn it has been argued more than once that the correct conclusion to draw from his discussion of the standard metre is that it too possesses an extraordinary property, namely the property of being necessarily a metre. He is not unaware that many people are convinced that the standard metre cannot but be a metre, there being no other length it can possibly have. Here, as usual, Wittgenstein aims to close off some avenues of inquiry; he does not purport to demonstrate that none can possibly succeed.

The key to understanding what Wittgenstein is attempting to achieve in the sections under discussion (and, I believe, elsewhere) is what he says at the end of §51 and in §52 (see also §5). In the case of the correspondence between words and things and 'countless similar cases', he tells us, 'we must focus on the details of what goes on; must look at them *from close to*' (§51). If we are to get clear about these matters, we must examine the phenomena of language more closely than we normally do and fight against what it is in philosophy that 'opposes such an examination of details' (§52). Only by exploring the various ways in which philosophers have defended the idea that words correspond to things in an objective, sublime fashion, bearing in mind language-games such as language-game (48), shall we manage to escape the grip this idea exerts on our thinking. By tracking down some of the many convictions that fuel the account of the *Theaetetus*,

Wittgenstein hopes to alert us to its power and the enormous difficulties that beset it. Whether he is successful or not will, of course, depend on how well he sketches 'the landscape' and the quality of the thoughts he manages 'to stimulate [in us]' (pp. ix and x).

Sections 55 to 64: Indestructible elements and analysed forms

The discussion of playing a game according to a definite rule in §54 is something of a digression, and Wittgenstein now returns to his consideration of the argument about analysis and genuine names introduced in §39. He explores the idea that the simples corresponding to genuine names are indestructible and takes issue with the all-important philosophical view that the real meanings of sentences are expressed by their fully analysed counterparts.

Section 55

You might think that names must have indestructible bearers and '*a name ought really to signify a simple*' (§39) if for no other reason than that 'it must be possible to describe the state of affairs in which everything destructible is destroyed'. 'Everything destructible has been destroyed' makes sense only if 'what corresponds to [the words of this sentence] cannot ... be destroyed'. And were it possible for their meanings to be destroyed along with everything else, it would be impossible to speak of everything having been destroyed. If the names of 'Everything destructible has been destroyed' did not signify simples, what they signify would be destructible, and we should end up in the absurd position of having to regard the sentence as meaningless. One cannot describe something using words which lack meanings any more than one can sit on a branch that has been sawn off. 'I must not saw off the branch on which I am sitting', and I must not undercut the meanings of the words I am using.

One problem with this argument is that the sentence 'Everything destructible has been destroyed' illegitimately 'except[s] itself from destruction'. Since sentences consist of sounds or signs, which are destructible, they too may be destroyed. Worse, the argument relies on the dubious assumption that 'what corresponds to the separate words of the description ... is what gives the words their meaning'. As Wittgenstein has already stressed several times, not even names of people become meaningless when they lose their bearers. To think 'a word has no meaning if nothing corresponds to it ... is to confound the meaning of a name with the bearer of a name' (§40).

There is indeed 'a sense' in which 'this man is ... what corresponds to his name'. Nobody denies it makes sense to speak of Mr N.N. as the individual corresponding to the name 'Mr N.N.'. But this hardly proves that the meaning of a name is its bearer. It is one thing to take Mr N.N. to 'correspond to his name', quite another to take his name to 'lose its meaning when the bearer [Mr N.N.] is destroyed'. If I say a man corresponds to his name, I am not saying that 'he is [not] destructible', nor am I saying his name becomes meaningless when its bearer no longer exists. (Compare §40: 'When Mr. N.N. dies one says that the bearer of the name dies, not that the meaning dies'.) Even when the meaning of a name is explained by pointing to someone or something, the name does not have to have a bearer to be usable.

This is not to suggest that names cannot lose their meanings when their bearers are destroyed. The meaning of a word may be given by a paradigm – 'sepia' might be an example – and a word may remain meaningful only so long as the paradigm it corresponds to is intact. (Compare §50, where Wittgenstein discusses 'the standard sepia', and §41, where he gives an example of a name for a tool becoming meaningless when the tool is broken.) It does not follow from this, however, that the things named by such names are indestructible. Paradigms – be they hermetically sealed samples of colours or whatever – are as destructible as tables and chairs.

Section 56

This last observation is unlikely to persuade those convinced that 'what the names in language signify must be indestructible' (§55). For one thing the relevant paradigms are more reasonably taken to be paradigms in our minds than to be hermetically sealed samples. We do not have to assume there is a sample of a colour stored somewhere. It is enough that we can '*bear in mind* the colour' the word stands for. Colours that can be conjured up at will are indestructible. 'When I imagine something red', one wants to say, 'I imagine it. Nobody can destroy that'.

But colour-words can be said to stand for indestructible samples we '*bear in mind*' only insofar as we always remember colours correctly. To count as an indestructible paradigm of a colour, a memory-image must always be an image of the same colour. But in the present context there is no reliable 'criterion of remembering it right'. When we forego using physical samples as independent checks, we cannot be sure that what seems red to us today is the same as what seemed red to us yesterday. While we sometimes judge whether a sample has changed colour 'by memory', this is not an infallible criterion. We do after all 'speak of a darkening (for example) of our memory-image'.

We are as much 'at the mercy of memory as of a sample'. The colour I painted yesterday might seem brighter today yet still be properly regarded as the same colour. It would, for instance, be perverse to think the colour had changed if now as then it matched the colour produced by combining two chemical substances. In such a case memory does not serve as the 'highest court of appeal', and the verdict of the chemical criterion takes precedence. True, we could take colour-words to stand for 'indestructible' samples we *'bear in mind'* were our memories always reliable. But they can let us down and we often 'judge ... by memory' incorrectly. (Wittgenstein discusses 'the criterion of remembering [something] right' in more detail later on; see especially §265. §§56–59, along with §§28–38, play an important role in his discussion in §§243–308 of the philosophical idea of a private language.)

Section 57

One might attempt to defend the idea that '[w]hat names in language signify must be indestructible' (§55) by noting that while individual red things may come and go, what 'red' signifies cannot be destroyed. Since the colour red cannot be 'torn up or pounded to pieces', it is absurd to think it destructible. Thinking it could be destroyed is like thinking the number two could be eradicated by writing down '2' and erasing it. (In the original text Wittgenstein emphasizes that he means the colour itself. He says 'color, nicht pigmentum'.) Moreover the colour red is sometimes spoken of as disappearing. For instance we speak of it as vanishing when a red light dims, a red pen runs out of ink or a bloodshot eye clears up.

Nor is it obvious that we could conjure up an image of red if everything red were destroyed. Assuming we could still do so is as unreasonable as assuming 'there would still always be a chemical reaction producing a red flame'. If everything red were destroyed and there were no longer chemical reactions producing red flames, all images of red might disappear and the word 'red' might 'lose its meaning for us'. 'Red' might become just a word – as 'sepia' now is for many people. There is no guarantee that we could 'play a particular language-game with it', and we could end up in the position of having lost a paradigm that serves as 'an instrument of our language' (see also the discussion of standard sepia in §50).

Section 58

Yet another way one might attempt to bolster the view that genuine names signify indestructible primary elements takes its cue from the idea, mentioned earlier, that 'existence cannot be attributed to an element' (§50). If we 'restrict the term "*name*" to what cannot occur in the combination "X exists"', we seem able to retrieve the idea that genuine names name indestructible things. On this view, red is an element since 'Red exists' cannot possibly be false. In the present restricted sense of the term 'name', 'red' is a name since 'if there were no red it could not be spoken of at all'. If redness can – in Plato's words – 'only be named, no other determination is possible, neither that it *is* nor that it *is not*' (§46), it makes no sense to deny that 'red' names an element.

It is not hard to find fault with this argument. One difficulty is that it is unclear how 'X exists' should be understood. If we take it to mean ' "X" has a meaning', which is perhaps the most natural way to take it, we are forced to conclude that the sentence says something about the word 'X', not something about the indestructibility of Xness. Construed this way, 'X exists' is not a proposition about the essential nature of things. It is 'a proposition about our use of language'.

When we say 'Red exists' makes no sense, we think we are 'saying something about the nature of red' and take the peculiar status of the sentence to indicate that red exists 'in its own right' (§46). We assume that 'Red exists' is 'a metaphysical statement about red', not merely a statement about the word 'red'. Similarly we are inclined to reason that the senselessness of 'Red exists' shows that the colour red is 'timeless', even 'indestructible'. (Presumably if things were capable of coming into and dropping out of existence without changing, 'Red is indestructible' would be stronger than 'Red is timeless'.)

But what 'we really *want*', Wittgenstein declares, 'is simply to take "Red exists" as the statement: the word "red" has meaning'. Better still, we should like to regard 'Red does not exist' as merely another way of saying ' "Red" has no meaning'. This is not something we can say straight-out, however. While 'Red does not exist' is senseless (since it 'contradicts itself in the attempt to say it'), ' "Red" has no meaning' is merely false (obviously the word 'red' has a meaning). We must instead speak of the first sentence as meaning the second one '*if it* meant anything'. But then are we not forced, once again, to regard red as existing 'in its own right'? If 'Red does not exist' does not mean anything, it would seem that red must be a very special sort of thing.

The error here is that the sentence 'Red does not exist' does not really 'contradict itself'. To the contrary, 'the only contradiction lies in something like this: the proposition looks as if it were about the colour, while it is supposed to be saying something about the use of the word "red"'. We are led astray by the fact that the sentence 'Red does not exist' seems to say something about the colour red (that there is no such colour) rather than about the word 'red' (that it has no meaning). 'In reality', when we 'say that a particular colour exists' all we are saying is that items of the colour exist. Saying 'Red exists' need be no less accurate than saying 'Red things exist'. And if I am referring to something that is 'not a physical object' – an image perhaps – 'Red exists' might even be better.

Section 59

Those who still think 'a *name* signifies only what is an *element* of reality' should ask themselves what sorts of things count as elements. The picture of 'an *element* of reality' that swims before our minds when we speak of 'what remains the same in all changes' does not derive from experience in the way that a picture of a chair or a person does. It is more like a picture of a perfect world (which we mistakenly take to be discernible in experience). What we obtain from experience is the concept of a component part, not the concept of a primary element. The fact that chairs comprise seats, backs and legs (and can change while their parts remain the same) does not show that they comprise elements that 'cannot be destroyed'. All that experience provides is 'the materials' from which we construct the picture of things as composed of simples.

Section 60

In §59 Wittgenstein suggested that the idea that 'a *name* signifies only what is an *element* of reality' is bolstered by the apparently anodyne picture of reality as comprising '*component parts*'. Now he turns his attention to the related idea, first broached in §39, that ordinary sentences can be broken down into sentences involving real names. How clear is it, he asks, that an analysed sentence expresses what the unanalysed sentence really says? (Recall that in §39 Wittgenstein outlines an argument that purports to show that the word 'Excalibur' must 'disappear when the sense [of each sentence in which it occurs] is analysed and its place be taken by words that name simples'.)

Consider the sentence 'My broom is in the corner'. Is this 'really a statement' about the component parts of the broom? (Wittgenstein is not suggesting analysis is always in terms of component parts; he examines this type of analysis since it is what we are apt to think of first of all.) On occasion 'My brush with broomstick fixed in it is in the corner' certainly counts as 'a further analysed form' of 'My broom is in the corner'. But what are we saying when we say this? Are we saying the sense of the analysed sentence is 'hidden in the sense of the [unanalysed] sentence' and *'expressed'* by it?

Wittgenstein makes two quick points to start with. The first is that a person who says 'The broom is in the corner' need not 'really mean' that the broomstick is there, the brush is there, and the broomstick is fixed in the brush. This person may not be thinking of the broomstick or the brush at all. Secondly if I were to call out 'Bring me the broomstick and the brush which is fitted on to it', you might well wonder what could have prompted me to say this rather than 'Bring me the broom'. Clearly you do not 'understand the further analysed sentence better'. (The issues Wittgenstein takes up here are related to the issues discussed in §§19–20. To say 'Bring me the broomstick and the brush which is fitted on to it' is hidden in 'Bring me the broom' is like saying 'Bring me a slab' is hidden in 'Slab!'.)

These two quick points do not settle very much. It is not unreasonable to think that requesting a broomstick with a brush fitted on to it 'achieves the same' as requesting a broom, albeit 'in a more roundabout way'. If you are convinced that 'Bring me the broomstick and the brush which is fitted on to it' is hidden in 'Bring me a broom' and expresses what it means, you are unlikely to be moved by the fact that the analysed sentence sounds odd. What matters, you will think, is that the analysed sentence reveals the meaning of the original sentence.

To explore this suggestion Wittgenstein introduces a new language-game, one in which someone is ordered to fetch and move objects composed of parts. (Here his strategy is similar to his strategy in §§1–2 and §§46–8. He first introduces a conception of language, then raises some preliminary difficulties for it, then provides a language-game to which the conception applies.) In the new language-game, which can be played two ways, marks are used either to signify composite objects or to signify parts of objects. In version (a) objects are marked – in the manner of §15 – with appropriate signs, e.g. '↕' for a broom, while in version (b) the parts of objects are marked, e.g. '↑' for a broomstick and '↓' for a brush. Wittgenstein wants us to consider when 'Bring ↑

and ↓' in (b) counts as 'an analysed form' of 'Bring ↕' in (a) and when the order in (b) is plausibly regarded as lying concealed in the order in (a). Everyone agrees that brooms consist of brushes and broomsticks, but how clear is that 'the order to bring the broom ["Bring ↕"] also consists of corresponding parts ["Bring ↑" and "Bring ↓"]'?

Section 61

A natural response to this last question is that 'a particular order in (a) means the same as [a particular order] in (b)'. 'Bring ↕' in (a) seems to mean the same as 'Bring ↑ and ↓' in (b) and to be 'an analysed form' of it. Certainly there can be no question of which orders in (a) corre-spond · to which in (b) and which in (b) contradict which in (a). Nobody can deny that 'Bring ↕' corresponds to 'Bring ↑ and ↓' or that 'Bring ↑' contradicts 'Bring ↕'. (If I ask for a broom, I want a broom, not just a broomstick.) In this sense an order in (a) can be said to have 'the same meaning' as one in (b) – they 'achieve the same' (§60). Still one may dispute the suggestion that 'Bring ↑ and ↓' means 'Bring ↕', to say nothing of the idea that 'the former lie[s] concealed in the latter, and is ... now brought out by analysis' (§60).

There is a world of difference between saying an order in (a) corre-sponds to one in (b) and saying it is hidden in it. You and I may agree about which orders in (a) correspond to which orders in (b) yet differ about 'the use of the expression "to have the same meaning" or "to achieve the same"'. (In §60 Wittgenstein allows that 'Bring me the broomstick and the brush which is fitted on to it' can 'achieve the same' as 'Bring me the broom'; here he scrutinizes the notion of achieving the same.) We may agree that certain orders achieve the same without having 'come to *general* agreement' about the matter. Even when there is no question of how orders in (a) and (b) are correlated, it may still make sense to ask whether (a) and (b) are 'merely two forms of the same game'.

(a) and (b) are 'forms of the same game' if they are comparable to ordering something in German and ordering the same thing in English. If the difference between (a) and (b) is as trivial as this, orders in (a) and (b) may indeed mean the same. But if (a) and (b) are more reasonably compared with the games of ordering and describing objects, they are not forms of the same game. Their respective mean-ings are – all things being equal – very different. The problem is it is not at all obvious that the first comparison is closer to the mark than the second one.

Section 62

In this section Wittgenstein develops the point that agreement regarding the equivalence of orders in (a) and (b) is different from '*general* agreement about the use of the expression "to have the same meaning" or "to achieve the same" ' (§61). He invites us to consider the case of a person who, given orders in (a) and (b), determines which object to fetch by looking at a table in the manner of the shopkeeper described in §1. Is this person doing '*the same* when he carries out an order in (a) and the corresponding one in (b)'? If games (a) and (b) are 'merely two forms of the same game', he is. 'Bring ↕' in (a) means the same as 'Bring ↑ and ↓' in (b) and it makes good sense to speak of 'the second [as] an analysed form of the first' (§61). But are (a) and (b) forms of the same game or are they different games?

The question of whether the person does 'the *same*' when he carries out the order 'Bring ↕' as when he carries out the order 'Bring ↑ and ↓' does not admit of a Yes or No answer. In one sense the person does the same thing – he brings a broom. But in another sense he does something different – he looks up one sign in a table when carrying out 'Bring ↕' and two signs when carrying out 'Bring ↑ and ↓'. (Compare counting a line of people starting from the right and starting from the left. Right-counting is different from left-counting, and neither game seems properly regarded as hidden in the other.)

It is no objection to this observation that '[t]he *point* of the two orders is the same'. While it is clear that the point of saying 'Bring ↕' and saying 'Bring ↑ and ↓' may be to have the broom brought, it is far from clear what counts as 'the "point" of an order'. Just as there may be agreement about particular uses of 'to have the same meaning' and 'to achieve the same' but no '*general* agreement' regarding how they are used (§61), so too there may be agreement about particular uses of 'the point of an order' without there being any general agreement regarding its use. If orders could be identified by their points and it were always clear what counts as the point of an order, we could perhaps say when one order is an analysed form of another. Unfortunately, however, 'it is not everywhere clear what should be called the "point" of an order'.

Orders need no more have a single point than artifacts need have a single purpose. An order like 'Bring ↕' may have a variety of 'points' – to get you to bring a broom, to determine whether you understand English, to verify whether you have strength enough to lift a broom – just as a lamp may have a variety of uses – to provide light, to fill empty space, to show off its owner's taste. In some language-games the essential is sharply distinguished from the inessential but not in all. The essential point of an order may be clear in language-game (2), but this is hardly a typical language-game.

Section 63

If we take an order in (b), say, 'Bring ↑ and ↓', to be 'an "analysed" form' of an order in (a), say 'Bring ↕', we should not regard it as 'the more fundamental form'. (Recall that in §60, Wittgenstein speaks of the former as 'a further analysed form' of the latter.) There is no good reason to suppose that it 'alone shews what is meant by [the unanalysed form]'. 'Bring ↑ and ↓' may tell us no more than 'Bring ↕', and a person who only has the form 'Bring ↕' need not be missing anything. (Compare §20, where Wittgenstein reminds us that Russians do not miss the copula.) In fact 'an aspect of the matter' may be lost in the analysed order as well as in the unanalysed order. Whereas the unanalysed order makes no mention of the parts of the broom, the analysed order fails to mention the fact that the parts constitute a unified whole.

Section 64

Wittgenstein concludes the present discussion of analysis by applying what he has been saying to the case of language-game (48) altered slightly so that 'U' names adjacent red and green squares, 'V' names adjacent green and white ones, etc. It is, he now observes, possible to imagine a people who have names for two-coloured rectangles but none for single-coloured squares. In their language, pairs of squares count as 'primary elements' just as single squares do in language-game (48). (Also recall Wittgenstein's remark in §48 about the possibility of a smaller area being ' "composed" of a greater area and another one subtracted from it'.)

In the 'U-V' language-game the rectangles are comparable to the French tricolor since they function as wholes that cannot be broken down further. One loses 'an aspect of the matter' (§63) when one regards a U-rectangle as comprising a red square and a green square in much the same way as one 'loses an aspect of the matter' when one regards the French tricolor as juxtaposed blue, white and red bands. A U-rectangle may function as a unit no less than what the French call the 'bleu, blanc, rouge' (the blue-white-red).

It is a mistake to regard the symbols of the 'U-V' language-game as being in need of analysis. While it may sometimes be possible to replace 'UUV' by 'RGRGGW' without loss, this is not always so (as the example of the French tricolor makes clear). Nor is it true that the U-V language-game can always be replaced by the 'R-G' language-game of §48. Actually the 'U-V' language-game is 'just *another* language-game', albeit one related in various ways to the 'R-G' language-game.

Interlude (10): 'It is just *another* language-game'

§§39–64 are mainly devoted to a critical examination of the view that meaningful sentences can be analysed and the ordinary names that figure in them can be replaced by words that name simple objects. After sketching an argument that purports to establish this view (§39), Wittgenstein criticizes the principle, central to the argument, that names are meaningful only if they name something (§§40–5), challenges the conception of primary elements as things that can only be named (§§46–50) and scrutinizes the philosopher's conception of how signs correspond to things (§§51–4). Finally, in the present instalment, he examines two other aspects of the idea of analysis: the conception of simple objects as indestructible (§§55–9) and the conception of analysed sentences as revealing the true meanings of the sentences they analyse (§§60–4).

Wittgenstein is not the first philosopher to take issue with the picture of language, thought and the world as being subject to analysis into fundamental units. Throughout the history of philosophy, there have been thinkers who have bucked tradition and argued that something is lost in the course of analysis. In the eyes of these philosophers, language, thought and the world cannot be broken down into parts since the whole is more than the sum of its parts, each sentence, each thought and each fact being a unified whole. From their standpoint Wittgenstein is right to ridicule the idea of asking someone to bring a broomstick and a brush when you want a broom, and he hits the nail on the head when he insists that an 'arrangement of colours (say the French tricolor) has a quite special character' (§64).

Nonetheless Wittgenstein's criticism is very different from the usual line of criticism, which rejects analysis on the grounds that it falsifies what is being analysed. Wittgenstein is no more sympathetic to the philosophical doctrine of holism, which takes sentences to be unanalysable units, than he is to the philosophical doctrine of atomism, which takes them to be built up out of linguistic atoms. For him it is just as big a mistake to think that wholes can never be analysed into their parts without loss as it is to think that they can always be so analysed. In fact Wittgenstein takes the picture of ordinary sentences as analysable into sentences, the names of which name simples, to be far more powerful and seductive than the picture of sentences as unified wholes. He never says or implies that wholes cannot be analysed without destroying their meanings. Indeed he recognizes that the atomistic picture of language and the world has application since he takes there to be languages for which 'the account of the *Theaetetus* ... is really valid' (§48). Nor should it be overlooked that Wittgenstein refrains from saying language (a) is better than language (b) and explicitly states that the U-V language-game is 'just *another* language-game' (§60 and §64).

Wittgenstein's approach is unusual and noteworthy mainly because he questions both the idea that unanalysed statements, orders or whatever are more fundamental than analysed ones and the idea that 'an "analysed" form is ... the more fundamental form' (§63). He stresses that what is simple and what is complex (and what is unanalysable and what requires analysis) depends on the nature of the language-game that is being played (and on our concerns and interests). Nothing counts as primary or fundamental in its own right. Whether something 'is composite, and what are its component parts ... depends on what [we] understand by "composite"'' (§47). Looked at one way the French tricolor is composite; looked at another way it is not. To the flag-maker it comprises three coloured stripes; to the French patriot it is the 'bleu, blanc, rouge'.

To put it another way, Wittgenstein questions the assumption, common to philosophical atomism and philosophical holism, that it makes sense to ask whether unanalysed sentences or their analysed counterparts are fundamental '*outside* a particular language-game' (§47). In opposition to the atomist he wants us to appreciate that there are language-games in which the whole counts as more than the sum of the parts; in opposition to the holist he wants us to appreciate that there are language-games in which the whole counts as equal to (or even as less than) the sum of its parts. (Recall that compound forces may be weaker than their component forces.) Taking 'philosophical problems [to] arise when language *goes on holiday*' (§38), he can consistently repudiate both lines of thought and regard atomism and holism as alternative solutions to a misformulated problem. To say, as he does, that it is the nature of the language-game in question that matters is not to solve the problem. It is to reject it.

The issues surrounding atomism and holism in philosophy are complex, and Wittgenstein does not claim to have shown the philosophical conception of analysis to be bankrupt. As noted in the last interlude, he would concede that there are many philosophical twists and turns he has not considered, never mind tracked down. Still he can claim to have shown that the conception of ordinary sentences as making sense only insofar as they are at some deeper level about simple objects is more problematic than its proponents usually suppose. And he can claim to have gone a considerable way towards showing we can get by without the ideas of 'real names', 'primary elements' and the panoply of other ideas that the conception of philosophical analysis brings in its wake. We do not have to regard sentences of everyday language as intelligible only if they are ultimately about primary elements. We can recognize them as making sense just insofar as they figure significantly in the language-games we play or might play.

If a commitment to analysis is characteristic of philosophy done in the analytic spirit, the *Investigations* cannot be classified, as it often is, as a work of analytic philosophy. Wittgenstein does, it is true, attend to language and logic as closely as most analytic philosophers, and like many others he thinks it important to examine carefully how we actually operate with words. But he is as critical as any holist of the idea that analysis reveals the real meaning of sentences and illuminates the essential nature of reality. Indeed in this respect he is one of the great opponents of philosophical analysis. There are few more trenchant critiques of analysis in the philosophical literature than the critique he mounts against it in §§39–64 (and in §§19–20 on 'real meaning'). Unlike other critics of analysis, he does not dilute his criticisms by coupling them with arguments for holism. As he sees it, we can set aside the philosophical conception of analysis while recognizing that it is more powerful than alternative philosophical conceptions. We do not have to commit ourselves to a still more disreputable philosophical doctrine.

Sections 65 to 70: Family resemblances

Wittgenstein exhorts us time and again to consider the functioning of particular language-games but never says what counts as one. All he does is describe and compare specific language-games. Is this good enough? In this instalment he confronts the objection that it is not.

Section 65

Wittgenstein begins by raising what he calls 'the great question that lies behind all these considerations [i.e. those of §§1–64]', the question of 'the *general form of propositions* and of language'. In the *Tractatus* Wittgenstein answered this question by noting that every genuine proposition says 'Such and such is the case'. But all he has done in the *Investigations*, at least so far, is mention some of the things he intends to call language-games and give examples (see, e.g., §7 and §23). He has said nothing about 'the essence of a language-game, and hence of language'.

This is not something Wittgenstein denies. He concedes he is letting himself 'off the very part of the investigation that once gave [him] most headache'. However, whereas he earlier took the task of characterizing the general form of a proposition to be exceptionally important, he now questions whether there is any such general form to be isolated. There is, he declares, nothing the phenomena of language have 'in common which makes us use the same word for all'. To the contrary, they 'are *related* to one another in many different ways'. What makes 'activities … into language or parts of language' is not that they possess 'something common to all that we call language' but that they are interrelated in various ways. '[I]t is because of this relationship, or these relationships, that we call them all "language"'.

Section 66

In §65 Wittgenstein observes that the phenomena of language (e.g. those referred to in §23) are called 'language' because 'they are *related* to one another in many different ways'. Now he explains what he means. He suggests that we can see how the phenomena are interconnected by examining 'the proceedings that we call "games"'. (That Wittgenstein should compare languages with games is unsurprising given his use of 'language-game' to stress the similarity of using a language to playing a game.) In neither the case of language nor the case of games does there have to be 'anything common'. It is not essential that there be 'one thing ... which makes us use the same word for all' (§65).

Consider board-games, card-games, ball-games, Olympic games, etc. Some of these are competitive, some not; some amusing, some not; some involve skill, some not. Even when we confine our attention to board-games, we find that they can differ significantly. Chess is different from snakes-and-ladders and snakes-and-ladders is different from monopoly. As we pass from one sort of game to the next 'much that is common is retained, but much is lost'. We do not discover something they all have in common but 'see a complicated network of similarities, overlapping and criss-crossing: sometimes overall similarities, sometimes similarities of detail'. (Wittgenstein is questioning whether there is a definition of 'game' of the sort mentioned in §3; he knows there are definitions of the word in dictionaries. Compare defining 'game' as an activity of 'moving objects about on a surface according to certain rules ...' with defining it, as my dictionary does, in terms of words like 'play', which are defined in terms of 'game'. Also compare §14 on defining 'tool'.)

Wittgenstein does not claim to prove there is nothing common to all games. Rather he exhorts us to do something – try to isolate something common to them. His thought is that if we investigate the matter for ourselves, we shall come up empty-handed. (Recall that he does not want 'to spare [us] the trouble of thinking' (p. x).) An examination of the phenomena *'from close to'* (§51) should, he thinks, disabuse us of our conviction that 'there *must* be something common [to all games], or they would not be called "games"'.

But how clear is it that if we 'look' rather than 'think', we shall find ourselves foregoing the idea of 'something that is common to *all*'? Games are complex and diverse, but so too are the motions of bodies. Since scientists have managed to find something common to the phenomena of motion, for all their complexity, it may seem perverse to discount the possibility of philosophers finding something common to games. Still the more we scrutinize the activities we call 'games' and fail to find something definitive of them, the less sense it makes to insist they must be alike, and the less reason we have to continue searching for something they have in common.

Section 67

Wittgenstein says he can think of no better expression than 'family resemblances' to characterize the similarities we see when we examine board-games, card-games, ball-games and the like. (Here we are to think of language-games as well as ordinary games.) The similarities between different sorts of games are like the similarities between members of a family. Just as there are resemblances between family members, so there are resemblances between games. In both cases there is 'a complicated network of similarities overlapping and criss-crossing' (§66).

When Wittgenstein speaks of games as resembling one another in the manner of family members, he is not saying that games have a special kind of property – that of being one of a number of interrelated activities. 'Family resemblance' is not something like black hair that each member of a family possesses. To speak of human beings or games or whatever as forming a family is to draw attention to the existence of similarities among them. It is not to isolate a common characteristic they possess, still less to provide an explanation of what makes them a family.

Wittgenstein elaborates the idea of family resemblance by observing that 'kinds of number form a family in the same way'. We call something a number 'perhaps because it has a – direct – relationship with several things that have hitherto been called number; and this can be said to give it an indirect relationship to other things we call the same name'. Consider the negative numbers. These seem to have come to be regarded as numbers because they function in important respects like the positive numbers, notably with regard to the possibility of being added together and subtracted from one another. They overlapped what were already regarded as numbers in much the same way as new fibres spun onto a thread overlap the fibres already there. (Here the relationship between the new and old numbers is 'direct'. Were another type of number introduced – say fractions – its relationship to the original numbers would be 'indirect'. Also note there are differences between negative and positive numbers as well as similarities. Unlike positive numbers, negative numbers do not function as quantities; there is no such thing as 'minus one moon'.)

But do not the individuals that form a family share 'the disjunction of all their common properties'? Consider chess, which is competitive and played on a board, football, which is competitive and played with a ball, and catch, which is played with a ball but non-competitive. Since each of these is either a competitive game or a ball-game, we can – according to the present suggestion – characterize them in terms of the disjunctive property of being either competitive or played with a ball.

This is 'playing with words'. There is a world of difference between a defining property and a disjunctive property. (Compare saying that whales have the property of being marine animals with saying whales and skyscrapers have the property of being either mammals or tall buildings.) Speaking of chess, football and catch as being either competitive or played with a ball is like speaking of there being something that 'runs through the whole thread, namely the continuous overlapping of [the fibres it comprises]'. It is not to say what makes them games. Activities, kinds of object or whatever are not characterized by 'the disjunction of their common properties'. Such disjunctions do not define what is common to them, never mind explain why we 'use the same word for all' (§65).

Section 68

You might try to breathe life into the idea that numbers share something in common another way. Instead of taking members of a family to share the disjunction of their common properties (as in §67), you might take them to belong to a disjunction of types of things. On this view the concept of number is defined as 'the logical sum of a corresponding set of sub-concepts', specifically as the disjunction of all the different sorts of numbers there are, 'cardinal numbers, rational numbers, real numbers, etc.'. (Cardinal numbers are the whole numbers – 1, 2, 3, 4, etc.; rational numbers are fractions – $^1/_4$, $^2/_3$, $^1/_1$, $^9/_2$, etc.; real numbers are numbers that can be expressed, roughly speaking, by infinite decimal expansions – 0.25387..., 1.0000..., 3.8686868..., etc.) And similarly for games; we are to think of a game as being either football or chess or catch or ....

While not implausible, this suggestion fares no better than the one canvassed in §67. A concept need not correspond to the logical sum of a set of sub-concepts if only because the list of things to which it applies may be open-ended and the possibility of the concept coming to embrace further sub-concepts is not excluded. When we say the numbers are 'cardinal numbers, rational numbers, real numbers, etc.', we are tacitly recognizing the possibility of adding other sorts of number later on. The word 'etc.' is not merely a time-saving device that relieves us of the effort of spelling out a fixed list of numbers.

We can, to be sure, give a concept 'rigid limits'. As Wittgenstein noted in §3, we 'can make [a] definition correct by expressly restricting it to [certain kinds of case]'. For instance we can limit the concept of a number to cardinal, rational and real numbers, and we can limit the concept of a game to football, chess and catch. But, equally clearly, concepts do not have to be so circumscribed.

In fact we typically use the word 'game' without fixing what it applies to. We use it 'so that the extension [what it applies to] is *not* closed by a frontier'. Our concept of a game is not bounded, and were we to specify a boundary for it, we would end up with a concept different from the one we actually use. Of course we 'can *draw*' a boundary around the concept of a game since 'none has so far been drawn'. But the fact that this concept is open-ended – and no boundary has been drawn – causes us very little trouble in everyday life.

At this juncture one may well wonder what makes one use of a particular word right and another wrong. If our concepts are 'unregulated' (and 'not everywhere circumscribed by rules'), what governs our meanings? In particular how can sentences in which the word 'game' figures – 'Games are played in every country' for instance – possibly mean something definite? (Here it is tempting to think that sentences that are 'unregulated' must be regulated at a deeper level and that analysis will reveal what is actually being said.) In response Wittgenstein limits himself to noting that while tennis is not regulated at every point by rules, it is 'for all that a game and has rules too'. The fact that the rules of tennis do not cover how high the ball is thrown hardly precludes our playing the game.

Does this retort settle matters? Presumably Wittgenstein does not believe it will satisfy philosophers who are convinced that our concepts must be bounded to be usable. Rather his aim is to get us to reflect on why we are so convinced that our concepts must be bounded. Far from trying to close down discussion, he expects what he has been saying to be questioned (and will pursue the issue in some detail in the sections that follow).

Section 69

If words do not have to be 'everywhere circumscribed by rules' (§68), how can we explain to other people how they are used? Is it not true that we can 'explain to someone what a game is' only because the word 'game' has a precise definition? Not if Wittgenstein is right. (Recall here his remarks in §31 about learning the rules of chess and his remarks in §68 in connection with the concept of number about learning the meanings of words by means of examples.) It is possible to explain words that do not have precise definitions by mentioning things they apply to. If someone wants to know what a game is, we 'describe *games* to him', adding perhaps 'This *and similar things* are called "games"'. Generally it is enough to give a list of examples and conclude by saying 'etc.' or 'and so on'.

It is not true that we know more than this and could, if we wished, give a definition. We are in no position to tell ourselves more than we can tell other people. As already noted, 'etc.' and 'and so on' are not merely time-saving devices; they signal that 'the concept is *not* closed by a frontier' (§68). Were we able to say more, we would not have to use such words. Given enough time and energy we could specify the concept explicitly. Nor do we say 'this, that and the like are games' rather than give a definition because of ignorance. We proceed as we do because there is no precise definition of 'game' for us to know. Even those who know English perfectly can do no better since the concept of a game plainly does not have 'rigid limits' (see §68). To repeat: we cannot know the boundaries since 'none have been drawn'.

A boundary can always be drawn 'for a special purpose' and it is often appropriate to draw one. Sports officials may find it useful to define what counts as a game for the purpose of deciding which activities should be included in the Olympics, and politicians may be forced to specify who counts as married for the purpose of determining eligibility for government benefits. None of this, however, means concepts must have sharp boundaries to be usable. We get by well enough most of the time with concepts that lack this kind of boundary.

Wittgenstein underscores the point that concepts can be serviceable without being rigidly delimited by noting that the notion of '1 pace' did not have to be defined precisely to have a use. '1 pace' was usable prior to being defined as '75 cm'. True, it makes good sense to say 'it wasn't an exact measure' beforehand. It may even be called 'an inexact [measure]'. But whatever one chooses to call it, the concept of '1 pace' is and was usable. Inexact or not, it can be used to specify a length of a particular object or how far something is from something else – and can do so perfectly adequately.

If you think '1 pace' is not 'an exact measure', you owe us 'a definition of exactness'. In what sense, we should like to know, are you taking it to be inexact? What standards of exactness do you have in mind? There is no more a single answer to the question of whether something is exact or inexact than there is a single answer to the question of whether something is simple or complex (compare §47).

Section 70

Wittgenstein has been addressing the worry that concepts would be inexplicable if they lacked sharp boundaries. Now he turns to the closely related worry of whether we 'really know what [we] mean' if our concepts are not 'everywhere circumscribed by rules' (§68). To know what a game is and what the word 'game' means, we must surely be able to do more than simply say 'this *and similar things* are called "games"' (§69). It seems impossible to convey what games are by the simple expedient of noting that they are like these or those particular games. (Socrates argues this way in many of Plato's dialogues. In the discussion of piety in the *Euthyphro*, for instance, he deprecates Euthyphro's suggestion that 'piety is ... prosecuting anyone who is guilty of murder, sacrilege, [etc.]' (5d); what is required, he tells Euthyphro, is an answer like 'piety is that which is dear to the gods' (7a), not a list of examples.)

To see that the present worry is unfounded, suppose I were to say 'The ground was quite covered with plants'. In the normal course of events it is absurd to say that 'I don't know what I am talking about until I can give a definition of a plant'. If I know that tulips, grass and the like are plants, nobody can accuse me of merely mouthing words. Certainly if I drew a picture to explain my meaning and said 'The ground looked roughly like this', you would have to concede I 'know what I am talking about'.

Nor is it a problem that I do not claim to provide more than a rough picture of what the ground looked like. The fact that I use the word 'roughly' is neither here nor there. I could just as well point to the picture and say '[I]t looked *exactly* like this'. It is irrelevant that the picture does not show the ground as it is, blade of grass for blade of grass. It does not have to count as an explanation of what I mean. To speak of a picture of the ground as looking exactly like the ground is not to imply that they are alike in every respect. The word 'exact' is not used this way. In the case of pictures 'is exactly like' does not mean 'is the very same thing as'. (See also §69 on the need to be clear about the use of 'exact' and §28 on the possibility of providing a 'perfectly exact' ostensive definition of 'two'.)

Note at the bottom of page 33

This note relates to the point, emphasized in the last few sections, that concepts do not have to be strictly circumscribed to be usable. If you were to say to me 'Shew the children a game', you would not have in mind every eventuality. You would in all likelihood not be thinking of the possibility of my teaching the children gaming with dice. But this hardly means you did not intend I should teach them something more salubrious. 'The exclusion of the game with dice' did not have to 'come before [your] mind' for you to use the word 'game' correctly.

Interlude (11): 'You take the easy way out!'

§65 is often thought to be an important turning point in the *Investigations*. Many commentators read Wittgenstein as shifting his focus at this juncture from criticizing themes that figure centrally in the *Tractatus* to providing a positive alternative to the views he previously held. As often as not, he is regarded as providing a new account of '*the general form of propositions* and of language' (§65). On this view the charge that he is 'tak[ing] the easy way out' carries no weight since he provides a new conception of 'the essence of a language-game, and hence of language', one in which the all-important notion of 'family resemblances' takes the place of the notion of a common property. We are to regard Wittgenstein as advancing a theory of meaning to replace the theory adumbrated in the *Tractatus* and to see his achievement as residing in large measure in the fact that he developed two radically different philosophical theories of language.

This way of reading Wittgenstein's remarks is not without merit. In the sections we have been examining, some of his statements about the meanings of words seem to encapsulate – albeit in a rough and ready way – an alternative to the conception of meaning promoted in the *Tractatus*. (Here I speak of Wittgenstein, as is usually done, as having provided a general philosophical theory of meaning in the *Tractatus*.) On the one hand he appears to make substantive negative claims. He states that there is 'no one thing in common [to all that we call language]' (§65) and insists that 'the "game" we play with [a word like "game"] is ... not everywhere circumscribed by rules' (§68; see also §69 and §70). On the other hand he seems to be advancing various positive claims about the meanings of words. He asserts that games and numbers are interrelated by 'complicated network[s] of similarities overlapping and criss-crossing' (§66) and unequivocally states that games and kinds of number each 'form a family' (§67).

Still it would be unwise to jump to conclusions. There are also important indications in §§65–77 that Wittgenstein did not intend to be understood as advancing positive or negative philosophical theses. It is not insignificant that he allows that he is letting himself off 'the part of the investigation that once gave [him] most headache' (§65). And why if he intended to provide a new account of 'the *general form of propositions* and of language' (§65), does he confine himself to pointing out that the phenomena of language have no one thing in common? Actually, as we have seen, he mainly scrutinizes suggestions about what is common to the phenomena and challenges our conviction that there must be something they all share. What he attempts to do is get us to examine our philosophical convictions '*from close to*' (§51). He thinks that reflection on the diversity of language-games should discourage us from trying to isolate 'the essence of a language-game, and hence of language' (§65).

If only for the sake of charity, we should hesitate before attributing to Wittgenstein a theory of meaning based on the idea of family-resemblance. To say the uses of words are related to one another in much the same way as members of a family are interrelated is not to say anything informative about their meanings. It is only to take issue with the idea that the meaning of words like 'game' can be captured by isolating common features of what they apply to. One does not explain what a game is by noting that it covers a variety of interrelated activities. Nothing is explained by stressing the existence of 'complicated network[s] of similarities overlapping and criss-crossing' (§66). Actually the opposite. This is tantamount to denying there is anything sufficiently well-behaved to be explained. (See also the remarks in the third interlude about philosophical explanation.)

In the sections of the present instalment, then, Wittgenstein is questioning whether there is anything philosophically interesting to say regarding 'the *general form of propositions* and of language' (§65). He is trying to get us to examine critically the philosophical project, on which philosophers have expended a great deal of effort, of saying what language, meaning, propositions and the like are essentially. He is asking whether the question 'What is language?' is any more likely to have a general answer than the question 'What is a game?'. For him the 'great question' of 'what the essence of a language-game, and hence of language, is' should not be uncritically accepted as a genuine question. We should not assume – as we usually do – that it must have an answer.

If Wittgenstein is attempting to get us to question the cogency of the 'great question' of the essence of language, the seemingly substantive remarks in this instalment need to be read as slogans rather than as theoretical principles, as summary statements rather than as allusions to a positive doctrine. Wittgenstein is not claiming to have shown that there is no one thing in common to all we call language, or to have proved that 'the "game" we play with [a word like "game"] is ... not everywhere circumscribed by rules'. Nor is he claiming to have demonstrated that nothing more can be said about games and numbers than that they form families and are interrelated by 'complicated network[s] of similarities overlapping and criss-crossing' (§65–§70). What he is doing is reminding us of undeniable facts about the phenomena that philosophers frequently overlook or discount as inconsequential. The remarks of this instalment, like the remarks of earlier instalments, are exploratory rather than explanatory, critical rather than theoretical.

It is even questionable whether the focus of Wittgenstein's attention shifts at §65. Not only is the discussion of §§65–70 closely allied to the discussion of analysis in §§60–4, the idea that there is nothing common to all we call language is closely allied to what Wittgenstein says about descriptions in §24 and to what he says about attending to the shape of a thing in §33. Moreover the issues broached in §70 are intimately related to those broached in §60. The oddness of a sentence like 'The ground was covered with 48 plants and 6000 blades of grass' is comparable to the oddness of a sentence like 'Bring me the broomstick and the brush which is fitted on to it'. (Also, as noted in the text, there are connections between §3 and §66, §31 and §69, and §28 and §70.) All in all, it seems clear that in §§1–64 and §§65–70 Wittgenstein is approaching 'the same or almost the same points ... afresh from different directions' (p. ix).

Sections 71 to 77: Seeing and understanding

In these seven sections Wittgenstein continues exploring the idea that we know what we mean only if our concepts are fully determinate. He examines the thesis that to be genuine a concept must have sharp boundaries, scrutinizes the suggestion that we are able to see what is common to a set of samples, and challenges the assumption that our knowledge of the meaning of a word is comparable to an unformulated definition.

Section 71

It is tempting to suppose that sentences are intelligible only insofar as their words are fully determinate. Consider saying there is a coin on the floor. If this is to mean anything, it would seem that 'What is a coin?', 'What is the floor?' and 'When is something on something else?' must have definite answers. Likewise if I were to ask you whether there is a coin on the floor, my question must have a determinate meaning; otherwise you could not tell me whether there is one there or not. Sentences that are indeterminate – an example might be 'There is a thing over there' – are uninformative. Indeed the determinateness of concepts would seem to be a straightforward matter of logic. If concepts were not determinate, a sentence like 'There is a coin on the floor' would be indeterminate and we could not regard 'There is a coin on the floor or there is not' as logically true. In other words, logical thought and smooth communication seem to require that words be – if not on the surface, at a deeper level – fully determinate. (Clearly, the requirement of determinate sense is closely connected with the idea of analysis understood as uncovering the determinate senses of sentences.)

While the idea that sentences must be determinate to be intelligible seems plausible enough, it is open to serious objection. For a start, as

Wittgenstein points out, it is a mistake to think that 'a blurred concept [is not] a concept at all'. A 'concept with blurred edges' – 'game' is an example – is no less a concept than a blurred photograph of me is a picture of me. Nor is it true that sharp concepts and sharp photographs are always preferable to blurred ones. Indistinct concepts and indistinct photographs may be 'exactly what we need'. A photograph of a criminal that leaves some of his or her features obscure may serve its purpose better than a more detailed sketch – the person may have aged since the photograph was taken. And the 'blurred' concept of 'a pace' may be more serviceable for specifying distances that the less blurred one of 'a centimetre'. If you were to tell me you live 100 paces from where we are standing, I would have a better sense of where you live than if you told me you live 7500 centimetres away.

It is no help to compare concepts with areas as Frege once did. (Frege put the idea this way: 'To a concept without sharp boundary there would correspond an area that had not a sharp boundary-line all round, but in places just vaguely faded away into the background. This would not really be an area at all; and likewise a concept that is not sharply defined is wrongly termed a concept'.[1]) While it is true that a concept covers things in much the same way as an area encompasses patches of ground, the analogy does little to bolster the thesis that genuine concepts are never 'blurred'. For one thing it is far from obvious that 'an area with vague boundaries cannot be called an area at all'. My telling you to say 'Stand roughly there' may make good sense even though I have not specified the exact area where you are to stand. Precision is sometimes important (as when an archer in a circus shoots an arrow at an apple on the head of a clown), but not always. (It is no argument against Wittgenstein that Frege's insistence on sharp boundaries does not stand and fall with the analogy of concepts with areas, which he introduces as a metaphor. Wittgenstein is aware that Frege takes the determinacy of sense to be an ideal, one to which scientific language should conform, and will return to the idea that ordinary language only approximates the ideal later on.)

The concept of a 'game' can be explained in much the same way as the position where someone is to stand. In the one case, one gestures at a certain spot; in the other, one gestures at appropriate examples. Thus I might explain the meaning of 'game' by mentioning that chess, football and catch are games, intending that cricket and monopoly be regarded likewise. My examples do not pin down what a game is precisely. But neither does my pointing to a particular spot pin down exactly where someone is to stand. Nevertheless my explanation may do the trick; a perfectly determinate explanation need not be necessary. (Wittgenstein is not claiming to have settled the matter. He knows that those who stress the importance of sharp boundaries are likely to insist one must be able to make one's instruction precise, that one must have something definite in mind, something retrievable by means of analysis.)

When I give examples of games intending you to use them a certain way, I am not attempting to get you 'to see in [them] that common thing which I – for some reason – [am] unable to express'. My object is not to have you see what chess, football and catch share along with all other games but to have you '*employ* those examples in a particular way'. What matters is the 'use [of the word] in the language' (§43).

Wittgenstein is not suggesting that we explain words by means of examples 'in default of a better [way of explaining them]' (compare §69). It is not his contention that 'giving examples is ... an *indirect* means of explaining' something one knows but cannot state. There is no more direct means of explaining 'game' than mentioning different sorts of games. No explanation of 'game' could be perfectly determinate since, however I explain it, I can be misunderstood. Even in cases in which definitions are possible, misunderstanding may occur. The definition of '1 pace' as '75 cm', for instance, works only when the meaning of 'centimetre' has already been fixed. Explanations of meaning are like ostensive definitions; they 'can be variously interpreted in *every* case' (§28). In everyday life, however, this is not a problem. We get by well enough using examples. As Wittgenstein reminds us, '*this* is how we play the game [i.e. the language-game with the word "game"]'. Normally our explanations explain what they are supposed to explain.

Section 72

In §71 Wittgenstein notes that when he says a person 'gives examples and intends them to be taken in a particular way', he does not mean that the person being addressed 'is supposed to see in those examples that common thing which [the person is] unable to express'. Now he scrutinizes the notion of '*seeing what is common*'. He observes that this notion, like the notion of a game, covers a family of interrelated cases. (Compare §53 and §54; in §53 he says that 'a rule of a language-game may have very different roles in the game', and in §54 he goes on to recall some of the ways in which a game may be said to be 'played according to a definite rule'. Here he notes some of the ways in which the notion of 'seeing what is common' alluded to in §71 is used.) In this connection he mentions three different ways in which I might get you to see what is common in pictures or samples.

In the first scenario, I tell you that variously coloured pictures have the colour 'yellow ochre' and you 'get to understand [my definition] by looking for and seeing what is common to the pictures'. In this case – unlike the case in §71 of giving examples of games one intends to be understood a certain way – you 'can look *at*, can point *to* the common thing'.

In the second scenario I show you figures of various shapes, each painted the same colour, and say 'What these have in common is called "yellow ochre"'. In this scenario, as in the first one, you 'can look *at*, can point *to* the common thing' but what is pointed to is different. Whereas in the first scenario I indicate one colour among others, in this one I indicate the same colour, and you have to know that it is the colour rather than the shape that is being singled out.

In the third scenario I show you various samples of different shades of blue and say 'The colour that is common to all these is what [is called] "blue"'. This scenario is more like the one provided in §71 since the person cannot 'look *at*' or 'point *to* the common thing'. Seeing a colour in a group of pictures of different shades of the colour is different from seeing a colour shared by a group of pictures of a single colour, and different again from seeing a colour in a group of multi-coloured pictures.

These differences are worth noting because we often forget that they exist. Wittgenstein thinks the 'complicated network' of uses of words (§66) is obscured when '*seeing what is common*' is taken to be one sort of activity, and he emphasizes that even the case of seeing the colours common to samples, which is about as simple a case as one can imagine, is far from straightforward. (Also compare the discussion of the notion of attending to the colour in §33.)

Section 73

Wittgenstein is not questioning the possibility of defining the names of colours by pointing to samples. As we have just seen, he thinks this can be done in various ways. Indeed, he stresses that defining the meanings of colour-words by pointing to coloured samples is similar 'in many respects' to providing a person with a table with words written underneath the coloured patches (recall the shopkeeper's table described in §1). Though there are differences between the two processes – when defining words ostensively we gesture towards the colour and say 'This is ...' or 'This colour is called ...' – words are correlated with things in much the same way in the two cases. Saying 'This colour is called "blue", this "green" ...' while pointing to colour-samples establishes a correlation between words and colours comparable to the correlation specified by a table.

Yet while it is true that colour samples can be used to explain the meanings of colour words, we need to be on our guard. We should not go on 'to extend the comparison' and assume that understanding the meaning of a word is a matter of coming 'to have in one's mind an idea of the thing defined'. Nobody can deny that we often provide samples or draw pictures when we teach people words – there is no easier way to explain the meanings of a large number of words than to draw pictures or to point to things. Still, taking words to be correlated with samples (as in a table) is altogether different from taking them to be correlated with mental samples or pictures. It should not be assumed that since we do not carry around material samples, we must carry around mental ones. (Compare §36 where Wittgenstein deprecates our tendency to postulate 'a *spirit*' whenever 'our language suggests a body and there is none'.)

Consider the word 'leaf'. Learning this word is not at all like acquiring a table. The meaning of 'leaf' cannot be equated with a mental picture one acquires, if all goes well, when one is shown a leaf and told 'This is called a "leaf"', shown another leaf and told 'This is called a "leaf"', shown a third leaf and told 'This is called a "leaf"', etc. While I may 'get an idea of the shape of a leaf, a picture of it in my mind' when you show me various different leaves, the picture I come to have in mind cannot be said to define 'leaf'. My image will be of something with a particular shape, not an image of 'what is common to all shapes of leaf'. (If you try to draw a picture of what is common to oak leaves, birch leaves, pine leaves, etc., you will end up with a picture of something shapeless.) The problem is that the word 'leaf' is a common noun that applies to differently shaped things.

For the same reason it is a mistake to equate the meaning of colours with mental pictures. There is no such thing as a picture of what is common to all shades of green as opposed to this or that particular shade of green. The 'sample in my mind' of the colour green has a particular shade. It is no more a 'sample of what is common to all shades of green' than a mental picture of a leaf is a sample of 'what is common to all shapes of leaf'. In this regard 'green' is like 'leaf' – its meaning cannot be equated with 'an idea of the thing defined'. (Wittgenstein is not going back on what he said at the end of §72. There he was discussing the case of someone seeing that samples of different shades of blue are all shades of blue; he was not assuming that the person acquires an idea or picture of something common to all shades of blue.)

You might think that Wittgenstein is overlooking the fact that 'general' samples are often used to specify what a leaf is or what green is. Surely nobody can deny that the meaning of 'leaf' is fixed by a 'schematic leaf' and the meaning of 'green' fixed by 'a sample of *pure* green'. In particular do not the schematic drawings and colour samples that are often included in dictionaries fix the meanings of the words they are coupled with? This is all undeniable. But it does not show Wittgenstein wrong. To the contrary, it reinforces what he has been saying. A leaf – or a drawing of a leaf – functions as a schema only insofar as it is 'understood as a *schema*', which 'in turn resides in the way the [sample] is used', not in what you or I or anyone else may have in mind. And similarly for a green patch. To be a sample of pure green the patch must be understood 'as a sample of all that is greenish'.

This becomes clearer when we ask '[W]hat *shape* must the sample of the colour green be?' The answer cannot be 'a regular figure (say, a rectangle)' but neither can it be 'an irregular figure'. A rectangular-shaped sample counts as a sample of a green-rectangular-shape no less than a sample of green while an irregularly-shaped sample also counts as 'a sample of irregularity of shape'. In fact the meaning of 'green' cannot be equated with any material sample or mental picture of green. We can learn the words for colours from pictures like those mentioned in §72 only when 'the post at which we station the word' has been fixed (§29).

Section 74

Wittgenstein now briefly considers an idea connected to his remarks about samples in the last section, namely that there is a difference between seeing a leaf 'as a sample of "leaf shape in general"' and seeing it 'as, say, a sample of this particular shape'. On this view he is wrong because seeing samples is coupled with a certain experience (that of seeing the leaf as a sample). The thought is that whoever sees a leaf (or drawing of a leaf) and has the requisite experience of seeing it as a sample would, no two ways about it, know what 'leaf' means.

Wittgenstein does not think that seeing a leaf (or a drawing of one) as a sample of 'leaf shape in general' is different from seeing it as a sample of 'this particular shape' but allows that 'this might well be so'. Even were there such a difference, he notes, all we could reasonably conclude is that 'as a matter of experience' people use the word 'leaf' a certain way when they '*see*' the sample as 'a sample of "leaf shape in general"'. It would simply be a fact that such-and-such experiences are correlated with using the word 'in such-and-such a way or according to such-and-such rules', which is not at all the same thing as knowing the use of the sample. Having a particular experience when shown a sample is altogether different from knowing that one is 'to *employ* [it] in a particular way' (§71). As Wittgenstein has noted more than once, what counts is not what experiences we have but how we proceed (see especially §6 and §35).

Of course 'there is such a thing as seeing in *this* way or *that*'. (Here Wittgenstein broaches an issue he discusses at length in section xi of part II of the *Investigations*.) I can look at the general outline of something or focus on the details. Moreover how we use a sample may depend on how we see it. Still Wittgenstein's point remains. Suppose you see a schematic drawing of a cube as a three-dimensional figure having twelve equal sides and I see it as a two-dimensional figure comprising a square and two rhombi (compare the schematic drawing on page 193 of the *Investigations*). In this case you and I would carry out the order 'Bring me something like this' very differently. You would bring a cube while I would bring three appropriately shaped flat objects. How we understand the schematic drawing would once again be reflected in how we proceed.

Section 75

Wittgenstein has been challenging the contention that understanding a definition 'means [having] in one's mind an idea of the thing defined' (§73). There is, he has been suggesting, an enormous difference between giving examples one intends to be taken a particular way and giving examples that supposedly share something in common that we can apprehend (§72). What goes on in us is neither here nor there; the meaning of a word such as 'game', 'leaf' or 'green' is fixed by 'its use in language' (§43). Now Wittgenstein takes up the question of how someone can know what something is without being able to say what it is.

It is tempting to think that whenever we cannot formulate a definition of something, our knowledge of what it is is 'somehow equivalent to an unformulated definition', one that we would recognize, were it formulated, as expressing what we know. (This is often assumed by cognitive psychologists and social scientists. Taking our knowledge of the meanings of words as 'tacit' and assuming that unformulated definitions are in some way or other 'represented' in us, these thinkers frequently take their task to be one of devising definitions that people will 'recognize ... as the expression of [their] knowledge'.) But how obvious is it that we know more than we can say and our knowledge is not 'completely expressed in the explanations [we] could give'? My knowing what a game is does not involve more than my being able to describe various games, my being able to provide examples of games, my being aware that games are played, and the like.

Section 76

Why is it unreasonable to think that my knowledge of what count as games is 'equivalent to an unformulated definition' (§75)? One reason is that were 'a sharp boundary' drawn around what I take to be a game, 'I could not acknowledge it as the one that I too always wanted to draw, or had drawn in my mind'. Apart from anything else, I have not 'want[ed] to draw [a boundary] at all'. No sharp definition could possibly coincide with my concept of 'game' for the simple reason that my concept does not have a well-defined boundary. (Compare the discussion of concepts that are '*not* closed by a frontier' in §68 and §69. Of course Wittgenstein allows that boundaries can be drawn 'for a special purpose' (§69).)

But while no strictly delimited concept corresponds exactly to my concept, it may well be akin to it. Most of the time 'the kinship is just as undeniable as the difference'. The concept of a game as consisting of 'moving objects about on a surface according to certain rules' (§3) is obviously similar to our own concept of it. The relationship between the two – and between other sharply defined concepts and the concepts we deploy in everyday life – is comparable to the relationship between pictures, 'one of which consists of coloured patches with vague contours, ... the other of patches similarly shaped and distributed, but with clear contours'. Just as blurred pictures differ substantially but not totally from sharp ones, so most concepts we use in everyday life differ substantially but not totally from sharply defined ones.

Section 77

The analogy between a concept like 'game' and a blurred picture can be developed further. Sharply defined concepts resemble ordinary concepts more or less closely just as sharp pictures resemble vague ones more or less closely – it depends on how vague the vague concepts or pictures are. And different sharp definitions may correspond equally well to a single ordinary concept just as different sharp pictures may be equally well imposed on a vague picture. Moreover it may be 'a hopeless task to draw a sharp picture corresponding to [a] blurred one' and a hopeless task to try to pick out a single definition corresponding to a concept. A best sharp picture corresponding to a blurred one may be out of the question, and a best sharp definition corresponding to an actual concept may not exist.

Wittgenstein suggests that we are in this position in the case of concepts in aesthetics and ethics (harmony and honesty would be examples). It is no more possible to isolate sharp definitions for these concepts than it is possible to isolate a sharp geometrical figure in a picture in which the colours merge 'without a hint of any outline'. And if 'you look for definitions corresponding to [such] concepts', you will find that '[a]nything – and nothing – is right'. (This is not to say one person's ethical and aesthetic opinions are as good as the next. Wittgenstein's point is not that there is no difference between right and wrong, only that if you look for precise definitions, you will come up empty-handed. To say it is futile to try to say precisely what counts as right is not to say that whatever a person deems right is right.)

To 'see that [the word "good"] has a family of meanings' it helps to consider how people learn its meaning. When we do this, we see that the word is applied in a host of different kinds of case – in phrases like 'a good person', 'a good life', 'a good tune', 'a good government', 'a good car', and so on. There is, it becomes clear, no one thing that good things have in common, only 'a complicated network of similarities' (§66).

Interlude (12): The requirement of determinate meanings

The discussion of this instalment carries on from and deepens the discussion of the last one. In §68 Wittgenstein notes a response one may be inclined to venture in opposition to his questioning whether games have anything in common. He imagines someone saying 'But then the use of the word [i.e. the word "game"] is unregulated'. After denying this is so, he considers one way the objection might be developed, the main thrust of which is that if games had nothing in common, it would be impossible 'to explain to someone what a game is' (§69). Unsurprisingly Wittgenstein denies this as well. It is, he notes, possible to explain what a game is by providing examples, specifically by 'describ[ing] *games* to [the person]'. This is a perfectly satisfactory way of proceeding, and it is wrong to think the lack of a 'sharp boundary' prevents our explaining the meaning of the word (see §70). Now, in the present instalment, he explores in detail our sense that when we explain words using examples, we must somehow convey their exact meanings notwithstanding the fact that they are not 'everywhere circumscribed by rules' (§68).

After reiterating that the concept of a game can be explained by 'giv[ing] examples and intend[ing] them to be taken a particular way' (§71), Wittgenstein scouts several suggestions regarding what happens when we learn concepts this way: first, that we come to see what is common to the examples (§72); secondly, that we acquire an idea of what it is that is being explained (§73); thirdly, that we catch on by virtue of taking the examples a certain way (§74). In addition he takes up the idea that when we come to know what a game is, we come to know something equivalent to an unformulated definition (§75 and §76). In each case he questions what is being suggested. Neither experience nor anything else is, he maintains, plausibly regarded as making up for the fact that giving examples falls short of giving a precise definition.

What is the upshot of this line of argument? Many readers have taken Wittgenstein's remarks to show something important about language, namely that our words and concepts are never determinate, that our sentences are irredeemably vague and that what we say is invariably surrounded by a penumbra of uncertainty. According to this interpretation, Wittgenstein is claiming – perhaps has managed to establish – that general terms like 'game', 'leaf' and 'green' are too amorphous to be explained or defined and the sentences in which they occur are only insignificantly different from vague sentences like 'Freedom is good'. He has even been read as attempting to show that language is in a profound sense limited and unreliable.

I think it clear this line of interpretation badly misconstrues Wittgenstein's remarks. Everything he says suggests that he believes that our sentences are mostly unambiguous and thinks our language is perfectly adequate for conveying what we want it to convey. If someone were to say 'Games are played in every country', he would not for a minute say that nothing definite is being asserted, still less contend that the speaker is not committed to anything. It is not his intention to deny the obvious. Like everyone else, he takes 'game' to cover certain kinds of activity and considers the other words of the sentence equally definite. Indeed, not only does he not suggest that what we say is nebulous, he explicitly states we can explain what we mean by means of drawings '*exactly*' (§70).

What Wittgenstein is challenging is the philosopher's principle of the determinacy of concepts, not our conviction that our sentences are mostly clear and determinate. He is attempting to get us to question the idea that concepts with blurred edges are not really concepts at all and the correlative idea that if we are to make sense our words must have 'real meaning' (§19). His target is the doctrine philosophers erect on the basis of the trivial fact that our sentences are normally neither vague nor equivocal. What troubles him is the philosophical view that our words and sentences must have definite senses somehow buried in them and must – since we mostly make good sense – at a deeper level be crystal clear. (In an early notebook Wittgenstein puts the idea this way: 'It seems clear that what we MEAN must always be "sharp" '; and in the *Tractatus* he equates 'the postulate of the determinateness of the sense' with 'the postulate of the simple signs'.[2]) There is, Wittgenstein would like us to agree, an enormous difference between the determinacy of sense as normally understood and determinacy construed philosophically. Here, as in the case of ostensive definition (see §§28–29), he thinks philosophers wrongly take a simple truth to underwrite a highly speculative philosophical theory.

But if the meanings of words are not fixed by ideas or unformulated definitions, how is it that our everyday discourse is as determinate as it is? How, for instance, is it possible – if my words can always be understood in various ways – that I can mean something definite when I say 'Games are played in every country'? Once again there is an echo of what Wittgenstein said earlier about ostensive definition (see §§30–31). He notes that practical determinacy does not require determinacy in the sense canvassed by philosophers. In the context in which I say 'Games are played in every country', misunderstanding may be out of the question. There is no need to postulate the existence of something that takes up the slack and fixes the meanings of our words since nothing whatever is needed to fix them. It is like the case of teaching the child gaming with dice mentioned in the note on page 33. Strange interpretations do not have to be ruled out in advance since they are rarely, if ever, entertained.

I conclude that in this and the last instalment Wittgenstein's aims are mainly critical. He is not advancing a new-fangled philosophical doctrine of the indeterminacy of sense but rather challenging the philosophical doctrine about its determinacy. He is taking issue with the assumption that 'a blurred concept [is not] a concept at all' (§71) and allied assumptions about the determinateness of our sentences. The question of how we can account for the fact that a person's sentences mean something given that they cannot be analysed in the way philosophers usually assume (and cannot be said to have real meaning somehow embedded in or underlying them) is not a question that needs to be answered. What philosophers regularly assume to be essential for intelligible thought and speech is no such thing, and the conception of linguistic determinacy they promote is a pipe-dream. As so often, the culprit is our craving for generality, and it helps break the picture that grips us to '*look and see*' how language actually functions (§66). (It is worth noting in passing that the sections of this interlude illustrate the interrelatedness of the various parts of the *Investigations*. What Wittgenstein says about indeterminate senses does not constitute a free-standing argument. It is only in the context of his earlier remarks about ostensive definition, exactness and simplicity that we can see what he is driving at and feel its full force.)

Sections 78 to 85: Definitions and rules

In this instalment, as in the last one, Wittgenstein concentrates on the idea that concepts are usable only if they have sharp boundaries. He draws attention to the fact that we cannot always state what we know, notes that proper names like 'Moses' are no more sharply definable than concept words like 'game', and explores the assumption that our use of language is at every point circumscribed by rules. Once again he emphasizes that it is neither remarkable nor problematic that the meanings of words are not determinate in the philosopher's sense.

Section 78

Wittgenstein has been reminding us that our knowledge of the meaning of words like 'game' (§75) and 'good' (§77) cannot be captured in definitions and we can know what such words mean without being able to define them. If this surprises us, it is because we are thinking of the sort of knowledge we have when we know the height of a mountain. (To know the height of Mont Blanc one must – unusual circumstances aside – be able to say how high it is.) We are not thinking of the sort of knowledge we have when we know how a clarinet sounds, which is describable only by means of phrases like 'the sound of a clarinet'. When we remember that we can be said to know the latter as well as the former, we shall not find it surprising that we can know the use of words like 'game' but not be able to specify it. Knowing that 'game' covers chess, football, catch and the like falls between the two extremes. If one knows the use of the word, one can say something about it, but one cannot specify what one knows in the way one can specify one's knowledge about the height of Mont Blanc. What counts as knowledge – like what counts as exactness (see §§69–70) – differs from case to case, and it should not worry us that knowing how a word is used differs from knowing a fact.

Section 79

The remarks of the last few sections about concept words like 'game' also apply to proper names like 'Moses'. Consider 'Moses did not exist'. This may 'mean various things' – e.g. '[T]he Israelites did not have a *single* leader when they withdrew from Egypt', '[T]heir leader was not called Moses' or '[T]here cannot have been anyone who accomplished all that the Bible relates of Moses'. This is uncontroversial and it is understandable why Russell would hold that the name 'Moses' can be said – e.g. as 'the man who led the Israelites through the wilderness' or 'the man who lived at that time and place and was then called "Moses"'. For him what we mean when we use a sentence involving 'Moses' depends on which description is being assumed. Moreover, Wittgenstein reminds us, if someone were to say 'N did not exist', we might well ask 'What do you mean? Do you want to say ...... or ...... etc.?'.

But is it true that names are always replaceable by descriptions? (Here it is important to keep in mind that Russell was of the view that sentences involving ordinary proper names – in contrast to 'genuine names' such as 'this' – are not fully analysed and the first step in their analysis is to replace each name in the sentence by a description.) If you were to ask me whom I mean when I say 'Moses married Zipporah', I may not be 'ready to substitute some *one* ... description for "Moses"'. I may only be prepared to say Moses is the person who did a good deal of what the Bible relates about him – that he led the Israelites through the wilderness, was as a child taken out of the Nile by Pharaoh's daughter, and so on. Nor is there any reason to suppose I must know in advance what would make me conclude that 'Moses married Zipporah' is false. I may have no clear idea of how much of the Biblical account would have to be wrong for me to conclude that there was no such person as Moses. (According to Russell 'Moses married Zipporah' is false if Moses did not exist because proper names are disguised definite descriptions and 'The man who ...' means 'There is exactly one man who ...'.)

To put it another way, the name 'Moses' does not have 'a fixed and unequivocal use for me in all possible cases'. I do not have one description (or collection of descriptions) that I am prepared to substitute for 'Moses', only 'so to speak, a whole series of props in readiness [that I] am ready to lean on' should the one I am leaning on be 'taken from under me'. Were it to turn out that someone other than Moses led the Israelites through the wilderness, I might forego thinking of him as 'the man who led the Israelites through the wilderness' and think of him instead as, say, 'the man who lived at that time and place and was then called "Moses"'.

Similarly when I say 'N is dead', I might be thinking of the person I once saw in certain places, who looked like a picture I am pointing to, who did such-and-such and who was generally called 'N'. If you ask me who N is, I might enumerate 'all or some of these points, and different ones on different occasions'. I might even say that 'N' can be defined as 'the man of whom all this is true'. Still I would not conclude, at least not immediately, that 'N is dead' is false if it turned out that some of what I took to be true of him is false. In particular I would hesitate to declare 'N is dead' false if 'it is only something which strikes me as incidental that has turned out false'. I might even change my mind about what is essential and what incidental. In fact 'I use the name "N" without a *fixed* meaning'.

This is not to say the meaning of a name changes as our knowledge of its bearer changes. Wittgenstein is not implying that 'N' acquires a new meaning when we discover N is a crook rather than a pillar of the community. He is restating what he said about 'Moses' – that the name has not 'got a fixed and unequivocal use ... in all possible cases'. His point is that we do not as a rule take the meaning of 'N' to be fixed by a definite description (e.g. as 'the person who did such-and-such' or even as 'the person to whom these or those descriptions apply'). Rather we enumerate various descriptions and different ones at different times.

Though not fully circumscribed, names are no less useless than words like 'game', for which we can only give examples. A name may serve its purpose even though the descriptions with which it is associated are not all true, just as a table with four legs may serve its purpose despite being unstable on uneven surfaces. A name 'without a *fixed* meaning' may not be less useful than one with a fixed meaning despite the fact that it may 'sometimes wobble'. Of course the meanings of names, like those of concept words, may be fixed 'for a special purpose' (§69). In a scholarly debate over the historicity of Moses, for instance, it might be helpful to specify at the outset whom one means by 'Moses'.

We may, if we wish, reserve the word 'sense' to cover names, the meaning of which can be specified precisely. But if we do, we should not conclude that people cannot be referred to using names that do not have '*fixed* meaning[s]'. I am not 'talking nonsense' when I use 'Moses' without being able to say exactly whom I have in mind. What matters is how names function in practice, not how we choose to speak of their use. We can say whatever we like as long as this 'does not prevent [us] from seeing the facts'. On the other hand when we 'see the facts', there is a 'good deal we will not say'. In particular we shall not say that statements make sense only if the meanings of their names can be precisely specified in advance.

Even in science, words may fail to have '*fixed* meaning[s]'. Here too 'the bounds of the incidental' are typically left open. Consider the definition of the word 'copper'. Whereas this used to be defined as a metal with a certain appearance, it is now defined as an element having an atomic weight of 63.54. That hardly makes it a useless word, however. Nor is its meaning unclear. The fact that a characteristic once regarded as definitive has been relegated to the status of 'observed concomitant' does not in any way affect the intelligibility of what chemists say about the metal.

Section 80

This section amplifies the point in §68 about our concepts not being 'everywhere circumscribed by rules'. Even in the case of a word like 'chair', we may find ourselves at a loss to know whether it applies to a particular object. If something we had used as a chair for years were suddenly to disappear, we would almost certainly think we had fallen prey to an illusion. But if the thing were to disappear and reappear at regular intervals and we were able to touch it and sit on it while it existed, we would not know what to say.

As matters now stand, however, the rules governing the use of the word 'chair' work well enough. The chairs we encounter in everyday life are invariably well-behaved, and it is neither here nor there that situations are conceivable in which we would be at a loss for words. We do not require rules specifying whether chair-like objects that disappear and reappear are chairs, nor do we 'miss [these rules] when we use the word "chair" '. The mere possibility of bizarre cases does not show that 'we do not really attach any meaning to this word'.

Section 81

We are inclined to think that a word like 'chair' has a meaning only insofar as we are 'equipped with rules for every possible application of it' (§80), in part at least, because we think of language as though it were a natural phenomenon governed by fixed general principles. We suppose that insofar as 'the use of words [can be compared] with games and calculi which have fixed rules ... someone who is using language *must* be playing such a game' and conclude that the application of their words must be determined in advance.

Frank Ramsey had a point when he spoke of logic as a 'normative science', which deals with how things ought to be rather than with how they actually are. Unlike the laws of natural science, which can only be conformed to, the rules of 'normative science' may be obeyed or violated. (Compare §54.) Still this way of talking about logic can easily mislead. If you regard logic as a science you are likely to think that 'our languages only *approximate* to [calculi with fixed rules]', and if you think this, 'you are standing on the very brink of a misunderstanding'. While there is indeed a sense in which languages '*approximate*' calculi – otherwise we could not 'compare' them – it should not be assumed that calculi with fixed rules are 'better, more perfect' than natural languages. We should not go on to conclude that there must exist 'an *ideal* language', one to which the language we actually speak only approximates. (It is important to notice that Wittgenstein does not disparage Ramsey's conception of logic. Indeed he speaks of himself as being unsure of what Ramsey had in mind. His view seems to be that Ramsey's remark is worth considering because it contains an important insight about the nature of logic.)

The idea of language as approximating an ideal and logic as concerned with language abstracted from the coarseness characteristic of natural languages like English and German is deeply problematic. Logic 'does not treat of language – or of thought – in the sense in which a natural science treats of a natural phenomenon'. It is not concerned with phenomena unencumbered by disturbing influences – 'our logic [is not] a logic for a vacuum'. While physicists can take credit for explaining the nature of motion, logicians cannot take credit for having shown people 'at last what a proper sentence look[s] like'.

Logicians do not reveal – by analysis or any other means – the real sentences lying hidden in our ordinary sentences. Rather they '*construct*' calculi with fixed rules to which natural languages can be compared. Ideal languages are subsidiary to natural languages, not more fundamental than them. They are of value just insofar as they clarify how we use words. (Wittgenstein is not extolling ordinary language. He is criticizing philosophers who 'sublime the logic of our language' (§38) and take ideal languages to reveal something hidden in the phenomena.)

If we are to see the role of logic 'in the right light', we need to consider how understanding, meaning and thinking function in our lives. Only then will it become clear what leads philosophers – including the author of the *Tractatus* – to suppose that when one says or thinks something (and '*means* or *understands* it') one is 'operating a calculus according to definite rules'. (Wittgenstein explores the nature of understanding, meaning and thinking in detail later in the *Investigations*.)

Section 82

To see that it is misleading to refer to speakers as 'operating a calculus according to definite rules' (§81), it is helpful to consider how we understand the phrase 'the rule by which [they proceed]'. There are several things we may have in mind. (Compare §54, where Wittgenstein lists some of the ways in which a game can be said to be 'played according to a definite rule'.) We may be referring to a 'hypothesis' to the effect that the person is using words in such-and-such a way (recall the shopkeeper in §1 who carries out the order 'five red apples'). We may be thinking of the rule – or table – the person consults to determine what he or she should do or say (recall that the shopkeeper uses a table to correlate 'red' with a certain colour). Or we may be alluding to the rule the person would claim to be following if asked (imagine the shopkeeper's saying he is following the rule 'Take an apple from the drawer marked "Apples" whenever you see the word "apple" on a shopper's slip').

But there are also cases in which a person's use of words does not accord with rules in any of these ways. There need not always be a 'hypothesis that satisfactorily describes [our] use of words', a rule or table that we consult, or a rule that we would specify if asked. Even when we can give a definition for a word, we may – as Wittgenstein noted in §79 in connection with names and scientific terms – 'withdraw and alter it'. In this case we do not know 'the rule according to which [we are] playing' and there is no reason to think anyone else is in a better position to 'determine [it]'. In fact you might well wonder whether 'the expression "the rule by which [someone] proceeds"' means anything here. In such cases it seems wrong to speak of a person 'operating a calculus according to definite rules' (§81).

Section 83

To reinforce the point that there are cases to which the phrase 'the rule by which he proceeds' does not apply (§82), Wittgenstein reverts to his comparison of language with games. A language-user who shifts from one language-game to another, interspersing unusual activities along the way, is no more plausibly regarded as following 'fixed rules' (§81) than a person who starts one game after another and proceeds aimlessly in between. In neither case is a single activity being pursued 'the whole time', and it makes no sense to say a 'definite rule' is being followed at every stage. Moreover we can 'make up the rules as [we] go along', even 'alter them' in midstream. (The case of poets changing the rules is instructive. Not only are they able to do this without lapsing into nonsense, their changing them may be what makes their work memorable.)

Section 84

Wittgenstein has been stressing that 'the application of a word is not everywhere bounded by rules'. (Recall that in §68 he dismissed the objection that he is committed to holding that 'the use of the word ["game"] is unregulated' on the grounds that its use 'is not everywhere circumscribed by rules'; in the German original he uses the same phrase here as before – 'überall von Regeln begrenzt'.) Now he questions whether our use of words could be completely bounded by rules. We can, it is true, always introduce a rule to eliminate a doubt about the use of a word. But what would it mean for the use of the word to be governed at every point by rules? To see that it is impossible to 'stop up all the cracks' and eliminate all conceivable doubts by introducing new rules, it helps, once again, to consider the case of a game. While we can introduce rules to remove specific doubts about how chess is played, doubts may arise regarding these rules, doubts that can be removed only by introducing still more rules – about which yet other doubts may arise. I can, for instance, remove a doubt about the ability of those playing chess to remember what they did by introducing a rule that determines who moved last, but to remove all possible doubts I would also have to introduce a rule specifying what is to count as the last move, and so on. (Elsewhere Wittgenstein asks: 'What do we mean by a complete list of rules for the employment of a piece in chess? Couldn't we always construct doubtful cases, in which the normal list of rules does not decide? Think e.g. of such a question as: how to determine who moved last, if a doubt is raised about the reliability of the players' memories'.[1])

The possibility of doubts arising hardly means there is something wrong with the games we play (or with our use of language). The fact that 'a doubt can creep in' is no reason to think it will creep in or has crept in. It is one thing to *imagine* a doubt', quite another to '[be] in doubt'. A person may think there is a huge hole outside his or her front door and always check to see whether there is (and may even prove to be right one day). But this is no reason for me to wonder whether there is a hole outside my door when I get up in the morning.

Section 85

Rules are like signposts. The grammatical rule that 'he' takes a singular verb is comparable to a signpost to Paris. It 'stands there' in much the same way as the signpost stands at the side of the road. Neither the rule nor the signpost says or does anything by itself. Grammatical rules do not force me to speak in a particular way any more than signposts force me to go in the direction they indicate. They do not grab me by the throat and make me do one thing rather than another. (Wittgenstein considers signposts because it is easier to get clear about them than about rules. For reasons that are not hard to fathom, we talk more lackadaisically about intangibles like rules than about concrete things like signposts. Also compare §14 and §73, where Wittgenstein shifts from talking about words and ideas to talking about tools and samples.)

In fact signposts – and rules – can invariably be understood in a variety of ways. I can interpret a signpost as telling me to go in the direction it points or as telling me to go in the opposite direction. Regardless of how many signs there are and how closely they are spaced, alternative interpretations are always possible. '→→→→' no more fixes once and for all the direction I am to go than '→' does.

The existence of alternative interpretations does not mean signposts are useless and we should never trust them. A signpost 'sometimes leaves room for doubt and sometimes not'. If you have reason to think a particular signpost has been turned around, you would be well advised to hesitate before following it. But if there is no reason to think this, you would be foolish to wonder how to proceed. Normally '→' can be sensibly understood only as saying we should go in the direction of the arrow. 'We are [not] in doubt because it is possible for us to *imagine* a doubt' (§84). And likewise for rules. (This passage is unclear. I take Wittgenstein to be asking whether the signpost leaves 'room for doubt' and saying that it may or may not. But other readings are possible. Also it is perhaps worth noting that Wittgenstein indicated that 'keinen' [no] in the text should be replaced by 'einen' [a].)

To say a signpost (or rule) 'sometimes leaves room for doubt and sometimes not' is to deny that there is anything philosophically interesting to say about the essential nature and interpretation of signposts (and rules). Whether doubt is reasonable or not depends on the political situation, the efficiency of the government, the interests of the inhabitants and other such facts. As Wittgenstein puts it, the proposition that there is sometimes room for doubt, sometimes not, is 'not a philosophical proposition, but an empirical one'. (Compare §47, where

Wittgenstein notes that it is 'not an answer but a rejection of the question' to say what counts as composite depends on how 'composite' is understood.)

Interlude (13): 'A rule stands there like a sign-post'

In the last instalment Wittgenstein took issue with the philosopher's conception of the determinateness of sense in two ways. On the one hand he questioned various considerations that seem to imply that sense must be fully determinate – notably the idea that the meaning of a word can sometimes be fixed by samples and the idea that our knowledge of its use is equivalent to an unformulated definition. On the other hand he noted that absolute determinateness of sense is not essential for thought and communication and reminded us that we are in the normal course of events able to get along perfectly well despite the fact that our concepts do not have sharp boundaries. In the present instalment he notes that the same goes for proper names like 'Moses' and emphasizes that rules are no more determinate than the meanings of words and no more problematic because they are not.

In connection with this last point it is important to notice that Wittgenstein is not challenging the idea that we follow rules. He is not committed to denying that using language and playing chess are rule-governed activities, still less committed to disputing it is a rule of English that 'he' is followed by 'is' and a rule of chess that kings move one square at a time. Nor, as §81 makes clear, does he think it wrong to compare 'the use of words with games and calculi which have fixed rules'. His target is the philosophical view that when we use language we '*must* be playing ... a game [with fixed rules]'. While agreeing that rules are comparable to calculi, Wittgenstein objects to identifying them and to thinking of the rules we follow as fixed in the way philosophers tend to assume. What bothers him is the idea that 'if anyone utters a sentence and *means* or *understands* it he is operating a calculus according to definite rules'.

Wittgenstein's central point is that meaning and understanding do not require our words to be fully regulated in the sense of being 'everywhere circumscribed by rules'. Just as it is a mistake to think 'a blurred concept [is not] a concept at all' (§71), so too it is wrong to think a 'blurred' rule is not a rule. It makes no sense to speak of games – or the application of words – as being determined in every possible situation by rules. Full regulation is out of the question since it is impossible to 'stop up all the cracks' (§84). Whenever a new rule is introduced to remove a doubt about the application of an old one, new doubts can arise – this time about how the new rule is to be applied. If full regulation were required for playing a game or for meaning something, games would be unplayable and language useless. To think of games, the uses of words or whatever as being completely fixed by rules is to step over 'the brink of a misunderstanding' (§81).

The thing to remember is that a rule simply 'stands there' (§85). There is no such thing as a rule that fixes how it is to be followed (or a self-interpreting signpost). Far from determining its own application, a rule can always be interpreted in more than one way. Not even a straightforward rule about the use of a word dictates how it is to be obeyed. 'Use the word "game" to apply to competitive activities involving skill, chance and endurance' no more fixes its own application than a signpost to Paris fixes how it is to be followed. The rule does not tell us that 'competitive' is to be understood as involving conflict, not cooperation, any more than the signpost to Paris tells us to go in the direction of the finger, not in the opposite direction. Like ostensive definitions, rules and signposts 'can be variously interpreted in *every* case' (§28). (It is no argument against this observation that signs that exert forces making us go where they point fix their applications. Following such a sign is a natural phenomenon on a par with the Moon's tracking the Earth as it goes around the Sun. It is not a phenomenon involving interpretation, never mind one that can be sensibly praised or blamed.)

This does not mean rule-following is a precarious business. The fact that there is always more than one way to interpret a rule is no reason to think that chaos constantly looms. Incomplete regulation in theory is fully compatible with complete regulation in practice. As in the case of concepts and names, difficulties do not normally arise, and there is rarely room for doubt (compare §85). The fact that we do not have rules ready for every eventuality does not mean we do not follow rules, and the mere possibility of misunderstanding detracts nothing from their usefulness (see especially §69 and §79). Mostly we do not 'interpret' rules (or signposts). We obey or disobey them, and the question of whether they should be understood this way or that is as distant from our minds as the question of whether there is an abyss outside our front doors. (Compare §201: '[T]here is a way of grasping a rule which is *not* an *interpretation*, but which is exhibited in what we call "obeying the rule" and "going against it" in actual cases'. Wittgenstein's remarks about ostensive teaching in §6 and about ostensive definition in §29 are relevant here, as is the discussion of the sixth interlude.)

I might put it this way. We follow rules (and signposts) as we do because we have a practice of following rules (and a practice of using signposts). We do not – at least not usually – first interpret rules, then do whatever we interpret them as telling us to do. As Wittgenstein stresses, if interpretations were always required, we would never do anything – every interpretation would have to be backed by another interpretation *ad infinitum*. Rather, we follow rules. Nothing is needed to link a rule that is being followed with an action that conforms to it since there is no gap to be bridged. Like assertion – see the discussion of §22 – following a rule is one thing, not two. While we may on occasion find ourselves in a position of having to interpret a rule, this is exceptional. Normally we do not interpret rules at all – we simply go by them. (In §201 Wittgenstein puts the point this way: '[T]here is an inclination to say: every action according to the rule is an interpretation. But we ought to restrict the term "interpretation" to the substitution of one expression of the rule for another'.)

But what are we to say about the case in which a rule or a concept fails us? What would happen if what we take to be chairs suddenly started going in and out of existence? Would we still call them chairs? Or – to take a more realistic example – what should we say about people who have been on life-support systems for long periods of time? Should we take them to be alive or dead? While Wittgenstein does not explicitly consider such questions, it is clear how he would answer them. He would point out that it makes no sense for us to rack our brains over the question of what our rules say about such cases, for the simple reason that they do not say anything about them at all. When a concept fails to cover a strange or unprecedented eventuality, all we can do is attempt to figure out as carefully and as intelligently as we can using all the resources at our disposal the best thing to say. We are on our own and have to decide matters for ourselves.

It should be clear by now that Wittgenstein's remarks about concepts, definitions and rules – as well as his earlier remarks about ostensive teaching – are very much of a piece. A discussion of application of concepts invariably involves an examination of what following a rule involves; a discussion of definitions naturally leads on to consideration of the rules governing the use of words; and a discussion of the process of ostensive teaching is inseparable from an examination of the rules connecting words with things and how they are inculcated. (Nobody should be surprised that Wittgenstein frequently returns to the topic of the nature of rules – see §54 and §82 and the extended treatment of rules in §§143–242.) Since these topics are interrelated Wittgenstein is obliged to go over the same ground more than once. To dispel philosophical confusion about meaning and language, he has to track it down wherever it manifests itself. He cannot afford to leave any significant stone unturned.

Sections 86 to 92: 'The essence of everything empirical'

Wittgenstein brings his examination of the philosophical requirement of determinateness of sense to a close with a discussion of tables, definitions and orders (§§86–9), then explores the philosophical idea of logic as transcending the exigencies of everyday life and as dealing with the most basic features of the world (§§90–2). There is a shift in focus between the two sets of remarks but they are not unrelated. The idea that determinacy of sense is essential for intelligible thought and speech goes hand in hand with the idea that logic deals with what we really or ideally mean.

Section 86

Having discussed the incompleteness of rules and the indeterminacy of sense, Wittgenstein now considers how tables can be used to determine the meanings of words. He introduces a variant of the builders' language-game described in §2 in which builder A gives builder B a written sign and builder B uses a table to determine which sort of building-stones to fetch. In this language-game builder B determines what he is to do by consulting a table that correlates signs with pictures of building-stones in much the same way as the shopkeeper determines what colour apple to pick out by seeing which colour is correlated with red (see §1). We are to think of the table as 'a rule which [builder B] follows in executing orders' and to imagine his having been trained to read it by 'learning to pass his finger horizontally from left to right'. (Whereas in §85 Wittgenstein focusses on the interpretation of rules, here he considers how someone uses a rule after 'receiving a training'. Also notice that in §1 he simply assumed the shopkeeper read his chart the usual way.)

Clearly, other ways of reading the table might subsequently be introduced. Instead of reading it 'horizontally from left to right', the builder might read it in such a way that 'block' is correlated with the picture of the pillar, 'pillar' with the picture of the slab, 'slab' with the picture of the beam, and 'beam' with the picture of the block. Moreover we can imagine the builder being supplied with a rule for reading the table, specifically a schema of lines showing how it is to be used. And we can imagine other rules being specified to explain this rule.

But while schemata showing how the rule is to be used may be supplied, they do not have to be. It is not true that 'the first table [is] incomplete without the schema of arrows' or that the other tables are 'incomplete without their schemata'. The builder who is trained to read his table one way does not need a second rule to explain the rule he has been taught – he will execute orders by proceeding as he was trained. Tables without schemata are no less complete than signposts. It is a mistake to think they are usable only when they are accompanied by rules explaining how they are to be read.

Section 87

Similarly the requirement of complete determinacy is out of place in the case of proper names. Even if I take the name to be replaceable by a single description – perhaps 'for a special purpose' (§69) – doubts may arise regarding what I mean. Suppose I explain what I mean by 'Moses' by saying that I take it to mean 'the man who led the Israelites out of Egypt' as in §79. You may still wonder how I understand 'Egypt' and 'Israelite'. And were I to define 'Egypt' and 'Israelite', doubts about the words I use in my definition would also be possible. Like rules and signposts, definitions lack the sort of determinacy philosophers take to be essential. (This is unsurprising since definitions are rules. When I explain what I mean, I specify a rule; I am saying ' "Moses" means "the man who led the Israelites out of Egypt" '.)

Not even definitions cast in terms of words like 'red' and 'sweet' are perfectly determinate. The meanings of colours and tastes can no more be fixed once and for all by means of samples than the word 'Moses' can be pinned down completely by means of definitions. When we point to a red sample, we are to all intents and purposes specifying a rule about how 'red' is used; we are saying it refers to things with the colour of the sample. And like all other rules, it can be variously interpreted. (See also §28 on ostensive definitions and §73 on defining colours using samples.)

Nor should it be thought that if there is no such thing as a 'final' explanation of a word, we 'don't understand what [a person who tries to explain the name] means, and never shall!'. This assumes that an explanation hangs 'in the air unless supported by another one' whereas in fact it may work perfectly well just as it is. What matters is whether the explanation serves its purpose, not whether it is supported by other explanations, still less whether it is 'final'. An explanation of a name is like a signpost; it 'sometimes leaves room for doubt and sometimes not' (§85). More explanation may be required, but not always or even usually. I may make myself clear – and you may understand me – if I say 'I take "Moses" to mean the man, if there was such a man, who led the Israelites out of Egypt'. This explanation is not 'in need of another – unless *we* require it to prevent a misunderstanding'. (Compare the discussion of ' "last" definition[s]' in §29.)

The possibility of doubts arising about what we mean does not reveal an 'existing gap in the foundations' of our thinking. '[S]ecure understanding' is not something that can be achieved only by 'first doubt[ing] everything that can be doubted and then remov[ing] all these doubts'. (Here Wittgenstein takes issue with the widely discussed philosophical view that we can be sure of something only if it resists all possible doubt and that it falls to philosophers to figure out which of our beliefs are securely grounded.) As the discussion of the word 'chair' in §80 makes clear, we can know what a word means even though the rules governing its use do not cover every eventuality. What we require of an explanation, definition or rule is not that it be fully determinate and immune to all possible doubt, only that it work in practice. A signpost, explanation, definition or rule is 'in order – if, under normal circumstances, it fulfils its purpose'.

Section 88

Wittgenstein's remarks about indeterminacy bear on the discussion in §71 of the expression 'Stand roughly there' and the discussion of exactness in §28 and §69. (In this section the German phrase, 'Halte dich ungefähr hier auf!', is translated as 'Stand roughly here'; in §71 it was translated as 'Stand roughly there'.) Wittgenstein first notes that the order 'Stand roughly here' may 'work perfectly' since an order may, like a signpost, 'under normal circumstances [fulfil] its purpose' (§87). It is no more surprising or lamentable that a person told to stand 'roughly here' may not know exactly where to stand than it is surprising or lamentable that a signpost may on occasion lead us astray. The mere possibility of an order not working perfectly is no reason to conclude the order is inadequate and no reason to think that an order could have been given that would work perfectly whatever the circumstances.

'Stand roughly here' might be called an inexact explanation of where the person is to stand. But if we call it inexact, we should not think it is 'unusable'. (Compare §69, where Wittgenstein warns against equating 'inexact' with 'unusable'.) Nor should it be thought that it is possible to provide an 'ideally exact' specification of where the person is to stand. 'Stand within this marked off area' is certainly more specific than 'Stand roughly here'. But it is not absolutely precise since the line marking off the area has breadth. Not even a colour-edge would fix the boundary 'perfectly exactly' since what counts as stepping over such a boundary and how this is to be determined would still be debatable. (When does a person's shoe count as being completely within the marked off area?) In the normal course of events, of course, we do not need to know any of this. The concern with perfect exactness does not arise in everyday life; it arises only when 'the engine [is] idling'.

Wittgenstein is challenging the philosopher's conception of 'ideal exactness', a conception which, like the conception of absolute simplicity, lies '*outside* a particular language-game' (§47). He is not denying that I can sensibly speak of setting my watch to the exact time and of your being exactly on time, only reminding us that what we ordinarily count as exact depends on the circumstances. If one is determining the time for dinner, a pocket-watch may give the exact time; if one is determining reaction-times of subjects in a psychology laboratory, a more sophisticated measuring device may be required. The fact that a scientist uses a device that gives times to a thousandth of a second hardly shows it is senseless to speak of a person turning up for dinner at the 'exact time' according to the clock on the wall. (Compare §17 on classifying chess pieces and §69 on inexact measures.)

If we take statements regarding exactness as commendations and statements regarding inexactness as reproaches, we shall be much less likely to become embroiled in the futile task of trying to figure out what counts as absolute exactness. Obviously nobody deserves to be reproached for not giving the distance to the sun to the nearest metre or praised for specifying the length of a table to the nearest hundredth of a millimetre.

We do not have a '*single* ideal' (or criterion) of exactness that applies in all cases, only a variety of cases each governed by its own standards – the case of setting a pocket-watch to the exact time, the case of coming to dinner punctually, the case of measuring astronomical distances accurately, etc. Nor would we be better off if we were to fix on a single standard. To the contrary. Everyday determinations of time would count as inexact were laboratory measurements of time taken to set the standard of exactness, while measurements of time in the laboratory that scientists deem inexact would count as exact were everyday measurements of time taken to set the ideal. In this regard it should not be forgotten that over-exactness can also cause trouble.

Section 89

Wittgenstein has been challenging the philosophical requirement of the determinacy of sense (and the definiteness of rules, definitions, explanations and the like). It is thus unsurprising that he should now turn to an examination of logic, a subject that deals with fully determinate senses. If everyday language lacks the sort of determinacy philosophers take to be essential for coherent thought and speech and it is a mistake to think of the logician's languages as being 'better, more perfect, than our everyday language' (§81), one may be forgiven for wondering 'In what sense is logic something sublime?' The difficulty is that Wittgenstein seems committed to denying that logic is immune from the contingencies of everyday life. Since he takes purity and exactness to depend on the language-game in question, how can he possibly account for the absolute purity and exactness of logic?

Wittgenstein begins his discussion of this issue by considering why one might think of logic as something sublime. He first notes that we are inclined to suppose that there 'pertain[s] to logic a peculiar depth – a universal significance'. The usual assumption is that logical propositions such as 'Everything is what it is and not another thing' refer to something that every science presupposes, something that is 'at the bottom of all the sciences'. When we say that everything is what it is and not another thing, we seem to be saying something about 'the nature of all things' – that each individual thing is essentially just what it is. (In an early notebook, Wittgenstein spoke of himself as attempting to 'giv[e] the nature of all being'.[1])

There is a kernel of truth in this conception. Logic is not concerned with particular 'facts of nature' such as the fact that it rained this morning or with 'causal connexions' such as smoking causes cancer. But while logical investigation 'takes its rise ... from an urge to understand the basis, or essence, of everything empirical', it should not be thought of as a kind of science that grasps the way things work in a deep sense. Philosophers are not scientists and their discoveries are not substantive discoveries. What they adduce are not new facts – that is the scientist's job – but 'something that is already in plain view'. When we do philosophy, it is this – what is already in plain view – that 'we want to *understand* [and] seem in some sense not to understand'.

For instance what Augustine aims to understand when he asks 'What, then, is time?' is something we are all familiar with. (The quotation is from Augustine's *Confessions*, Book XI, chapter 14.[2]) It is characteristic of philosophical questions that one can say, as Augustine does, 'Provided that no one asks me, I know. If I want to explain it to an inquirer, I do not know'. This is not the sort of thing a scientist would say. No physicist would say 'Provided that no one asks me what the specific gravity of hydrogen is, I know. If I want to explain it to an inquirer, I do not know'. To be incapable of saying what one knows when one is asked is to be in a philosophical predicament, not a scientific one.

The fact that we cannot explain things like time despite being able to talk about them in everyday life is something we need 'to *remind* ourselves of' and something that is 'for some reason ... difficult to remind [ourselves of]'. Our inability to explain concepts rarely prevents our trying to fathom 'the nature of all things'. As Wittgenstein notes in §52, something in philosophy opposes 'an examination of details'.

Section 90

Instead of thinking of logical investigation as trying 'to *penetrate* phenomena' we should think of it as concerned with 'the "*possibilities*" of phenomena', with what we can sensibly say about the phenomena. What Wittgenstein takes the liberty to call 'our investigation' focusses on the '*kinds of statement*' we make about phenomena, not on the phenomena themselves. In the case of time, for instance, we should devote our efforts to examining how we talk and think about time rather than to advancing views about its essential nature. We should examine statements about time flying by, one event occurring before another, the past being fixed, its taking time to do something, and the like. Since such statements are 'not *philosophical* statements', they do not help us understand the essence of time. But that does not matter as long as they dissuade us from attempting 'to *penetrate* phenomena'.

Philosophical investigation that attends to 'the "*possibilities*" of phenomena' rather than the phenomena themselves is 'grammatical' in nature. (Compare §47, where the question of what to count as a complex object is referred to as a '*grammatical* question'.) Whereas 'logical investigation [as traditionally construed] explores the nature of all things' (§89), grammatical investigation attempts to clarify how we speak and think. It strives to clear away 'misunderstandings concerning the use of words, caused, among other things, by analogies between the forms of expression in different regions of language'. An example would be the analogy between expressions about the passing of time and expressions about the flowing of rivers. This fools us into thinking of time as something that moves from one place to another like water.

When Wittgenstein observes that misunderstandings of the sort he has in mind can sometimes be removed by 'analysis' he is not going back on what he said earlier. Analysis as he now envisions it is not a matter of replacing a less 'fundamental form' by a more fundamental one (§63). Rather it involves 'substituting one form of expression for another' for the purpose of removing a particular philosophical confusion. He is not claiming this sort of analysis always does the trick, only that 'some' misunderstandings can be cleared up by 'an "analysis" of our forms of expression'. (Notice that Wittgenstein speaks of such analysis as being 'sometimes' like taking things apart and puts the word 'analysis' in quotation marks.)

Section 91

Wittgenstein's suggestion that we should engage in grammatical investigation can easily be misconstrued. You might think – especially if you 'feel as if [you] had to *penetrate* phenomena' (§90) – that if statements can be analysed (and particular misunderstandings removed), it makes sense to speak of them as being fully analysed and of all possible misunderstandings as having been anticipated. There must, you might reason, be 'a *single* completely resolved form of every expression', a completely determinate 'final analysis'. Since analysis brings more to light, it ought to be possible to obtain expressions that are 'completely clarified'. If the process of eliminating misunderstanding by making our expressions more exact involves 'moving towards … a state of complete exactness', 'the real goal of our investigation' would seem to be no different from the goal of traditional logical investigation.

Wittgenstein does not explicitly reject this line of argument. He expects us to appreciate that the suggestion that we can or should be aiming at 'a state of complete exactness' runs counter to almost everything he has been saying up to now. (See especially the discussion of real meaning in §§19–20 and the discussion of analysis in §§60–4.) For him the idea of 'a state of complete exactness' is another philosophical myth. All that can be safely said is that 'some [misunderstandings] can be removed by substituting one form of expression for another' (§90).

Section 92

Yet another misunderstanding regarding the kind of analysis involved in grammatical investigation concerns the sense in which philosophy is concerned with 'the *essence* of language, of propositions, of thought'. Wittgenstein is not disparaging all questions concerning essences. '[W]e too are in these investigations', he explicitly declares, 'trying to understand the essence of language – its function, its structure'. What he is challenging is not the conception of philosophical investigation as concerned with the essence of language understood as something 'that already lies open to view and that becomes surveyable by a rearrangement'. His target is rather the idea of philosophy as attempting to reveal the essence of language understood as 'something that lies *beneath* the surface'. What he objects to is the idea of there being 'something that lies within [language], which we see when we look *into* a thing, and which an analysis digs out'.

If you proceed as philosophers traditionally proceed and take the 'essence of language' to be '*hidden from us*', you will ask ' "*What is* language?", "*What is* a proposition?" ' (and '*What is* simplicity?', '*What is* exactness?', etc.). You will assume there are answers to be given 'once and for all', answers of the sort Socrates describes in the quotation given in §46 when he notes he has heard it said that 'the essence of speech is the combination of names'. If, on the other hand, you proceed as Wittgenstein recommends, you will bend your energies to rearranging what everyone already knows with the object of exposing philosophical misunderstanding.

Interlude (14): 'We feel as if we had to *penetrate* phenomena'

What Wittgenstein says about tables, definitions and orders in §§86–8 should seem familiar given his discussion of rules in the last instalment. In these sections he mainly extends his critique of the 'determinacy of sense' to these three topics. The burden of his remarks is that tables can fulfil their purpose even though they can be variously interpreted; definitions can explain meanings even though misunderstanding is always possible; and orders can work perfectly even though they are never ideally exact. As before, his contention is the double one that it is a mistake to suppose that a practice can ever be fully regulated and a mistake to suppose that without regulation anarchy threatens at every turn. The only problem is that there no longer appears to be any place for logic. Can Wittgenstein really be denying that in logic sense is fully determinate? Surely here, if nowhere else, meanings are fixed, the rules are complete, and there are no gaps in the foundations.

Wittgenstein approaches the problem indirectly. In §§89–92 he clarifies the nature of logical investigation by reminding us how it has been traditionally understood and by sketching how it appears when construed as a grammatical investigation. In particular he draws our attention to the widely-held conception of logic as 'explor[ing] the nature of all things' (§89) and as '*penetrat[ing]* phenomena' (§90). On this view a logical law like 'Everything is what it is and not another thing' reveals something profound about the world. It tells us that individual things are essentially just what they are. For Wittgenstein, on the other hand, logical investigation is concerned with 'the "*possibilities*" of phenomena', i.e. 'the *kinds of statement* we make about the phenomena' (§90). He would have us discount the question of what 'lies *beneath* the surface' (§92) and treat logical principles like 'Everything is what it is and not another thing' as belonging to what in §50 is called 'our method of representation'.

The target of Wittgenstein's remarks in §§89–92 – the idea of logic as a kind of super-physics concerning 'the nature of all things' (§89) – is one that Wittgenstein himself initially embraced. In 1913 in some notes on logic he observes that 'philosophy consists of logic and metaphysics: logic is its basis', while in an entry in a notebook in 1916 he states that his 'work has extended from the foundations of logic to the nature of the world' (also compare Russell: 'Philosophy is the science of the possible').[3] Now by contrast Wittgenstein takes Frank Ramsey's characterization of logic as a 'normative science' (§81) to be closer to the mark. He deprecates the conception of logic as lying at 'the bottom of all the sciences' (§89), as providing a general account of the essential character of the world, as revealing the innermost secrets about the nature of things. It is, he insists, a mistake to picture logical investigation as taking us beyond physics, which deals with contingent matters of fact, to metaphysics, which deals with the nature of all being.

When philosophers ask '*What* is language?' or '*What* is a proposition?' they are looking for answers that are 'given once and for all; and independently of any future experience' (§92). They take philosophical investigation to be like scientific investigation in that it reveals something about the world but different from it in that its theories are, if true, necessarily true (and hence immune to refutation by new empirical findings). For them logical investigation aims to explain how things are no less than scientific investigation. The only difference is that logic provides much deeper explanations. The philosophical question '*What is* language?' (§92) is similar but more profound than the scientific question 'What is the specific gravity of hydrogen?' (§89) since it applies – in much the same way as the picture of human language adumbrated in §1 – to every conceivable case.

In contrast to logical investigation understood as a form of super-physics, which purports to be explanatory, grammatical investigation is straightforwardly descriptive. It does not assume that an explanation of what a language is essentially can be given (where this is understood as referring to something that – as Wittgenstein puts it in §92 – 'lies within'). Rather it explores the 'countless different kinds of use of what we call "symbols", "words", "sentences"' (§23) with the goal of resolving philosophical quandaries. We should not attempt to provide an explanation of language, only make a concerted effort to get clear about what we seem 'in some sense not to understand' despite the fact that it 'is already in plain view' (§89). Consider the question 'What is knowledge?'. Unlike Socrates – who in the *Theaetetus* (147a) compares this question to the question 'What is clay?' and expects to be given an account of the nature of knowledge comparable to the scientist's account of the nature of clay (not a list of different sorts of clay) – Wittgenstein advocates that we bend our energies to examining what we count as knowledge. As he once put it, 'our answer' consists in giving what 'Socrates doesn't regard as even a preliminary answer to the question', namely an enumeration of cases of knowledge – along with a 'few analogies'.[4] (Also recall Socrates's remarks about piety quoted in the comments on §70.)

To avoid misunderstanding I should stress that Wittgenstein is not saying we should be attempting to provide a comprehensive descrip-tion of language, nor even suggesting that such a description could be devised. He is not recommending we forego the search for a general explanatory theory of phenomena in favour of the less ambitious project of developing an overview – or descriptive theory – of language, one that gives its essential 'grammar'. Actually far from assuming the existence of an underlying grammar of our language, he attempts to disabuse us of the idea of such a grammar by stressing the multiplicity of language-games. He even questions the possibility of sharply distinguishing between grammatical and empirical facts. For one thing 'what to-day counts as an observed concomitant of a phenomenon [may] tomorrow be used to define it' (§79).

But where does this leave the problem of how logic can be 'sublime' (§89)? This problem is not explicitly addressed in this instalment. Still it is not hard to guess how Wittgenstein would treat it He would try to convince us that the problem disappears once we have a proper conception of logical investigation, one disentangled from traditional ideas about what it involves. In this regard it is significant that after noting that logic does 'not treat of language – or of thought – in the sense in which a natural science treats of a natural phenomenon', Wittgenstein observes that 'the most that can be said is that we *construct* ideal languages' (§81). This suggests that he thinks logic appears sublime because it deals with constructed languages. The tension between the nature of logic and his remarks about the indeterminacy of sense is more apparent than real. Logic is sublime for the simple reason that we construct it to be sublime.

Sections 93 to 103: 'We are not striving after an ideal'

The themes of this instalment are closely related to those of the last one. §§93–6 focus on our conviction that propositions are a special kind of thing while §§97–103 explore the conception of logic as something inflexible and perfectly clear.

Section 93

The question '*What is* a proposition?' (referred to in §92) has the same general character as Augustine's question 'What is time?' discussed in §89. Viewed one way '[a] proposition is the most ordinary thing in the world'; viewed another way it can seem 'very queer'. In everyday life we are able to recognize and use propositions without difficulty but when we try to explain what they are, we end up floundering. We find ourselves wondering what sort of thing a proposition is and how it can achieve what it does. Consider saying 'N'Djamena is the capital of Chad' in response to someone's asking about the capitals of countries in Africa. While there is nothing at all odd about saying this, one might still wonder how a proposition can be about something thousands of kilometres away. (Wittgenstein initially thought propositions deserved special attention. 'My *whole* task', he wrote in 1914, 'consists in explaining the nature of the proposition'.[1])

This worry is without foundation. We lose sight of how propositions 'really work' because 'the forms that we use in expressing ourselves about propositions and thought stand in [the] way'. Propositions are 'remarkable' in the sense that they play an enormously important role in everyday life but there is no reason to regard them as 'very queer'. We should not let ourselves be 'seduce[d]' by how we talk about propositions – and how we talk about thought – into regarding them as remarkable in the sense that they achieve 'something extraordinary, something unique'. To think of them as unlimited in their reach because we can speak and think of things that are not present is 'a *misunderstanding*'. As Wittgenstein puts it, 'a misunderstanding of the logic of language' – i.e. how we use words – 'makes it look to us as if a proposition *did* something queer'. (Also see §38, where Wittgenstein draws attention to our 'tendency to sublime the logic of our language'.)

Section 94

The idea that a proposition is a 'queer thing' fuels our tendency to sublime 'our whole account of logic'. When we take propositions to achieve 'something extraordinary, something unique' (§93), we overlook how we operate with words. We treat language as something apart from how we use it in everyday life and suppose there must be objective meanings or unadulterated thoughts that mediate between signs and facts. Taking the sentence 'N'Djamena is the capital of Chad' to be connected with the fact that N'Djamena is the capital of Chad, we postulate a 'pure intermediary' to do the job. Even worse, we 'sublime' the spoken or written sentence itself and conclude that the connection is effected directly rather than with the help of an intermediary. On this view the six written words of the propositional sign 'N'Djamena is the capital of Chad' possess the remarkable property of being able to reach out to the fact of N'Djamena's being the capital of Chad on their own.

What misleads us into thinking that propositions are 'queer thing[s]', Wittgenstein repeats, is our ways of speaking, 'our forms of expression'. Since it makes sense to speak of sentences as having meaning and as expressing thoughts, we are inclined to suppose there must be objective meanings and unadulterated thoughts. How we speak prevents us from seeing that 'nothing out of the ordinary is involved' and we set out 'in pursuit of chimeras'. Noticing that 'N'Djamena is the capital of Chad' states that N'Djamena is the capital of Chad, we imagine it somehow reaches out to this fact, whereas it is simply a sentence someone might use to inform someone else of something, display his or her knowledge of geography or the like.

Section 95

It is hard to shake the feeling that 'thought must be something unique'. When I say 'N'Djamena is the capital of Chad', my sentence seems to get me face to face with whatever it is I say is true. As Wittgenstein observes, 'when we say, and *mean*, that such and such is the case', it appears that 'we – and our meaning – do not stop anywhere short of the fact'. The proposition 'N'Djamena is the capital of Chad' seems to mean '*this–is–so*'; it seems to mean the very fact that N'Djamena is the capital of Chad.

That there is something amiss here becomes clear the moment we remember that '*thought* can be of what is *not* the case'. (The reason Wittgenstein refers to this as a 'paradox' which 'has the form of a truism' is that thought about what is not the case seems to be about what is the case.) Whatever one wants to say about the thought that N'Djamena is the capital of Chad, the thought that N'Djamena is the capital of Burkina Faso clearly does not reach out to the fact of N'Djamena's being the capital of Burkina Faso. It makes no sense to speak of the meaning of a mistaken thought as 'not stop[ping] anywhere short of the fact'. There is no fact for it to stop short of. The thought that N'Djamena is the capital of Burkina Faso means something despite being of 'what is *not* the case'. (Nor does it help to postulate non-existent facts. To assume the existence of facts that do not exist is hardly a step forward.)

Section 96

The illusion that 'a proposition is a queer thing' (§94) and 'thought must be something unique' (§95) is allied with other illusions. For instance it is tempting to suppose that 'N'Djamena is the capital of Chad' and 'N'Djamena est la capitale de Chad' share a single meaning, even that they name or describe the same proposition. We are easily fooled into positing the existence of meanings that capture what sentences mean regardless of the language in which they are expressed. It escapes us that 'N'Djamena is the capital of Chad' and 'N'Djamena est la capitale de Chad' mean the same because they are used by English and French speakers in similar circumstances and for similar purposes.

If we are bewitched by this sort of illusion, we are likely to take sentences, thoughts and facts to line up 'one behind the other, each equivalent to each' and to think of 'thought, language, ... as the unique correlate, picture of the world'. The most natural assumption, the one to which we are drawn to first of all, is that the sentence 'N'Djamena is the capital of Chad' corresponds to the thought that N'Djamena is the capital of Chad, and this in turn corresponds to the fact of N'Djamena's being the capital of Chad. In the *Tractatus* Wittgenstein puts the idea this way: 'The gramophone record, the musical thought, the score, the waves of sound, all stand to one another in that pictorial internal relation, which holds between language and the world. ... They are all in a certain sense one'.[2]

While the picture of sentences, thoughts and facts as 'each equivalent to each' is suggestive, its use is still in need of explanation. The words 'sentence', 'thought' and 'fact' are – to borrow a phrase from §38 and §94 – being 'sublime[d]' since '[t]he language-game in which they are to be applied is missing'. While a language-game could doubtless be supplied for them, none has been supplied. (Compare §2 where an application was supplied for Augustine's picture of language, and §48 where an application was supplied for the picture of names naming primary elements.) Moreover it would not help to provide an application. This would only show that the picture is appropriate for a narrowly circumscribed region (compare §3). Indeed showing how sentences, thoughts and facts can be regarded as 'each equivalent to each' would mainly serve to remind us that sentences, thoughts and facts – as these are normally thought of – are far from 'equivalent'. For one thing, as Wittgenstein noted in §95, thoughts and facts need not coincide since thoughts can be 'of what is *not* the case'.

Section 97

If we take logic to deal with 'the nature of all things' (§89) and sublime our 'whole account of logic' (§94), we are likely to think that '[t]hought is surrounded by a halo' and to regard logic as revealing 'the *a priori* order of the world: that is the order of *possibilities*, which must be common to both world and thought'. (In 1915, soon after he began the work that led to the *Tractatus*, Wittgenstein wrote 'The great problem around which everything I write turns is: Is there an order in the world *a priori*, and if so what does it consist in?'.[3]) We shall suppose that logic describes something 'utterly simple', something '*prior* to all experience', something of 'the purest crystal', something that cannot be mutilated, transgressed or subverted. Consider the logical law of identity, which states that everything is identical to itself. It is hard to imagine anything more definite, more secure, more 'concrete'. The fact that each thing is identical to itself does indeed seem to be 'the *hardest* thing there is'. (The passage in the *Tractatus* to which Wittgenstein refers states that 'our problems are not abstract but perhaps the most concrete that there are'.)

When we think of logic as revealing 'the a priori order of the world', we take there to be 'a *super*-order between – so to speak – *super*-concepts' and ignore the mundane order that obtains between concepts as they figure in everyday life. Instead of attending to how our concepts are actually related, we think of them separately from the particular language-games to which they belong and take them to be intrinsically related. For instance the relationship between the concepts of existence and identity delineated by the logical principle that everything is what it is and not another thing is often thought to tell us something important about 'the incomparable essence of language'.

To think of 'language', 'experience' and 'world' as '*super*-concepts' is to think of them as having to do with the way things are essentially. But why regard them differently from other words? Insofar as they have a use, it is the use they normally have. The order among them is no more exalted than the order among 'table', 'lamp' and 'door'.

Section 98

In this section Wittgenstein explores the idea, mentioned in §97, that logic deals with 'the a priori order of the world'. On the one hand '[i]t is clear that every sentence in our language "is in order as it is" '. (This harks back to the *Tractatus* 5.5563: 'All propositions of our colloquial language are actually, just as they are, logically completely in order'.) We are not '*striving after* an ideal', and it is a mistake to think of the sentences of ordinary language as pale reflections of sentences in a still to be constructed perfect language. On the other hand it also seems clear that 'where there is sense there must be perfect order'. It seems undeniable that even a vague sentence like 'There is something on the table' must have a 'perfect order' buried in it, one that pins down its meaning exactly.

These two thoughts are not equally cogent. While the first 'is clear', the second only 'seems clear'. It is one thing to say 'every sentence in our language "is in order as it is" ', quite another to say 'where there is sense there must be perfect order'. The fact that ordinary language lacks the definiteness philosophers aspire to is no strike against it. Sentences that fall short of perfection in the philosopher's sense are not unusable. Ordinary sentences should not be regarded 'as if [they] had not yet got a quite unexceptionable sense'. They do not have to have a perfect order of the sort philosophers envision to make perfectly good sense in the normal course of events.

Section 99

In §98 Wittgenstein notes that it is tempting to suppose that 'where there is a sense there must be perfect order' and to conclude from this that 'there must be perfect order even in the vaguest sentence'. Now he draws attention to an equally dubious related assumption, namely that even a sentence that is not perfectly precise 'must nevertheless have *a* definite sense'. While the sense of a sentence may leave certain things open, it must surely be perfectly definite. Consider 'The watch is on the table'. This leaves open which watch and which table is meant, but whatever is not left open must be, according to this view, perfectly definite. (In an early notebook, Wittgenstein put the idea this way: '[I]f possibilities *are left open* in the proposition, *just this* must be *definite: what* is left open. What I do not know I do not know, but the proposition must show me WHAT I know'.[4]) 'An indefinite sense [is not] a sense *at all*'. To say a sentence can have an indefinite sense is like saying an area can have 'an indefinite boundary'. Fuzzy senses are as incongruous as fuzzy numbers. Senses, like numbers, are all or nothing.

Unsurprisingly given his criticism in §71 of Frege's contention that concepts must be sharply delimited, Wittgenstein takes issue with this view of sense. Not only does the sentence 'The watch is on the table' leave this and that open, it has an indefinite sense. Inevitably some possibilities will not have been excluded. (Compare the note on page 33 regarding teaching children gaming with dice.) The thing to bear in mind is that a sentence may serve its purpose even though it is indefinite just as a boundary that is indefinite may mark off an area well enough in practice. Insisting that '[a]n indefinite sense ... would really not be a sense *at all*' is as unreasonable as insisting that '[a]n indefinite boundary is not really a boundary'. A country with vague boundaries may still have a seat at the United Nations, collect taxes and go to war, and a sentence with an indefinite sense may convey all one wants it to convey.

Thinking that 'an indefinite sense' is not a real sense is like thinking that confining someone in a room with an unlocked door is always 'a sham'. While a room with an unlocked door would normally serve poorly as a prison, in special circumstances it may do the job well enough. If it kept someone who was threatening me at bay sufficiently long for me to escape, it would not matter whether it was completely secure or not. Likewise it is not always true that 'an enclosure with a hole in it is as good as *none*'. (Also compare §88, where Wittgenstein stresses that telling someone to 'stand roughly here' may serve its purpose and 'work perfectly'.)

Section 100

It might be thought that on Wittgenstein's own reckoning 'an indefinite sense … would really not be a sense *at all*' (§99). If languages are, as he himself suggests, comparable to games, an indefinite sense would appear to be a contradiction in terms, games being playable only if they have definite rules. In response, Wittgenstein repeats that 'vagueness *in the rules*' need not 'prevent its being a game'. (Recall that in §68 he notes that games can be played despite being 'not everywhere circumscribed by rules'.) Nor are games that have 'some vagueness *in the rules*' less than 'perfect games'. Ordinary games, the rules of which are not entirely precise, are not imperfect, and to speak of them as imperfect is to 'misunderstand the role of the ideal in our language'. Tennis is no less 'the pure article' because its rules do not cover every eventuality. Indeed, as noted in §84, no game can possibly be 'everywhere bounded by rules'.

Games may be less than ideal because the rules are vague but vagueness in the rules does not in and of itself mean that they are not ideal. When we say a game is not ideal, we are saying it could be made more interesting to watch, safer to play, easier to teach or something similar. This might prompt us to modify its rules but not necessarily. It may be better to design new equipment or change where the game is played. (It makes no sense to complain that tennis falls short because it does not – see §68 – include a 'rule for how high one throws the ball'. Also recall §88: ' "Inexact" is really a reproach, and "exact" praise'.)

Section 101

Wittgenstein now observes that we find ourselves wanting to say 'there can't be any vagueness in logic'. Not without reason, we suppose that logic is not in the least vague but rather of 'the purest crystal' (§97). This in turn inclines us – Wittgenstein thinks wrongly – to believe that the ideal that logic encapsulates ' "*must*" be found in reality'. We take it to be virtually self-evident that the concreteness, the hardness, of logic referred to in §97 has to do with the way things are essentially. For instance, we tend to think that things are what they are and not anything else because of their essential nature. It does not bother us that we do not know how this 'ideal' occurs in the world, never mind what it means to say that it '*must*' be lodged there. We are convinced a thing has to be just what it is because 'we think we already see [this ideal in reality]'.

Section 102

In this section Wittgenstein continues his exploration of our conviction that 'the ideal "*must*" be found in reality' (§101). We are, he points out, apt to think the rules governing meaningful speech and thought are in some way or other hidden in the 'medium of the understanding'. It seems obvious to us that 'the a priori order of the world' which logic presents (§97) must in some way or other derive from and reflect how our minds work. Since 'propositional signs' (i.e. spoken sounds or written words) provide information about what we see and what is happening, we think we should be able to grasp the essential nature of reality by reflecting on 'the strict and clear rules of the logical structure of propositions'. The reason I am convinced that things are what they are and nothing else is that every time I think or speak about things I seem to affirm that they are the very things they are.

Section 103

It is easy to persuade oneself that 'the strict and clear rules of the logical structure of propositions' (§102) constitute an 'unshakable' ideal since there seems to be no escaping the requirements and constraints of logic. One wants to say that logic fixes what is sayable and that beyond the limits it sets there is only nonsense. 'Outside', there is no air and it is impossible to breathe. Outside, nothing is sayable.

The conception of logic as fixing the limits of sense is bolstered by the picture of it as functioning like a pair of glasses. My thoughts about the world seem to be filtered through a set of concepts in much the same way as my perception of the passing scene is filtered through the glasses I wear. I seem to be stuck within the confines of logic no less than I am stuck within the confines of my glasses. I cannot transcend logic and think A is not A. There is no such thing as illogical thought; a thought is a thought only insofar as it makes sense.

When we think of logic as defining an ideal, we are inclined to go on to regard it as built into the very nature of things. We forget that this ideal is not 'unshakable' and we are no more bound by it than we are bound by our glasses. While there can be no denying that we require concepts to think and speak, it is far from obvious that we can only think and speak within the framework of a set of 'strict and clear rules of the logical structure of propositions ... hidden in the medium of the understanding' (§102). To recognize that we need concepts to speak and think is not to embrace the picture of an unshakable ideal hidden in the medium of understanding. Saying that we cannot think or speak without concepts is very different from saying that we are somehow trapped within them in the way philosophers suppose. While there is much to be said for the comparison of language with a pair of glasses, it is a mistake to think of people as carrying around rules of logic with them as though they were glasses glued to their noses.

Interlude (15): Subliming the logic of language

We tend to overlook that logic is a human construction. All too often we sublime it and regard it as something apart from all language-games. For one reason or another, we view it as above or beyond our everyday linguistic practices rather than as woven into them. We think of it as built into the nature of things or as God-given and take ourselves to be responsible to it rather than the other way around. It is not that we do not know any better. We know how language functions in everyday life and are perfectly capable of recognizing the difference between proceeding logically and proceeding illogically in particular cases. Still we are convinced that there must be more to it than this. Even though we believe our sentences to be in order as they are, we feel there must be a perfect order hidden in them, one that only logic can describe. It seems shallow to focus on the language-games to which our words belong, and we set out in search of something seemingly much deeper – 'the incomparable essence of language' (§97).

The subliming of logic takes many forms and is buttressed by a variety of considerations and illusions. We assume there must be a 'pure intermediary' between sentences and facts (§§93–94). We think of propositions as 'something remarkable' because they can be used to say something about the world, to 'mean: *this–is–so*' (§95). We picture thought as unique, as 'surrounded by a halo', and we misconstrue logic as something out of the ordinary, something '*prior* to all experience' and free of all 'empirical cloudiness or uncertainty' (§97). We think that 'an indefinite sense ... would not really be a sense *at all*' (§99) and conclude that 'the ideal [of sharp senses] "*must*" be found in reality' (§101). Moreover it seems to us obvious that what we think and say is mediated by 'the strict rules of the logical structure of propositions' just as what we see is mediated by our glasses (§103).

In §§93–103 Wittgenstein questions these conceptions by probing two pictures that more or less surreptitiously inform how we are inclined to think about the logic of language. The first, discussed in §§93–6, is that the contents or meanings of our sentences line up with and are equivalent to the facts; the second, discussed in §§97–103, is that our sentences must be perfectly in order and perfectly clear if they are to mean anything at all. (Actually §§93–6 began life as a single section.) In opposition to the first picture Wittgenstein notes that it makes no sense to speak of our thoughts as coinciding with the facts since they can be of 'what is *not* the case' (§95). In opposition to the second picture he insists that the conception of sentences as having definite senses regardless of how much they leave open presupposes a faulty understanding of 'the role of the ideal in our language' (§101). He points out that there is no good reason to treat thought as 'the unique correlate, picture, of the world' (§96) and no good reason to take an indefinite sense to be 'really not ... a sense *at all*' (§99).

Both pictures of language can be defended in various ways. Wittgenstein would not need to be told that those convinced of the need for contents or meanings will resist what he says in these few brief sections. The author of the *Tractatus*, for one, would not have been swayed since he took the principle that sense is determinate to be unimpeachable and believed himself to have managed to account for the fact that '*thought* can be of what is *not* the case'. (In the *Tractatus* genuine names are said to reach out to simples and propositions are held to be true, roughly speaking, just when the configuration of their names corresponds to the configuration of the simples they reach out to.[5]) What Wittgenstein is questioning in the present instalment is certain specific ways philosophers construe logic, not all of them.

This is not to belittle what Wittgenstein is saying about logic, only to draw attention to the nature of his campaign to get us to change how we think about it. Wittgenstein is not arguing for substantive conclusions. He is urging us, as he so often does, to consider more closely our philosophical convictions. It is not by chance that he speaks of our being 'seduced' into thinking that propositions are queer (§93), regards us as pursuing 'chimeras' (§94), refers to the 'illusions' that lead us to think of language, thought and the world as equivalent (§96), takes us to be 'trying to grasp the incomparable essence of language' (§97) and holds that we are 'dazzled' by the ideal of a language without empirical cloudiness or uncertainty (§100). Time and again he uses language of the sort we use when we are trying to coax others into setting aside pictures they hold. Presumably nobody wants to be thought of as having been seduced into a certain way of thinking, or as being under an illusion, or as trying to grasp an incomparable essence, or as being dazzled by an ideal.

Wittgenstein hopes that if we think carefully enough about how we operate with words, we shall come to see that we do not have to embrace the idea of a super-realm of meanings. He wants us to recognize that it is far from obvious that something extraordinary 'must' be achieved by propositions (§93), that thought 'must' be something unique (§95), that the order of possibilities 'must' be utterly simple (§97), that there 'must' be a perfect order even in the vaguest sentence (§98), that sentences 'must' have definite senses (§99), and that the ideal of perfection 'must' be found in reality (§101). Is any of this, he would like us to ask ourselves, as clear as philosophers are inclined to suppose? Are we obliged to embrace these conclusions or are we being misled by 'our forms of expression' (§94)? Do we even 'understand the nature of this "must"' (§101)?

As Wittgenstein sees it, we deceive ourselves when we take the philosophical ideas he has been discussing to go without saying. Instead of leaping to conclusions and subliming the logic of our language, we should consider carefully how we operate with words. If we look at how we use language, we shall, he thinks, come to appreciate that there is nothing remarkable about the way our propositions are correlated with the world. We shall see that the apparent queerness of propositions is an artefact of the way our fact-stating language-game works, and we shall end up conceding that there is nothing odd about thinking of 'what is *not* the case'. Likewise we shall see that the ideal of logical perfection is not somethng that "*must*" be found in reality but rather something we project onto it (§101). We shall come to appreciate how little there is to be said for the idea of a realm of definite senses and the idea of a '*super*-order' between '*super*-concepts'. Moreover we shall find ourselves regarding with suspicion the idea of a perfect language awaiting construction and agreeing that we have no clear conception of what we mean by an unshakable ideal hidden in the nature of things.

Sections 104 to 114: 'Back to the rough ground!'

This instalment takes up where the last one left off. Wittgenstein continues his discussion of the traps into which we are apt to fall when we do philosophy and emphasizes the insidious influence of our forms of expression on our thinking. Again his aim is to curb our tendency to sublime the logic of our language.

Section 104

Having questioned the conception of logic as a straight-jacket that confines thought and speech, Wittgenstein now takes issue with the widespread assumption that the world must have certain general features corresponding to how we think and speak about it. He warns us against projecting onto a thing our 'method of representing it'. It is, he insists, a mistake to think reality must – given how we talk and think about it – have these or those essential characteristics. We should not assume that each individual thing must have the property of self-identity and be in some deep sense fundamentally identical to itself. That things should seem to have this property is unsurprising since we represent them as being self-identical. Saying they have the property of self-identity is like saying what we see through a pair of yellow-tinted glasses looks yellow. (Compare §50, where Wittgenstein reminds us that means of representation are not representations and 'what looks as if it *had* to exist, is part of the language'.)

Nobody should be 'impressed by the possibility of compar[ing]' sentences with the world. When I determine that 'The book is blue' is true by comparing it with the way things are, I am not 'perceiving a state of affairs of the highest generality'. The fact that we use sentences with subjects and predicates is no reason to conclude that the world must comprise objects and properties. My speaking truly of a certain book as blue does not entail or presuppose anything metaphysically interesting about reality. After all I could say the same thing using the language of events or by means of equations.

Section 105

If we take there to be a logical order embedded in language, we are likely to think there is something unsatisfactory about 'what are ordinarily called "propositions"', what are ordinarily called 'words' and what are ordinarily called 'signs'. We shall deem ordinary propositions, words and signs excessively crude and hanker after ones that are crystal clear. Recall the example in §39, 'Excalibur has a sharp blade'. It is tempting to think that 'Excalibur' is not a genuine name (since Excalibur can be broken up without the sentence losing its meaning) and that the sentence itself is misleading (since it seems to assert that a certain sword has a certain property whether or not there is such a sword). According to the view at hand, only in a logically perfect language are names always genuine and propositions always transparent. In contrast to ordinary language, 'the proposition and the word that logic deals with are supposed to be something pure and clear-cut'. Real sentences are analysed sentences of the sort referred to in §39, the names of which are all '*real* sign[s]'.

If we think we have to uncover 'the ideal' in our language, we shall find ourselves 'rack[ing] our brains over the nature of the *real* sign'. We shall ask ourselves what sort of sign figures in fully analysed propositions. Is it 'perhaps the *idea* of the sign' or 'the idea at the present moment'? While this question seems subtle, it is far from obvious we should be 'dissatisfied with what are ordinarily called "propositions", "words", "signs"'. The more reasonable view is surely that attempting to determine 'the nature of the *real* sign' is a pointless exercise (except perhaps as an aid to helping someone appreciate the sterility of the question).

Section 106

It is hard to shake the conviction that logic 'presents ... the a priori order of the world' (§97) and the important thing is 'the *real* sign', not 'what are ordinarily called ... "signs"' (§105). It is not by chance that we set off 'in pursuit of chimeras' (§94) and attempt to 'grasp the incomparable essence of language' (§97). When doing philosophy, we find it difficult 'to keep our heads up' and 'stick to the subjects of our every-day thinking'. We think we have 'to describe extreme subtleties', subtleties that we are 'quite unable to describe with the means at our disposal'. For example we suppose we should be trying to clarify the nature of real names, simples, indestructibility, correspondence and the other notions linked with analysis mentioned in §§39–64. Philosophical problems seem so difficult that 'we feel as if we had to repair a torn spider's web with our fingers'. Taking ordinary language to be insufficiently refined to capture what we want to say, we imagine ourselves as having to create something exceedingly delicate using the coarsest of tools. A good example of this is the difficulty we experience when we try to explain how a 'genuine name' manages to link up in an unmediated fashion with the thing it names.

Section 107

As long as ordinary language goes unexamined, the degree to which it departs from the ideal of perfect determinateness is likely to pass unnoticed. But when we scrutinize our everyday ways of speaking and thinking and attend to 'the details of what goes on ... *from close to*' (§51), the disparity is hard to miss. On the one side there is ordinary language with its 'empirical cloudiness' and 'uncertainty'; on the other side there is the picture of language as presenting 'an order of possibilities ... of the purest crystal' (§97).

Ordinary language is in conflict with the logical requirement of crystalline purity for the simple reason that logic is designed to be 'the *hardest* thing there is' (§97). Logic can no more fail to be solid and pure than description can fail to describe. Its adamantine character cannot be discovered in the way that the composition of a chemical can. It is 'not a *result of investigation*' but a 'requirement' of it, one that is built into our conception of logic. The fact that names are used to name objects, for instance, is not something that could have been otherwise; it is presupposed from the outset.

When we notice how different the language we use in everyday life is from the sort of language logicians are concerned with, the conflict seems intolerable. Worse, the requirement of crystalline purity appears to be 'in danger of becoming empty'. Language ideally construed is so far from ordinary language, it can come to seem totally disconnected from our usual ways of speaking. Indeed insofar as logic concerns itself with language unsullied by 'empirical cloudiness' it seems to have the character of 'slippery ice where there is no friction' – though ideal, it is useless. (This echos Kant's comparison of the metaphysician who aims to escape the world of the senses with 'the light dove that cleaving the air in her free flight and feeling its resistance imagine[s] that its flight would be easier still in empty space'.[1])

We cannot get from place to place if the ground is perfectly smooth, and we cannot use logic when it is completely divorced from our everyday affairs. In both cases the solution is the same: to return to 'the rough ground'. We need traction to walk, and we need the roughness of ordinary language to think and speak. (Elsewhere Wittgenstein says: 'How strange if logic were concerned with an "ideal" language and not with *ours*. For what would this ideal language express? Presumably, what we now express in our ordinary language; in that case, this is the language logic must investigate'.[2])

Section 108

Sentences and language do not have the 'formal unity' that Wittgenstein thought when he wrote the *Tractatus*. Rather they form a 'family of structures more or less related to one another'. The search for 'the *general form of propositions* and of language', which once gave Wittgenstein 'most headache', is futile (§65). Instead of assuming propositions have something in common, we should think of them as comprising 'a complicated network of similarities overlapping and criss-crossing' (§66).

Does this mean philosophers and logicians are wrong to think of logic as 'something sublime' (§89), as something of 'the purest crystal' (§97)? (Recall that in §89 Wittgenstein raised the question 'In what sense is logic something sublime?' but did not answer it.) The answer, he now tells us, is both Yes and No. Yes because the '*preconceived* idea of crystalline purity' is bankrupt. No because it is impossible to bargain 'any of [the] rigour [of logic] out of it'. Logic does not lack rigour; there is no such thing as logic without rigour.

What we need to do is turn 'our whole examination around'. Instead of thinking of the rigour of logic as deriving from the way the world is, we should think of it as deriving from the fact that we put it there. As noted in §107 its crystalline purity is not a '*result of investigation*' but a 'requirement' of it. Logic is an adjunct to our everyday language, and the answer to the question 'What has become of logic now?' is simply that it should be thought of as a resource, as something that is, somewhat like morse code, occasionally very useful. Rather than regarding logic as underpinning ordinary language, we should regard it as yet another language. Its value lies in the light it sheds on the 'grammar' of the expressions we use (see the note on page 18 and §90), not in the fact that it reveals the essence of language, reality or anything else.

To rotate 'the axis of reference of our examination ... about the fixed point of our real need' is to take the 'philosophy of logic' to be concerned with sentences and words in their ordinary use. Whereas the old inquiry focussed on a sublime 'non-spatial, non-temporal phantasm', the new one focusses on the 'spatial and temporal phenomenon of language'. This is not to suggest that philosophers should start examining the 'physical properties' of words and sentences. Studying physical properties is a job for scientists. In 'philosophy of logic' we focus on the rules of language we follow in everyday life just as when studying games we focus on the rules of chess, football and the like.

Note at the bottom of page 46

This note has to do with the 'physical properties' of language referred to in §108. Wittgenstein probably inserted it to remind us that scientists mean something different from philosophers even when they use similar language. Saying, as Michael Faraday does, that water is an individual thing that never changes is quite different from saying that things are essentially unique and unchanging. Whereas Faraday is stating what he takes to be the case, philosophers are concerned with what must exist or happen. What concerns them is 'the *hardest* thing there is' (§97).

Section 109

The considerations Wittgenstein is advancing are not scientific considerations. He is not concerned with finding out 'empirically "that, contrary to our preconceived ideas, it is possible to think such-and-such" – whatever that may mean'. It is of no interest to him that people are, let us say, able to think of being ten feet tall or of becoming millionaires. However one characterizes what Wittgenstein is doing, he is not engaged in a quasi-empirical investigation of possibilities, still less attempting to apprehend what is thinkable by rummaging in an ethereal realm. (As Wittgenstein reminds us in a parenthetical remark, the idea of philosophers investigating possibilities is closely allied with 'the conception of thought as a gaseous medium'. Whereas scientists explore the material world, philosophers are supposed to explore an ethereal mental world.)

In philosophy as Wittgenstein understands it, there are no empirical theories and no philosophical hypotheses verifiable by experiment. Philosophy is not a branch of science, and philosophers should not be trying to explain phenomena by subsuming them under all-encompassing general principles. Properly conducted philosophical inquiry confines itself to describing the phenomena. It arranges what is already known to remove confusions (compare §90). Its aim is to provide a clear view of the 'workings of language: *in despite of* [our] urge to misunderstand them'. In contrast to science, the task of which is to provide new information, '[p]hilosophy is a battle against the bewitchment of our intelligence by means of language'. (This remark may be read as saying that language is the means we use in the battle or that it bewitches us. Elsewhere Wittgenstein says: 'Philosophy, as we use the word, is a fight against the fascination which forms of expression exert on us'.[3])

Section 110

The philosophical contention that 'language (or thought) is something unique' mentioned in §95 is 'a superstition (*not* a mistake!)'. It is not an error that can be rectified but a picture that 'makes clear vision impossible' §5 (Also recall §93, where Wittgenstein points out that a misunderstanding of the logic of language 'seduces us' into thinking that a proposition achieves 'something extraordinary, something unique'.) Regarding language and thought as unique and regarding them as not unique are equally senseless. What we ought to conclude is that both views – that language and thought are unique and that they are not unique – are 'produced by grammatical illusions'. Think of how we speak of ourselves as being mentally in the future. This way of speaking makes it seem as though language has the unique property of anticipating what is to come. As Wittgenstein once remarked: 'If one does not understand the grammar of the proposition "I am mentally in the future" one will believe that here the future is in some strange way caught in the sense of a sentence, in the meaning of words'.[4]

The reason that philosophical discussions of the uniqueness of language and thought are impressive is not that they concern deep questions about reality. Their 'impressiveness' stems rather from the depth of the 'grammatical illusions' that fuel them. The misunderstandings of the great philosophers are of a different order from the misunderstandings of pundits, politicians and ideologues, to say nothing of the ramblings of the mentally deranged. They are misconceptions of the greatest of minds.

Section 111

Philosophical problems stemming from 'misinterpretations' of how we think and speak have 'the character of *depth*' because they derive from features of our language. Their depth is comparable to the depth of a grammatical joke. (In an earlier version of the *Investigations* Wittgenstein gave the example of a person's asking someone who writes 100 as 001 to count up to 001.)

Section 112

Part of the reason philosophy is difficult is that we are led astray by similes absorbed into our language. When reflecting on language, we are often deceived by idioms and other turns of phrase into thinking that something has to be a certain way even though we are sure that it is actually not this way at all. All too often we think that '*this* is how it has to *be*' even though we know '*this* isn't how it is'. An example – one Wittgenstein mentions in an earlier draft of this section – is the idea that time cannot be measured even though we measure it using clocks and watches. On the one hand it seems obvious that time can pass; on the other hand it is impossible to compare the beginnings and ends of happenings since the one is always gone by the time the other comes around. (Elsewhere Wittgenstein notes that we are like the philosopher Schopenhauer when he declared that 'man's real life span is 100 years'. 'Yes, that's how it is', we are inclined to say, 'because that's how it *must* be!'. We no more ask how we actually operate with words than Schopenhauer asked '[H]ow long do men actually live?'. This 'strikes [us] as a superficial matter; whereas [we] have understood something more profound'.[5])

Section 113

When we do philosophy we often think 'But *this* is how it is ──' (compare §112). We suppose that were we to 'fix [our] gaze sharply enough', we would be able to figure things out and 'grasp the essence of the matter'. Thus we think that were we to make the necessary effort, we could '*penetrate* [the] phenomenon' of time (§90), that we could apprehend the true nature of the past, present and future. By contrast, Wittgenstein would have us 'keep our heads up' and stop imagining that 'we have to describe extreme subtleties' (§106). We should be on our guard for grammatical illusions (§110) and refrain from treating idiosyncrasies of our language – and our means of representation – as metaphysically significant.

Section 114

Philosophers tend to say to themselves over and over such things as 'The general form of propositions is: This is how things are'. (C.K. Ogden translates the passage as 'The general form of proposition is: Such and such is the case'.) It seems undeniable that all genuine propositions say how things happen to be and I can well imagine Wittgenstein repeating this to himself when writing the *Tractatus*. Certainly nobody can deny that 'N'Djamena is the capital of Chad', 'The watch is on the table', 'Napoleon was a French general' all say 'This is how things are'.

But while this remark – 'The general form of propositions is: This is how things are' – seems to have the 'character of *depth*' (§111) and to reveal 'the essence of the matter' (§113), it merely states a trivial truth about how we think and speak about the world. The illusion that something metaphysically grand is being conveyed derives from the forms of expression we use (see §112). Without realizing it we are alluding to our method of representing a thing. Far from 'tracing the outline of that thing's nature', we are 'merely tracing round the frame through which we look at it'. We are not referring to the world, only to the 'frame' – i.e. the form 'This is how things are' into which words and phrases like 'N'Djamena' and 'the capital of Chad' can be slotted. (See also §104 on our tendency to 'predicate of the thing what lies in the method of representation'.)

Interlude (16): The illusion of philosophical depth

This instalment covers a lot of ground. Wittgenstein first criticizes the idea that logic delineates the principles underlying speech and thought and urges us 'to stick to the subjects of our every-day thinking' (§106). Next he suggests that the rigour of logic comes about because we put it there and declares that 'the *preconceived idea* of [the crystalline purity of logic] can only be removed by turning our whole examination round' (§108). This is followed by some remarks on the theme that philosophical problems are not 'empirical problems' but rather problems to be solved 'by arranging what we have always known' (§109). Finally, in the last four sections, Wittgenstein discusses the illusion of philosophical depth and traces the impressiveness of philosophy to the complexity of the grammatical muddles and misunderstandings that kindle it. These points are not unrelated; each is a salvo in Wittgenstein's on-going battle against traditional ways of doing philosophy.

As in the sections in the last instalment Wittgenstein tries to dissuade us from believing that language has what in §97 he calls an 'incomparable essence' (see §§104–7). The fundamental features of the world that logic has traditionally been thought to reveal are, he insists, reflections of the kind of language we use. We take our 'method of representation' to represent how things are and project onto the world how we speak and think about it. So – to take a simple example – instead of thinking of reddish-green as impossible because of how we use colour-words, we suppose nature in some profound way abhors this colour. Our assumption is that statements like 'Nothing is reddish-green' are representations concerning the essential order of things rather than part of a system of representation. We take it for granted that the world divides up the way our language categorizes it and forget that, as Wittgenstein puts it later in the *Investigations*, grammar 'tells us what kind of object anything is' (§373).

This is not to say that formal logic is limited or misguided. Wittgenstein has no objection to logic understood as an endeavour devoted to the examination of common uses of logical particles such as 'and', 'or', 'not', 'all' and 'some'. As he sees it, formal logic is as precise and as uncontroversial as mathematics, and it is senseless to try to bargain 'any of the rigour out of it' (§108). He agrees that 'George either is or is not two metres tall' is true given the normal understanding of the meanings of 'or' and 'not' but questions what many philosophers make of such a sentence. He is challenging the conception of 'the philosophy of logic' as a subject devoted to gleaning facts about the essential nature of the world from logical truths. It is, he is stressing, far from clear that the truth of 'George is either two metres tall or not two metres tall' tells us something about George, specifically that it is essential to him that he is or is not two metres tall. Wittgenstein's central point is that the philosophy of logic deals with 'sentences and words in exactly the sense in which we speak of them in ordinary life' (§108).

Wittgenstein's target is the conception of philosophy as a science of 'the a priori order of the world' (§97). He allows that the problems of the philosophy of logic – indeed of philosophy in general – are not empirical problems, which can be explored scientifically. Moreover, like the traditional philosopher, he takes philosophical investigation properly so-called to be altogether unlike scientific investigation. What he abandons is the assumption, embraced by most philosophers if only surreptitiously, that it is possible to have philosophical knowledge about the world in addition to scientific knowledge. As he sees it, it is questionable whether philosophy provides information and questionable whether it makes sense to speak of knowledge that is necessarily true. The idea of necessary truth as a particularly strong kind of truth – as something much 'hard[er]' than empirical truth (§97) – is in Wittgenstein's eyes yet another philosophical conception in need of detailed examination. There is a world of difference between Faraday's empirical claim – quoted in the note on page 46 – that 'Water is one individual thing – it never changes' and Schopenhauer's metaphysical claim that 'Water remains water … [I]n every case it is true to its character, and always reveals that alone'.[6] From a philosophical point of view Faraday's claim is intelligible but uninteresting, Schopenhauer's interesting but unintelligible.

Wittgenstein sums up his conception of the relationship of philosophy to science in §109 by noting that whereas science is conjectural, '[t]here must not be anything hypothetical in our considerations'. Instead of thinking of philosophy as an enterprise that aims to provide a general account of the inner workings of the world, we should think of it as an enterprise that presents facts that everyone knows. When we proceed as Wittgenstein would have us proceed, we 'do away with all *explanation*, and description alone [takes] its place'. Philosophy is important because it exposes confusions that surround how we think about language, thought, reality, the human condition and the rest, and philosophical description 'gets its light, that is to say its purpose, from the philosophical problems'. Unlike science, which advances theories, philosophy 'is a battle against the bewitchment of our intelligence by means of language' and philosophers should try to help us to understand the workings of language despite our tendency to misunderstand it.

The picture of philosophy as a super-science dealing with 'the a priori order of the world' is an anathema to Wittgenstein. In the passages in this instalment he insinuates that this kind of philosophy is misguided and that an account of language of the sort philosophers aspire to is neither available nor needed. There is nothing to recommend the conception of philosophical theories as more or less warranted by evidence. Philosophical theories cannot be confirmed or disconfirmed by the facts; they are 'superstition[s]' not 'mistake[s]' (§110). The problems of philosophy arise because 'language produces a false appearance' (§112) and we should devote our efforts to figuring out how it misleads. If we look more carefully at the forms of expression embedded in our language, we shall understand why we are 'disquiet[ed]' and see more clearly why we are being drawn into thinking '*this* is how it has to *be*' despite knowing full well that '*this* isn't how it is' (*ibid*).

Two other points about what Wittgenstein is saying are worth noting to avoid misunderstanding. First, in recommending that we 'keep our heads up' (§106) and refrain from stepping into the philosophical arena, Wittgenstein is not saying that we cannot know anything or that there is no such thing as empirical investigation. He is not suggesting we do not know a lot about the world, only disputing the philosopher's claim to provide knowledge about its essential nature. Secondly, in recommending that we 'stick to the subjects of our every-day thinking' (*ibid*), he is not saying that everyday usage is clear and fixed, even less suggesting that technical language should always be eschewed. He allows that our language may let us down (see, e.g., §80), and he is not at all averse to introducing new terminology – a good example is his use of the notion of a language-game. What he is doing is altogether different. He is trying to get us to confront squarely our tendency to avert our eyes from how we operate with words in the vain hope of fastening on to a deep philosophical truth.

Sections 115 to 123: 'Your scruples are misunderstandings'

The central theme of this instalment is that '[w]e must do away with all explanation' (§109). Wittgenstein deplores our tendency to think of logic separately from how language is used in everyday life, explains the conception of philosophy as a critical endeavour, questions the possibility of providing a philosophical account of philosophy itself, and underlines the importance of a clear understanding of the way we operate with words for allaying philosophical worries.

Section 115

In §114 Wittgenstein suggested that when we specify what we take to be '[t]he general form of propositions', we are not 'tracing the outline of the thing's nature' but merely 'tracing round the frame through which we look at it'. Now he notes that we are misled because 'a *picture* [holds] us captive'. We take propositions to line up with facts and go on, naturally enough, to conclude that they all say 'This is how things are' (see §96 and §114). There is, we think, no escaping the fact that language harmonizes with reality and our propositions correspond, when true, to facts. If I say 'N'Djamena is the capital of Chad', I am saying 'This is how things are'. I cannot 'get outside' the picture of propositions saying what is the case; my language seems 'to repeat it to [me] inexorably'. Another example is the 'picture of the essence of language' referred to in §1; our language also seems to say: 'Every word has a meaning. This meaning is correlated with the word. It is the object for which the word stands' (§1).

Section 116

Wittgenstein next returns to a point he made earlier about our being apt to ignore the ordinary uses of words when we do philosophy (see

§97 and §108). We should, he says, always ask whether the words that figure centrally in philosophical discussions – words like 'knowledge', 'being', 'object', 'I', 'proposition' and 'name' – are used in everyday life the way philosophers use them. If we do this, we shall see that philosophers use them differently from people in the street. The philosopher's use of the word 'I', for instance, is quite unlike its use 'in the language-game which is its original home'. Normally we use 'I' to refer to ourselves; we do not use it to refer to a shadowy ego occupying our bodies, the owner of our thoughts and feelings. If I say 'I feel ill', I mean that I, Andrew Lugg, feel ill; I am not referring to an ego or a self. (While the original text has 'Sprache' [language] rather than 'Sprachespiel' [language-game], Wittgenstein is clearly thinking of language in action; the sections in this and the next instalment derive from material that was drafted in the early 1930s before he had coined the phrase 'language-game'.)

Our task, as Wittgenstein sees it, is to bring the words philosophers use – 'knowledge', 'being', 'object', 'I' and the rest – 'back from their metaphysical to their everyday use'. Instead of trying 'to grasp the *essence* of the thing[s]' that such words are supposed to name we should be investigating how the words themselves are used. In the case of 'I', for instance, we should not be racking our brains over what it refers to but rather focussing on its function in our language. The better our appreciation of how the word is used, Wittgenstein thinks, the less apt we shall be to think there is an *'essence* of the thing' to be grasped. (It is not a problem that psychologists and theologians often take 'I' to refer to an inner object. In Wittgenstein's view what goes for philosophy also goes for psychology and theology. Here too we should ask ourselves whether words are being used the way they are normally used.)

Wittgenstein does not take ordinary language to be sacrosanct. He is not assuming everyday use is transparent, still less assuming philosophical disputes can be straightforwardly resolved by examining how words are typically used. He recognizes that the language we use in everyday life requires scrutiny and would not deny for a moment that what counts as a word's 'original home' is often hard to discern. As he sees it, the ordinary has to be tracked down; it is not something that hits us in the face.

Section 117

But how clear is it that philosophers use words like 'knowledge', 'being', 'object', 'I', 'proposition' and 'name' in a metaphysical sense

(§116)? One may be forgiven for thinking these words are used in philosophy in a 'sense [we] are familiar with' and we understand philosophers' writings perfectly well. On the other hand, it is important to notice that words do not carry their meanings with them from context to context. The meaning of a word is not like 'an atmosphere' that accompanies the word (in the way my net worth accompanies me and yours accompanies you). Actually the opposite. There is every reason to think that philosophers use 'I' differently from how it is normally used. As already noted, they use it to refer to a shadowy ego, and it is not at all obvious that this makes sense.

Wittgenstein explains his point about words not carrying their meaning around with them by considering the example of someone saying 'This is here' while pointing to an object in full view. You might think that a thing's being here counts as an item of knowledge no less than my being 183 centimetres tall. Indeed it is tempting to treat 'This is here' as a particularly secure item of knowledge. Still we should hesitate before accepting this conclusion. It is far from clear that 'knowledge' is being used the same way in the two contexts. Whereas 'Andrew Lugg is 183 centimetres tall' is informative and could be wrong, 'This is here' is uninformative and cannot be false. My saying 'This is here' to someone who can see the thing in question just as well as I can serves no useful purpose. I am not saying anything; my sentence is empty. (Some philosophers would argue in response that it is immaterial that 'This is here' is empty and obvious. For them it is true and nothing is gained by denying it counts as knowledge.)

The 'special circumstances' in which a sentence like 'This is here' is 'actually used' are different from the circumstances in which something is in full view. Sometimes – consider the case of a children's game of hunt the thimble – saying 'This is here' conveys information and it makes sense to wonder whether the speaker is right or wrong. Wittgenstein's point is simply that this is so only in unusual cases, not always.

To say 'This is here' does not count as knowledge when the thing is in full view is not to say it is not known where the thing is. Wittgenstein is noting that talk of knowledge in such circumstances is inappropriate, that 'This is here' cannot sensibly be said to be known or not known. We should think of it as part of the framework within which we speak of where things are, not as something expressed within this framework. Speaking of an object that is in full view as being here is like speaking of the standard metre in Paris as a metre. 'This is here', like 'This is a metre', is 'an observation concerning our language-game – our method of representation' (§50).

Section 118

Wittgenstein's conception of philosophical investigation does not 'destroy everything interesting, that is, all that is great and important'. Nothing of interest is being sacrificed – what is being destroyed deserves to be destroyed. Wittgenstein is recommending the destruction of 'houses of cards', not the destruction of sturdy buildings. Losing the illusions that grip us when we do philosophy is like losing the fear of the dark we had as children. It is not something to be lamented. (Here Wittgenstein is more strident than usual. Elsewhere – see especially §110 – he stresses the depth of the illusions which grip us.)

It should not be thought that Wittgenstein is saying that philosophy is valuable because it provides a clear account of our use of words. He does not speak of philosophy as having a positive as well as a negative role, never mind regard it as clarifying the hidden structure of language. Rather he takes 'our investigation' to be directed at clearing up 'the ground of language on which [the houses of cards] stand'. This is, he thinks, a good antidote to philosophical superstition; it is not a first step towards developing a general account of language.

Section 119

If the aim of philosophy is to pull down 'houses of cards' and clear up 'the ground of language on which they stand' (§118), the 'results of philosophy' are not what they are usually taken to be. Philosophy is important because it pinpoints places where we mistakenly try to get beyond the limits of language, not because it provides new information. Whereas traditional philosophy attempts to transcend language and answer questions '*outside* a particular language-game' (§47), philosophy of the sort Wittgenstein favours labours 'to bring words back from their metaphysical to their everyday use' (§116). Uncovering the senselessness of 'This is here', for instance, counts as a philosophical result in Wittgenstein's sense because it exposes a 'piece of plain nonsense' and helps us to stop running our heads against 'the limits of language'. (This echoes a remark of the Austrian satirist Karl Kraus, a writer Wittgenstein respected: 'When I don't make any progress, it is because I have bumped into the wall of language. Then I draw back with a bloody head. And would like to go on'.[1])

Section 120

When we talk about language, we 'must speak the language of every day'. An explanation of the use of the word 'I' has to be expressed in language that the person being addressed understands (compare how I explained the use of 'I' when commenting on §116). English is not 'too coarse' for what we want to say, and any special terminology we introduce must itself be explained. Somewhere along the line, the language we use in everyday life has to make an appearance. Moreover would it not be remarkable, if philosophers were right, that we can do so much with the language we have? We do not need a '*constructed*' language to explain the use of 'I', and it is hard to imagine much that ordinary language could be used for if we did.

Explanations of the use of language are not couched in a 'preparatory, provisional [language]' of the sort promoted by philosophers. When we talk about language we 'have to use language full-blown'; we cannot but avail ourselves of 'the language of every day'. Explaining our use of the language is not like explaining the motions of bodies. Whereas we can discuss the phenomenon of motion before we understand it, we have to understand the phenomenon of language before we can discuss it. Of course the development of grammar in children, the neurological basis of speech and such like can be explained in much the same fashion as the motion of bodies. What cannot be explained this way is how language is used. To understand an explanation of the use of language, one already understands how language is used. (It is no objection to this observation that, as Russell once put it, '[t]here may be another language dealing with the structure of the first language, and ... to this hierarchy of languages there may be no limit'.[2] This does not help since sooner or later we 'have to use language full-blown'.)

There are no facts about the intrinsic character of language, only 'exterior facts' about it, facts such as Dutch is spoken in Antwerp and more people speak Spanish than Russian. Saying 'I' is used to refer to the speaker is not an empirical fact – one cannot discover the use of 'I' the way one can discover that a certain language is spoken in a certain city. Normally it is as senseless to say to a native English speaker 'The word "I" is used to refer to the speaker' as it is to say 'This is here' to someone who has an object in full view (§117). Outlandish cases aside, knowing English means knowing that 'I' refers to me when I say 'I feel ill'.

Certainly explanations of how people use words can on occasion 'satisfy us'. Wittgenstein is not denying that one person may get a second person to understand the use of 'I' by noting that it is used to refer to the speaker. He is claiming that there are no interior facts about language. One does not satisfy people who are confused about particular uses of language by citing facts; one does so by elucidating, describing, clarifying the uses in question. If I am puzzled about how the word 'I' is used and you tell me that it is used to refer to the speaker, you are not adducing a fact. You are attending to my worry by alerting me, using my language, to how the word is used. My request was cast in language, and you are responding in kind.

Our 'scruples' about language – about its being 'somehow too coarse and material for what we want to say' – 'are misunderstandings'. We think we need a language free of 'empirical cloudiness [and] uncertainty' (§97) but mostly our language works well enough. If our scruples mean anything, and our worries about language are not idle, we must, as noted, already understand language. To answer a question that 'refer[s] to words [we] have to talk about words'. There is no escaping language, and no need to escape it. Elsewhere Wittgenstein puts the point this way: 'We are not justified in having any more scruples about language than the chess player has about chess, namely none'.[3]

At this juncture it may be objected that it does not matter that we have to refer to words when talking about them since we are interested in their meanings. On this view, what words mean can be discussed in much the same way as the motions of bodies, meanings being, like motions, outside language. Instead of discussing words, we can discuss their meanings; we can focus on something 'of the same kind as the word, though also different from the word'. Undoubtedly philosophers who embrace the picture sketched in §1 will think we should be concentrating on what words stand for.

Wittgenstein responds to this objection by questioning, once again, the conception of meanings as things separate from words. He notes that the relationship between words and meanings is like the relationship between money and what it can be used for. Our being able to buy a cow for a certain amount of money is an exterior fact – this can be discovered and we can be right or wrong about the cost. Our being able to use money to buy things, by contrast, is not a fact at all – it is simply a matter of grammar (compare §90). To say money is used to buy things is like saying rulers are used to measure things. And likewise for words. The word 'I', for instance, gets its significance from how it is used (from our using it to refer to the speaker), not from what, if anything, it is correlated with (a self or an ego). '[T]he meaning of a word is its use in language' – at least '[f]or a *large* class of cases' (§43).

Section 121

But do not philosophers provide interesting answers to 'questions refer[ring] to words' despite their having to 'talk about words' (§120)? It seems undeniable that 'there must be a second-order philosophy', which deals with philosophy, and there are facts about language other than 'exterior facts' (§120). Nobody can deny that 'philosophy speaks of the use of the word "philosophy"' and philosophers say interesting things about the word (and the nature of the philosophical enterprise). If one can worry about the application of the word 'philosophy' and explore the question of what philosophy is, philosophy must, it would seem, be a fit subject for investigation. Indeed the possibility of 'a second-order philosophy' would seem to have been demonstrated in practice many times over.

Whether this poses a problem for Wittgenstein is, however, doubtful. The use of the word 'philosophy' (and the nature of the enterprise) is a philosophical problem, one that can be resolved only by doing philosophy. While it is possible to adduce empirical facts about the history of philosophy, where it has been taught, its social consequences and such like, it is not possible to provide an account of the meaning of 'philosophy' and the nature of the discipline from a standpoint outside philosophy (compare §120). Philosophy is like orthography, which deals, among other things, with the spelling of the word 'orthography'. Discussing the use of the word 'philosophy' is philosophy just as spelling the word 'orthography' is orthography.

Section 122

Wittgenstein has been suggesting that we get into trouble because we use words in ways that depart from how they are ordinarily used and that we should try 'to bring words back from their metaphysical to their everyday use' (§116). Now he adds that 'a main source of our failure to understand [and our finding ourselves in difficulty when doing philosophy] is that we do not *command a clear view* of the use of our words'. Consider again the question of why we can see reddish-blue but not reddish-green. According to the present suggestion, we can clarify this phenomenon (and cast doubt on the idea that it tells us something important about the nature of the world or our perceptual systems) by considering how the words 'reddish-blue' and 'reddish-green' are used. When we do this – perhaps with reference to a colour wheel, a device that provides us with a 'perspicuous representation' of important connections among colour words – we see that while red and blue are compatible colours, red and green are not. The thought is that a study of the grammar of colour words shows that reddish-green is no more a possible colour than transparent white.

It is hard to overstate 'the importance of finding and inventing *intermediate cases*' for 'seeing connexions' among ways words are used. We shall, for instance, appreciate better how the phrases 'attend[ing] to the colour' and 'seeing what is common' function and how '*knowing* and *saying*' differ if we consider such cases (see §33, §72 and §78).

The reason that '[t]he concept of a perspicuous representation is of fundamental significance for us' is that we are fooled by the forms of expression embedded in our language. Were our grammar clear, we should not require representations of how we use words. But since – for good reason – '[o]ur grammar is lacking in this sort of perspicuity', we need a corrective. (It is important to bear in mind that our language is not primarily used for philosophical purposes, let alone designed to preclude philosophical confusion.) Perspicuous representations contribute to removing philosophical confusion caused by pictures embedded in our language because they help us get straight about the language we use when doing philosophy.

The concept of a perspicuous representation 'earmarks the form of the account we give'. A representation of the sort Wittgenstein envisions can perhaps be said to constitute a 'Weltanschauung' since it draws attention to 'the way we look at things'. It does not, however, add up to – or contribute to – a philosophical theory of the world, the mind, language or anything else.

Section 123

Philosophical problems arise because we fail to '*command a clear view of the use of our words*' (§122). When we grapple with philosophical problems, we are in the situation of not knowing our way about. We are lost and need to figure out where we are. Small wonder, then, that Wittgenstein should encourage us to ask whether words like 'knowledge' and 'being' function in philosophy as they do in everyday life (§116), exhort us to bend our energies to 'clearing up the ground of language on which [the houses of cards] stand' (§118) and urge us to try to expose the 'plain nonsense and [the] bumps that the understanding has got by running its head up against the limits of language' (§119). It is by such means that we can recover our bearings.

Interlude (17): Pictures and representations

The remarks of this instalment accord well with what was said in the last interlude about how Wittgenstein conceives the philosophical enterprise. The burden of what he says here is that philosophers are held captive by pictures (§115), that they use words in idiosyncratic ways (§§116–17) and that the main role of philosophy is to expose nonsense masquerading as sense (§§118–19). In addition Wittgenstein takes issue with the conception of ordinary language as something that can be treated without presupposing ordinary language (§120), and he critically scrutinizes an argument for the idea of 'second-order' philosophy (§121). Finally he recommends the development of 'perspicuous representation[s]' as an aid to removing confusions created by the forms of language we use and stresses that '[a] philosophical problem has the form: "I don't know my way about"' (§§122–3). Throughout the instalment, I think it pretty clear, Wittgenstein is concerned to emphasize the critical nature of philosophy.

The idea that we are held captive by pictures is central to Wittgenstein's thinking. Time and again he opens his discussion by describing a picture to which we are inclined to gravitate when we think about language. Thus in §1 he introduces a 'picture of the essence of human language'; in §46 he mentions a picture of names as naming primary elements; in §60 he directs our attention to the picture of analysed sentences hidden in the sense of unanalysed ones; and in §96 he refers to the picture of propositions, thoughts and facts as lining up one behind the other. In each case, he believes we allow our thinking to be dominated by a simple conception. We do not control the picture – and see that it has or can be given this or that application – but allow ourselves to be controlled by it. We take it to be 'appropriate ... for the whole of what [we are] claiming to describe' (§3). Later Wittgenstein will say: 'The picture is there. And I am not disputing its validity in any particular case. —— Only I also want to understand the application of the picture' (§423).

As a corrective to our tendency to be held captive by philosophical pictures, Wittgenstein advises us to consider how words function 'in the language-game[s] which [are their] original home[s]' (§116). He would have us remember that 'know' applies only when there is a possibility of error, that 'is an object' is a very different sort of predicate from 'is blue', that 'I' is used to refer to oneself, that 'proposition' is in many instances interchangeable with 'sentence', and that 'name' covers labels for things that do not exist as well as things that do. He thinks the extraordinary extent to which we are bewitched by language when we do philosophy becomes clear when we focus on the language-games to which these and similar words belong (compare §109). Consider 'object'. If we remember that it is mostly used in sentences like 'There are four objects in the box', we shall be less likely to take it to function like 'blue' and less likely to suppose objects are intelligibly characterized as being objects. (Saying 'This is an object' is more like saying 'This is here' to someone next to you than like saying 'This is blue' to someone across the room.)

But is it really a problem that philosophers do not operate with words the way we typically operate with them? It is sometimes thought Wittgenstein is making a mountain out of a molehill since philosophy is itself a language-game, different only in trivial ways from the language-games listed in §23. I have even heard it argued that Wittgenstein fails to appreciate that metaphysics is itself 'a form of life'. Whether this is something that should worry Wittgenstein, however, is again far from obvious. To answer him one would have to show that metaphysicians do not err in thinking they can say something meaningful '*outside* a particular language-game' (§47) and respond to his complaint about philosophers treating words as though they carried their meanings around with them (see §117). It is not enough to note that philosophy is a practice and that philosophers engage in metaphysical speculation. What has to be established is that philosophy is an intelligible practice and philosophers' contentions can be thought through, the very thing Wittgenstein is questioning.

Of course Wittgenstein does not deny it is possible to make sense of the metaphysician's words. He would allow that the metaphysical claim that objects exist can be understood in a way that makes perfectly good sense. He is certainly not saying this claim would be meaningless if it were understood as a claim to the effect that a particular box has something in it. His target is the supposed cogency of the metaphysician's contention, which is hardly so prosaic. Wittgenstein's thought is that metaphysical speculation about objects existing is nonsensical and there is nothing to be said for the idea that objects have existence in a deep philosophical sense (compare §50, where he discusses the idea of elements having 'being'). As he sees it, the metaphysician's claims are either incomprehensible or uninteresting. It is possible to make sense of them but only at the expense of changing the subject and missing what is driving the metaphysician.

Nor is it possible to circumvent this last conclusion by resorting to a metalanguage, one that can be used to discuss our normal use of words. As Wittgenstein notes in §120 and §121, one cannot stand outside language and determine its structure in the way that one can stand outside motion and study its nature. The idea that we can discuss the intrinsic nature of language from an external point of view is, Wittgenstein insists, incoherent. To assume there are metaphysical facts embedded in language is to assume that there are facts about language other than exterior facts and that language can be explained, as well as elucidated, from the inside. It is to take there to be facts about the essential nature of representation (for instance that all sentences, when properly understood, consist of names for simples). In particular Wittgenstein warns us against regarding elucidations of the forms we happen to use as revealing something about the fundamental nature of the world. These are uninformative and we are misled when we take them to be philosophically significant.

Wittgenstein recommends that philosophers devote themselves instead to uncovering 'one or another piece of plain nonsense and [the] bumps that the understanding has got by running its head up against the limits of language' (§119). Nobody is more distrustful of the idea of philosophy as a source of philosophical knowledge, and nothing he says is supposed to convey information properly so-called. The 'considerations' he adduces are not 'scientific ones' (§109) and he deprecates metaphysical speculation. To his way of thinking, claims about the essential nature of the world, thought or language are not false – if they were, their opposites would be true. They are 'superstition[s]' (§110). It is as futile to attempt 'to grasp the incomparable essence of language' (§97) as it is to attempt to grasp the occult powers of numbers. While the philosopher's confusions about language are more consequential and more disquieting than the numerologist's confusions about numbers, they are no less the result of the bewitching effect of language on our thinking. Later in the *Investigations* Wittgenstein puts the matter this way: 'My aim is: to teach you to pass from a piece of disguised nonsense to something that is patent nonsense' (§464).

Sections 124 to 133: 'There is nothing to explain'

In this instalment, the last one I shall discuss, Wittgenstein continues to clarify his conception of the aims and methods of philosophy. As in the last few instalments, the discussion is very compressed. Matters deemed easily grasped are passed over and we are left to work out the details.

Section 124

Philosophers should not meddle with the use of language. While allowing the value of technical terminology, Wittgenstein insists that 'philosophy can in the end only describe [language]'. Rather than try to explain the grammar of our language, we should confine ourselves to presenting it in a perspicuous way (see §122).

In particular we should refrain from trying to ground or justify language. Speaking and thinking are no more in need of philosophical foundations than walking, eating and other sorts of activities that make up 'our natural history' (§25). To provide a foundation for language, one would have to be able to stand outside it, which is something no one can possibly do (see §120). If I have described the relevant grammatical connections, I have – to borrow a phrase from later in the *Investigations* – 'reached bedrock, and my spade is turned' (§217). Far from providing a foundation for our use of language, philosophy 'leaves everything [more specifically, our use of language] as it is'.

Likewise philosophy 'leaves mathematics as it is'. It cannot provide mathematics with a foundation any more than it can provide any other means of representation with one. Indeed mathematics and philosophy are two separate enterprises. '[N]o mathematical discovery can advance [philosophy]' since there is nothing mathematicians have discovered or could discover that would solve a philosophical problem. It is a mistake to think, as some philosophers do, that transfinite number theory – the theory of numbers beyond the finite numbers – settles the philosophical debate over whether there could be an actual (as well as a potential) infinity of things. Philosophical conclusions can be obtained from mathematical premises only given additional philosophical assumptions.

Not even problems of mathematical logic are philosophical problems. (The phrase 'a leading problem of mathematical logic', which Wittgenstein quotes, is due to Frank Ramsey.) The question of whether a system of logic does all it should, for instance, is a technical question of mathematical logic. It is no more a question for philosophy than the question of whether in Euclidean geometry the internal angles of triangles always add up to 180°.

Section 125

Having stressed the independence of philosophy and mathematics in §124, Wittgenstein briefly examines an argument to the contrary, namely that it is one of the tasks of philosophy to eliminate contradictions in the foundations of mathematics. On this view contradictions – e.g. the contradiction Russell uncovered in the theory of sets when he proved there is no set of sets that are not members of themselves – are philosophical problems. (The difficulty Russell identified is that the seemingly anodyne principle that predicates of English define sets conflicts with the fact that there is no set corresponding to the predicate 'is a set that is not a member of itself'.) As Wittgenstein sees it, such problems are not in any interesting sense philosophical. Philosophers should not take it upon themselves to resolve contradictions in the foundations of mathematics 'by means of a mathematical or logico-mathematical discovery'. Rather they should attempt to provide 'a clear view of the state of mathematics that troubles us'.

If mathematics is viewed as a theory comparable to a scientific theory, the discovery of a contradiction in its foundations will seem to show it is faulty and in need of new foundations. But if it is viewed, as Wittgenstein would have us view it, as a method of representation, the discovery of such a contradiction would merely reveal that some of its rules do not apply in every circumstance. It would not show that mathematics is in some way or other incorrect, only that we are 'entangled in our own rules'. The conclusion we should draw is that we need 'a clear view of the state of mathematics that troubles us', one that delineates the rules mathematicians are working with '*before* the contradiction is resolved'.

The point Wittgenstein is making is much the same point as he made in §80 about our concept of a chair. Just as our everyday concepts may fail to cover novel situations, so the mathematician's concepts may fail to apply in unusual cases. There is no guarantee in either case that things will invariably 'turn out as we had assumed', and it no more falls to philosophers to develop new mathematical concepts than it falls to them to develop new concepts in everyday life. Problems about ordinary usage are problems for the people using the language, and problems in mathematics are problems for mathematicians.

Wittgenstein is not objecting to the technical arguments of thinkers like Russell, even less 'sidestepping a difficulty'. He is stressing that it is up to mathematicians – in their capacity as mathematicians – to determine what to do about mathematical contradictions. It is for them to decide whether to forbid the use of a rule in a particular context or to introduce a new rule. They are the ones to figure out – given their special concerns – whether it would be better to revise the principles of mathematics, cordon off the contradiction in question, or deal with it in some other fashion. Consider obtaining '1 = 0' by dividing '1 × 0 = 0 × 0' throughout by zero. Wittgenstein is not for a moment suggesting that it may be better to accept '1 = 0' than to proscribe division by zero. His point, transferred to this case, is that the decision is properly made on mathematical, not philosophical, grounds.

Nor should Wittgenstein be criticized for regarding mathematics as free of philosophical confusion or for ignoring that mathematicians were led to important results because of metaphysical beliefs. He knows there is a great deal of fog in mathematics and mathematicians often insist on the reality of numbers and other mathematical objects. (One of the things Wittgenstein is concerned with in *Remarks on the Foundations of Mathematics* is the infiltration of metaphysics into mathematics.) What he would like us to consider – on a case by case basis – is whether mathematical results are inextricably interwoven with philosophical ideas. As he sees it, mathematics appears to presuppose or entail philosophical assumptions because mathematical language, like ordinary language, *'goes on holiday'* (§38). Mathematical results no more depend on the metaphysical beliefs of the mathematicians who discovered them than the theory of gravitation depends on Newton's theological beliefs.

A consideration of how we can become entangled in our rules also 'throws light on our concept of *meaning* something'. The possibility of discovering contradictions in mathematics shows that the rules governing what we mean may fail to work as expected and 'things [may] turn out otherwise than we had meant, foreseen'. While nothing is '*hidden from us*' (§92), meaning is not transparent. There is nothing '*beneath* the surface' governing the meanings of words but it is not always clear where our rules lead.

What makes a contradiction interesting for philosophers is its 'civil status ..., or its status in civil life'. The question of how we should understand a paradoxical statement like 'I am lying' or a self-stultifying order like 'Stay where you are but leave the room' is a philosophical question. It is right and proper for philosophers to try to figure out how a contradiction undermines itself and how it functions in a language-game. The status of contradictions is puzzling, and it is the job of philosophers to disperse the fog that surrounds them. Elsewhere Wittgenstein says: 'We shall see contradiction in a quite different light if we look at its occurrence and its consequences as it were anthropologically .... That is to say, we shall look at it differently, if we try merely to *describe* how the contradiction influences language-games'.[1])

Section 126

As Wittgenstein sees things, philosophers are not in the business of explaining and justifying. It is not their task to account for a phenomenon using the smallest number of assumptions or to deduce something from allegedly self-evident first principles such as 'I think' or 'Everything is what it is and not another thing'. Nor should they be attempting to elaborate a theory of the essential nature of language, the world or anything else. '[W]hat is hidden' – the physiological mechanism of speech, the physics of the atom and such like – is of no philosophical interest. Philosophy is concerned with 'what is possible *before* all new discoveries and inventions'. It aims to remove misunderstandings by putting 'everything before us' and we should focus on how language is used, something that 'lies open to view'. (Compare §122 where Wittgenstein stresses the importance of 'perspicuous representation[s]' for clarifying '[o]ur grammar'.)

Section 127

If we proceed as Wittgenstein recommends, we shall limit ourselves to 'assembling reminders for a particular purpose'. Our investigation is 'a grammatical one' aimed at relieving philosophical confusion (§90), and the particular reminders we shall assemble will depend on the nature of the misunderstandings we are trying to remove. Thus to dispel confusion about time we may find it helpful to note how we speak about the past, present and future.

Section 128

The only theses the philosopher who 'assembl[es] reminders' (§127) will advance are *'theses'* that everyone agrees on, 'theses' like the past precedes the present and the word 'I' is used by speakers to refer to themselves. Such theses, if this is the right name for them, differ radically from the theses philosophers usually defend. They are trivial grammatical observations, not substantive doctrines about the reality of the world, its ideal nature, its essential materiality and the rest. 'We must', Wittgenstein declares, 'do away with all *explanation*' (§109).

Section 129

When we do philosophy, what is important is 'hidden because of [its] simplicity and familiarity'. The 'aspects of things' that we have to deal with – the multiplicity of language-games, the different uses of words and such like – are difficult to see because they are staring us in the face. For one reason or other 'we seem in some sense not to understand' what is 'already in plain view' (§89). In fact 'the real foundations' of our inquiry – what is basic to philosophical inquiry construed as a 'grammatical [investigation]' (§90) – 'do not strike [us] at all'. The trouble is that 'we fail to be struck by what, once seen, is most striking and most powerful'.

Section 130

Wittgenstein is not suggesting that 'our clear and simple language-games are ... preparatory studies for a future regularization of language'. He did not introduce language-games in §2, §6, §8, etc., as a first step on the road to a full-scale account of language. Such language-games are not approximations – ignoring friction and air resistance – to be embellished later on. They are *'objects of comparison'*. (This does not conflict with what I said about §2. There my point was that Wittgenstein's models of language are primitive in much the same way that the physicist's models of phenomena are primitive, not that they are 'first approximations'.)

Language-games construed as objects of comparison 'throw light on our language by way not only of similarities, but also of dissimilarities'. An examination of how our language differs from a primitive language like the builders' language may be as valuable for clarifying how we operate with words as an examination of how they line up. It is like introducing a simple example of the sonata form to throw light on a work by Beethoven; the differences between the work and the example may be as revealing as the similarities.

Section 131

Only by presenting the 'model' of a simple language-game as 'an object of comparison' can we avoid 'ineptness or emptiness'. Construed as 'preparatory studies for a future regularization of language' (§130), language-games are of little, if any, interest. Their force derives solely from the views they illustrate. The discussion of the builders' language-game in the early sections of the *Investigations*, for instance, is interesting just to the extent that it illuminates the picture of the essence of human language described in §1. If this picture did not hold us 'captive' (§115), there would be no point discussing the builders' language-game. It is worth considering only because it is 'a language for which the description given by Augustine is right' (§2).

A 'model' like the builders' language functions like a measuring-rod. It tells us that a language has this or that feature in much the same way that a measuring-rod tells us that a given object has a certain length. In neither case do we obtain information about the essential nature of anything.

In philosophy it is easy to pronounce dogmatically on this or that. Our thinking is dominated by philosophical pictures to such a degree that we take it for granted that 'reality *must* correspond' to our 'preconceived idea[s]' even though we know full well that there are many ways it could be (compare §112). For instance we do not hesitate to see in Augustine's remarks quoted in §1 a particular picture of what is essential to language despite knowing there are 'countless different kinds of use of what we call "symbols", "words", "sentences"' (§23). Something opposes 'an examination of details in philosophy' (§52) and we are disinclined to look at what actually goes on *'from close to'* (§51).

Section 132

When we philosophize in the manner Wittgenstein recommends, we 'order our knowledge of the use of language' with a 'particular end in view' – specifically that of destroying 'houses of cards' (§118). The order we choose is 'one out of many possible orders; not *the* order', never mind the order to which 'reality *must* correspond' (§131). In philosophy we proceed with an eye to what we want to achieve much as we do when assembling books on shelves. As Wittgenstein notes in another work, 'some of the greatest achievements in philosophy could only be compared with taking up some books which seemed to belong together, and putting them on different shelves, nothing more being final about their positions than that they no longer lie side by side'.[2]

Ordering our knowledge in a way that 'give[s] prominence to distinctions which our ordinary forms of language easily make us overlook' is not the same thing as reforming language. The question of whether a language needs reforming has to be answered in practice. (See also §23 and §124.) We do not highlight distinctions as a first step towards establishing a better, clearer language. We highlight them to dispel confusion. Where there is no confusion, focussing on a distinction makes no sense and might even be counterproductive.

Section 133

After noting, once again, that '[i]t is not our aim to refine or complete the system of rules for the use of words in unheard-of ways', Wittgenstein stresses that 'the clarity' we seek in philosophy is '*complete* clarity'. Our task is to make 'the philosophical problems … *completely* disappear' by 'assembling reminders' (§127), 'giving prominence to distinctions' (§132), and the like.

'The real discovery', as Wittgenstein sees it, would be one that enables us to stop doing philosophy when we want to, 'one that gives philosophy peace, so that it is no longer tormented by questions which bring *itself* into question'. (Elsewhere Wittgenstein says: 'Thoughts that are at peace. That is what someone who philosophizes yearns for'.[3]) But a discovery of this kind is out of the question. We shall be tormented as long as 'the forms of our language produce a false appearance' (§112). Nothing Wittgenstein or anyone else could say could possibly settle the problems of philosophy once and for all. (Wittgenstein is reported to have said 'In my book I say that I am able to leave off with a problem in philosophy when I want to. But that is a lie; I can't'.[4])

The clarity we seek can only be achieved piecemeal. All we can do is explore what bothers us using Wittgenstein's method of giving examples one after another. We can indeed stop at any time since we can break off giving examples. But we cannot hope to find ourselves in the position of no longer being tormented by philosophical worries. While this or that specific worry can be eased or relaxed, it is not possible to resolve 'a *single* problem' – for instance the problem of the nature of the proposition. However much we chip away at the problems and eliminate difficulties there will always be worries requiring attention, and we shall always be racked by doubts about what we are doing. Indeed Wittgenstein once hazarded the opinion that philosophical questions will become 'superfluous' only when there has been 'a change in the way people live'.[5]

When Wittgenstein speaks of himself as 'demonstrat[ing] a method', he is not claiming to have found a method of resolving philosophical confusions that applies across the board. 'There is not *a* philosophical method', only methods that are appropriate for particular philosophical problems. The method of 'assembling reminders' referred to in §127 can, for instance, take the form of 'the method of §2' (§48), that of 'finding and inventing *intermediate cases*' (§122) and that of 'giving prominence to distinctions' (§132). The therapy appropriate for an intellectual disorder, no less than the therapy appropriate for an illness, depends on the nature of the disorder itself. (Also compare §255: 'The philosopher's treatment of a question is like the treatment of an illness'.) There is not one disorder and there is not one treatment.

Interlude (18): The proper aim of philosophy

Given Wittgenstein's remarks in earlier instalments, it is unsurprising that he should declare that philosophy 'puts everything before us, and neither explains nor deduces anything' (§126). Nor is it at all odd that he should conclude that 'if one tried to advance *theses* in philosophy, it would never be possible to debate them, because everyone would agree to them' (§128). Indeed the theme that philosophy, in contrast to science, deals with what lies 'open to view' and 'is possible *before* all new discoveries and inventions' (§126) can be traced back not only to §109 or to §89 but to the remark in the opening section of the book about 'explanations com[ing] to an end somewhere'. What is controversial about Wittgenstein's discussion is not so much how it should be understood as whether it can possibly be right. In the view of many readers, what he says in this instalment is highly questionable, if not obviously false.

One common criticism of Wittgenstein's remarks focusses on his suggestion that mathematics has nothing to contribute to philosophy and philosophy nothing to contribute to mathematics. Wittgenstein cannot, we are told, know that technical mathematical discoveries will never be relevant to philosophers' traditional concerns or that philosophy will never have anything positive to offer foundational studies in mathematics. This is not an unreasonable complaint, especially given the stridency of some of Wittgenstein's comments. On a more sympathetic reading of his remarks, however, it is clear he is not prejudging the course of inquiry, only taking issue with 'the dogmatism into which we fall so easily when doing philosophy' (§131). Far from closing down discussion, he wants us to engage in it more. (In §124 and §125 Wittgenstein is alerting us to issues he thinks require exploration, issues he originally intended to discuss at greater length later in the book.)

Similarly Wittgenstein's suggestion that philosophy 'can in the end only describe [language]' (§124) is less contentious than often supposed. He is not saying what is already in place is better than anything we could possibly invent. As I noted when discussing §116, Wittgenstein does not take ordinary language to be of special philosophical significance. His contention is that philosophy 'cannot give [the actual use of language] any foundation', not that we should always stick with the linguistic practices we have. The reason philosophers are confined to describing language is not that our language never needs reforming but rather that our use of words lies open to view and 'there is nothing to explain' (§126). We may find that our linguistic practices could be improved, even that they should be radically reformed, but this is a practical matter; it is not anything 'we [as philosophers] have to do with' (§132).

Nor is Wittgenstein open to the charge that he undervalues philosophy. Though philosophy of the sort he defends cannot be compared to the great systematic philosophy of the past with regard to its theoretical pretensions, it may still contribute to clarifying our thinking about the world and our place in it. The task of clearing away 'houses of cards' (§118) is certainly very different from the task of constructing new buildings, but it may well result in something equally important, an unencumbered landscape. Despite leaving everything of substance as it is, philosophy geared to dispelling fog and confusion can be enormously valuable, especially in an age when speculation, ideology, sophistry and pseudoscience are rife. Intellectual delusions, like mental delusions, are often debilitating, and the value of exposing them can hardly be overstated.

Again Wittgenstein should not be criticized for promoting, if only unwittingly, relativism, subjectivism, irrationalism or something equally bad. He does indeed deny there is 'a preconceived idea to which reality *must* correspond' (§131) and inveighs against philosophical absolutism. But he never says or implies or assumes that different ways of regarding the world are equally good or claims that there is nothing to choose between different language-games. Certainly he does not think the builders' language-game is as serviceable as our own.

Actually the opposite, he challenges the philosophical conception of a neutral standpoint from which ways of looking at the world and ways of talking about it can be judged. Whereas relativists, subjectivists and irrationalists think the foundations of language are too weak to discriminate between conflicting representations or different language-games, Wittgenstein takes issue with the very idea of language having a foundation. Philosophy cannot, he tells us, give language 'any foundation' (§124).

Finally Wittgenstein should not be chided for engaging in a futile attempt to negotiate a way between the Scylla of scepticism and nihilism and the Charybdis of the anti-sceptical and anti-nihilistic doctrines traditionally championed by philosophers. He had little time for half-way measures and would have agreed that the prospects for such a compromise are exceedingly dim. In fact he seems to have taken the traditional doctrines to be the only ones worth entertaining and proceeds mostly on the assumption that if these are unworkable, nothing will work. What concerns him is what he refers to in §308 as 'the decisive movement in the conjuring trick'. The focus of his criticisms is on the step into philosophy, the one that gets us to engage in philosophical speculation in the first place. He does not attempt to pull a rabbit out of a hat but tries to get us to consider why we think there is a rabbit there to be pulled out.

The thing to remember when reading Wittgenstein's remarks on philosophy is that he is not against explanation as such. Though less impressed by the modern world than many of his contemporaries (this is clear from his Preface and his choice of motto from Nestroy), Wittgenstein does not deny that scientists have figured out a great deal about the way the world works. His target is our tendency to sublime the logic of language and pass off prejudice as scientific fact. It is speculation in the guise of explanation that bothers him, and his efforts are largely directed towards exposing pseudo-explanations, the pseudo-explanations of philosophy most of all. One can well appreciate his distaste for philosophical works that involve, as he sees it, 'a kind of idol worship, the idol being Science and the Scientist'.[6] He really does think, as he puts it later in the *Investigations*, that '[w]hen we do philosophy we are like savages, primitive people, who hear the expressions of civilized men, put a false interpretation on them, and then draw the queerest conclusions from it' (§194).

In the remaining sections of the *Investigations* Wittgenstein continues to comment on what he takes to be the proper aim of philosophy. Even when discussing particular philosophical issues, he remains concerned with the question of what philosophy is and what it can achieve. Still §133 is reasonably regarded as bringing Wittgenstein's main discussion of the nature of philosophy to a close. In the rest of the book the emphasis is more on the confusions that arise when the 'engine [is] idling' (§132). §§134–42 reconsider the general form of a proposition; §§143–242 examine in more detail the notion of following a rule; §§243–308 discuss the philosophical idea of a completely private language; and §§309–693 investigate important issues surrounding concepts we use to talk about our mental lives. (Part II deals with a motley of issues, many of which are touched on in Part I.) In these sections, as in the sections we have been considering, Wittgenstein devotes his efforts to trying to get us to reflect on our philosophical prejudices and to forego our convictions about the fundamental nature of language, the world, the mind and other philosophical staples.

Conclusion

I began by saying I believe Wittgenstein is best read as attempting to get us to change our stance with regard to philosophical problems rather than as advancing philosophical theses, distinctions or methods, and I am hoping this will now seem more reasonable. I do not claim my examination of §§1–133 establishes that Wittgenstein must be read as trying to disabuse us of our philosophical preconceptions but I should like to think I have gone some considerable way to showing that he is most naturally read this way. As we have seen, in §§1–88 Wittgenstein confines himself to taking issue with particular philosophical suggestions, while in §§89–133 he inveighs against the idea of philosophy as providing knowledge. The aphoristic style that Wittgenstein favours can make it seem as though he is advocating philosophical views, but what he actually says shows this is not his intention. In this connection a remark he wrote in 1933, which did not make its way into the *Investigations*, is revealing: 'All that philosophy can do is destroy idols. And that does not mean creating a new one – for instance as in "absence of an idol" '.[1]

Also I hope it will now be agreed that it is essential to pore over Wittgenstein's text to appreciate what he is driving at. It is futile to try to reconstruct §§1–133 as a series of arguments for general philosophical doctrines, if only negative ones, and we miss what is most fascinating and important about the book if we read it as comprising premises and conclusions that can be isolated and evaluated. Wittgenstein's summary statements can hardly be improved on, and his discussion becomes flat and uninteresting if we take these statements out of context and elevate them to the status of philosophical theses. To do justice to what he is saying, we must regard it as an investigation aimed at uncovering and probing philosophical prejudices and biasses. It is not by chance that Wittgenstein speaks of himself as travelling 'over a wide field of thought criss-cross in every direction' (p. ix) and to get something out of his remarks we have to make the journey with him.

Nothing in §§1–133 shows Wittgenstein thinks he can establish that philosophical theorizing is irredeemably speculative, even less that he believes he can prove philosophical problems to be misformulated and philosophical solutions to be nonsensical. He never asserts or implies anything as unsubtle (and as self-refuting) as the doctrine that philosophical theses are gibberish. He knows full well that all he, or anyone else for that matter, can do is prod us into considering whether the problems that trouble philosophers are genuine problems and whether their theses are as intelligible as they would have us believe. His aim is to break the spell of philosophical speculation by whittling away at our conviction that there is something to be said '*outside* a particular language-game' (§47), by exposing the extent to which philosophical opinions are presupposed rather than demonstrated. As he himself is reported to have acknowledged in a lecture, he is 'in a sense making propaganda for one style of thinking as opposed to another'.[2]

In characterizing Wittgenstein as trying to persuade us to examine the cogency of philosophical problems, I do not mean to suggest that his philosophy is entirely free of substantive philosophical remarks, only that this is the intention. As I noted at the time, one might dispute Wittgenstein's pronouncement in §117 about its being senseless to say 'This is here' about something in full view, and there can be no denying that in §109 and elsewhere he speaks of philosophy as being totally distinct from science. However I think it beyond doubt that he would, if pressed, remind us of what he said in §128 – 'If one tried to advance theses in philosophy, it would be impossible to debate them, because everyone would agree to them'. He would not continue to argue that 'This is here' is meaningless rather than merely false nor would he stubbornly insist that the conceptual is altogether distinct from the empirical. To the contrary, he would scout the narrowly circumscribed regions where his opponents' theses have application and challenge their alleged philosophical significance. He thought guarding against '[t]he dogmatism into which we fall so easily in doing philosophy' important (§131) and battled against it until the end of his life.

Throughout §§1–133 Wittgenstein resists the conception of philosophy as a theoretical enterprise comparable to science. Nothing is more central to his outlook than his distrust of the idea that philosophy should be informed by the scientific method, to say nothing of the idea that it should be based on scientific results. While he has no quarrel with science rigorously pursued – it is a common mistake to read his writings as anti-scientific – he is adamantly opposed to scientific thinking in philosophy. Nothing riles him more than the easy assumption that our philosophical worries can be assuaged by developing explanatory theories and the allied idea that philosophy can make progress only if it emulates science. He has as little time for ordinary science philosophy as he has for ordinary language philosophy. In his view, it is as much a mistake to regard what scientists say and do as a starting point (or final court of appeal) for philosophy as it is to privilege what people in the street ordinarily say and do. As he sees it, philosophers go wrong because they 'constantly see the method of science before their eyes, and are irresistibly tempted to ask and answer questions in the way science does'; '[t]his tendency', he tells us, 'is the real source of metaphysics, and leads the philosopher into complete darkness'.[3]

While antagonistic to philosophical explanation, Wittgenstein does not doubt the possibility of reformulating philosophical problems so that they become amenable to scientific treatment. He is not averse to philosophers setting aside the questions that concern their predecessors – and that concern him – in favour of empirical questions that can be submitted to rigorous scientific investigation. Where he differs from the scientific philosopher is mostly over the value of closely examining traditional philosophical doctrines and the worries such doctrines are supposed to address. He takes philosophers' speculations to require careful scrutiny because of their power and 'impressiveness' (§110) and believes our philosophical qualms need to be confronted, not dismissed as false or farmed out to the sciences. In fact few philosophers have been more respectful of the impulse to philosophize than Wittgenstein. To his way of thinking, philosophers' attempts to say something substantive, while 'absolutely hopeless', are 'a document of a tendency in the human mind which [he] personally cannot help respecting deeply', one that he 'would not for [his] life ridicule'.[4]

Having emphasized the critical character of Wittgenstein's philosophy, I should reiterate the point briefly touched on in the last interlude, about its being liberating. While radically negative in form, aim and achievement, the remarks of the *Investigations* induce us to think about the world and our place in it less dogmatically than we usually do. Far from leaving us with nothing, the 'long and involved journeyings' reported in the *Investigations* (p. ix) teach us something important; one might say they embody a powerful vision – in a sense a 'Weltanschauung' (§122). Wittgenstein's assault on philosophical speculation encourages us to figure out what we should think and how we should live our lives for ourselves. If philosophers' views about meaningful thought and action are, as he insinuates, superstitions, they are constraining, even coercive, and we would do well to set them aside and try to see things as they actually are.

In a lecture in the early 1930s, when beginning the work that was to culminate in the *Philosophical Investigations*, Wittgenstein is said to have suggested that there is 'now, in philosophy, a "kink" in the "development of human thought" comparable to that which occurred when Galileo and his contemporaries invented dynamics'.[5] Taking a new way of doing philosophy to have been found, he saw himself as engaged in a 'new subject', not just as opening another stage in a 'continuous development', one that involves a different 'sort of thinking'. By now, I trust, it is clear why he might have thought this. §§1–133 provide a good indication of the nature of the philosophical approach he was pioneering, what he took himself to have achieved and how he thought it could change the course of philosophy. However here too we must exercise care. It is all too easy to misconstrue Wittgenstein's contention that philosophy in its latest guise 'takes the place' of earlier philosophy and provides us with 'what [we] really wanted'. He does not pretend to have settled the vexed question of what philosophy is once and for all. In his eyes the new conception of philosophy is no less in need of exploration than the old one.

Notes

Wittgenstein's Preface

1   L. Wittgenstein, *Philosophical Investigations*, second edn, G.E.M. Anscombe and R. Rhees (eds), translated by G.E.M. Anscombe (Oxford: Basil Blackwell, 1958).
2   See N. Malcolm, *Ludwig Wittgenstein: A Memoir* (Oxford: Oxford University Press, 1958); B. McGuinness, *Wittgenstein: A Life* (London: Duckworth, 1988); R. Monk, *Ludwig Wittgenstein: The Duty of Genius* (London: Jonathan Cape, 1990); and R. Rhees (ed.), *Recollections of Wittgenstein* (Oxford: Oxford University Press, 1984).

Sections 1 and 2

1   L. Wittgenstein, *Culture and Value*, G.H. von Wright (ed.), translated by P. Winch (Oxford: Blackwell, 1980), p. 57.
2   L. Wittgenstein, *Philosophical Grammar*, R. Rhees (ed.), translated by A.J.P. Kenny (Oxford: Blackwell, 1974), p. 56.
3   L. Wittgenstein, *The Blue and Brown Books* (Oxford: Blackwell, 1958), p. 77.

Sections 3 to 7

1   *The Blue and Brown Books*, p. 77.

Sections 8 to 17

1   *The Blue and Brown Books*, p. 7.

Sections 18 to 20

1   *The Blue and Brown Books*, p. 77.
2   *The Blue and Brown Books*, p. 78.
3   *The Blue and Brown Books*, p. 78.

Sections 21 to 25

1   L. Wittgenstein, *Notebooks 1914–1916*, G.H. von Wright and G.E.M. Anscombe (eds), translated by G.E.M. Anscombe, second edn (Oxford: Blackwell, 1979), p. 96.

2   L. Wittgenstein, *Lectures and Conversations on Aesthetics, Psychology and Religious Belief*, C. Barrett (ed.) (Berkeley: University of California Press, 1970), p. 2.
3   See L. Wittgenstein, *Tractatus Logico-Philosophicus*, translated by C.K. Ogden (London: Routledge and Kegan Paul, 1933), 4.5.
4   I. Kant, *Critique of Pure Reason*, translated by N. Kemp Smith (New York: St Martin's Press, 1965), B131/132.
5   *The Blue and Brown Books*, pp. 58–70.

Sections 33 to 38

1   *Tractatus Logico-Philosophicus*, p. 27.
2   B. Russell, 'The Philosophy of Logical Atomism', in *Logic and Knowledge, Essays 1901–1950*, R.C. Marsh (ed.) (London: George Allen and Unwin, 1956), p. 203.

Sections 39 to 47

1   *Tractatus Logico-Philosophicus*, 3.221 and 2.021; *Philosophical Grammar*, p.208.
2   *Notebooks 1914–1916*, p. 3.

Sections 48 to 54

1   B. Russell, *Introduction to Mathematical Philosophy* (London: George Allen and Unwin, 1919), p. 178.
2   *Tractatus Logico-Philosophicus*, 3.21.

Sections 71 to 77

1   *The Frege Reader*, M. Beaney (ed.) (Oxford: Blackwell, 1997), p. 259.
2   *Notebooks 1914–1916*, p. 68; *Tractatus Logico-Philosophicus* 3.23.

Sections 78 to 85

1   L. Wittgenstein, *Zettel* (Oxford: Basil Blackwell, 1967), §440.

Sections 86 to 92

1   *Notebooks 1914–1916*, p. 39.
2   Augustine, *Confessions*, translated by H. Chadwick (Oxford: Oxford University Press, 1991), p. 230.
3   *Notebooks 1914–1916*, p. 106 and p. 79; B. Russell, 'On Scientific Method in Philosophy', in *Mysticism and Logic* (London: George Allen and Unwin, 1917), p. 84, italicized in the original.
4   *Philosophical Grammar*, pp. 120–1.

Sections 93 to 103

1   *Notebooks 1914–1916*, p. 39.
2   *Tractatus Logico-Philosophicus* 4.014.
3   *Notebooks 1914–1916*, p. 53.
4   *Notebooks 1914–1916*, p. 63.
5   *Tractatus Logico-Philosophicus* 3.2–3.24.

Sections 104 to 114

1   *Critique of Pure Reason*, A5/B9.
2   L. Wittgenstein, *Philosophical Remarks*, R. Rhees (ed.), translated by R. Hargreaves and R. White (Oxford: Blackwell, 1975), p. 52.
3   *The Blue and Brown Books*, p. 27.
4   *Philosophical Grammar*, p. 155.
5   *Culture and Value*, p. 26.
6   A. Schopenhauer, *The World as Will and Representation*, volume I, p. 139, quoted in G. Hallett, *A Companion to Wittgenstein's 'Philosophical Investigations'* (Ithaca: Cornell University Press, 1977), p. 190.

Sections 115 to 123

1   K. Kraus, *Half-Truths and One-and-a-Half Truths*, translated by H. Zohn (Chicago: University of Chicago Press, 1990), p. 67.
2   B. Russell, Introduction to L. Wittgenstein, *Tractatus Logico-Philosophicus*, p. 23.
3   *Philosophical Grammar*, p. 121.

Sections 124 to 133

1   L. Wittgenstein, *Remarks on the Foundations of Mathematics*, revised edn, G.H. von Wright, R. Rhees and G.E.M. Anscombe (eds), translated by G.E.M. Anscombe (Oxford: Basil Blackwell, 1978), p. 220.
2   *The Blue and Brown Books*, pp. 44–5.
3   *Culture and Value*, p. 43.
4   G. Hallett, *A Companion to Wittgenstein's 'Philosophical Investigations'*, p. 230.
5   *Culture and Value*, p. 61.
6   *Lectures and Conversations on Aesthetics, Psychology and Religious Belief*, p. 28.

Conclusion

1   L. Wittgenstein, 'Philosophy', in *Philosophical Occasions 1912–1951*, J. Klagge and A. Nordmann (eds) (Indianapolis: Hackett, 1993), p. 171.
2   *Lectures and Conversations on Aesthetics, Psychology and Religious Belief*, p. 28.
3   *The Blue and Brown Books*, p. 18.
4   L. Wittgenstein, 'Lecture on Ethics', in *Philosophical Occasions 1912–1951*, p. 44.
5   G. E. Moore, 'Wittgenstein's Lectures in 1930–33', in *Philosophical Occasions 1912–1951*, p. 113.

Index